TOXIC AIR POLLUTION

PAUL J. LIOY
JOAN M. DAISEY

A Comprehensive Study of Non-Criteria Air Pollutants

 LEWIS PUBLISHERS, INC.

Library of Congress Cataloging in Publication Data

Toxic air pollution.

    Includes bibliographies and index.
    1. Airborne Toxic Element and Organic Substances Project
(N.J.) 2. Air—Pollution—Toxicology—New Jersey. 3.
Air—Pollution—New Jersey. I. Lioy, Paul J. II. Daisey, J. M.
III. Airborne Toxic Element and Organic Substances Project (N.J.)
[DNLM: 1. Air Pollutants—toxicity. 2. Air
Pollution—analysis—New Jersey. WA 754 T7545]
RA576.6.N5T68 1987   363.7′3922′09749 86–20136
ISBN 0-87371-057-6

LEWIS PUBLISHERS, INC.
121 South Main Street, Chelsea, Michigan 48118

PRINTED IN THE UNITED STATES OF AMERICA

Dedicated to all of the ATEOS scientists

Preface

Industrial success commonly results in relatively high population density, and has produced the concomitant and, at times, synergistic problems of air, water, and soil pollution. Petrochemical facilities, motor vehicles, metal processing industries, and home space heaters are just a few of the litany of pollution sources that have led to contamination in the environment. In aggregate, these problems are widely thought to be related to elevated cancer mortality.

The State of New Jersey, being an industrial leader, is intensely interested in this vital area. The state continues to play an important role in the development and growth of our nation, as it has since colonial times. One of the manifestations of that role in today's world was its active support of the Airborne Toxic Element and Organic Substances project (ATEOS).

Although notable improvements in New Jersey air quality have been brought about by shifts in the types of fuels used, a reduction in industrial production, and environmental regulatory actions, there is a continuing concern across a wide spectrum of groups about the role of air quality in cancer mortality incidence. It is with this backdrop that the ATEOS project evolved.

Historically, scientists attempting to link concentrations of air pollutants to lung cancer mortality incidence have been constrained by the quantity and quality of data used to estimate exposure. For example, due to the lack of more direct measures of carcinogenicity, sulfur dioxide, total suspended particulate matter, and smoke-shade measurements have been inappropriately utilized in various epidemiological studies as surrogates for human exposure to airborne carcinogens. As air quality improves, more specific information is necessary to understand the role of air pollution in lung cancer mortality incidence. Further, it has become possible to develop a better understanding of the possible role of specific airborne pollutants in lung cancer mortality incidence, due to the evolution of air quality monitoring and analytical techniques. Thus, the ATEOS project was developed to begin to establish quantitative information related to human exposures to airborne carcinogens and to answer the following questions related to selected air pollutants in the New Jersey atmosphere:

1. What are the levels and distribution of biologically active pollutants?
2. What are the potential impacts of environmental factors on the atmospheric concentration?

v

3. What are the major source types contributing to ambient levels?
4. What are the health risks associated with exposure to specific substances?

As can be seen in the eight chapters comprising this volume, virtually all goals of the ATEOS project were achieved. Because of these accomplishments, the evolution of more focused governmental regulatory, enforcement, and monitoring efforts can be undertaken to begin to reduce exposures to outdoor airborne carcinogens and to quantify the degree of success of such efforts. Completion of the project does not mean that further research efforts are unnecessary. In fact, the ATEOS project proves the need for additional research and already has precipitated the following efforts in New Jersey:

- total exposure studies
- source-specific VOC studies
- combustion source characterization studies
- investigation of airborne mutagens in extractable organic matter

Through the completion of these new initiatives and other studies, a more complete understanding of the role of airborne carcinogens in cancer mortality incidence will be documented. While an overall increase in the understanding of exposure to airborne carcinogens in the New Jersey environment is important, the technical tools available to accurately estimate health risks are very crude at best, and new epidemiological studies must be designed for other significant problem areas.

The purpose of this book is to: (1) summarize and present the major findings of the ATEOS study, which in turn (2) makes available, as averages, the concentrations of the many toxic, mutagenic, and carcinogenic pollutants measured, in a convenient and accessible form, for scientists, regulators, educators, and students in air pollution.

It is our hope that this book will provide a historical data base of ambient toxic air pollutant measurements for future trend analysis, as well as for assessing total exposure and indoor air pollution relationships, and that it will provide a comprehensive major resource for designing and implementing future studies.

Paul J. Lioy
Joan M. Daisey
Ronald D. Harkov

Authors

Thomas Atherholt is a graduate of Gettysburg College. He received his PhD degree from Rutgers University in 1978. Following work at Cappel and Cannon Laboratories, he joined the Department of Microbiology at the Coriell Institute for Medical Research in 1980, where he currently heads the Environmental Mutagen Research Laboratory. Dr. Atherholt is involved in research and development on detection and characterization of environmental mutagens.

Joseph Bozzelli received a bachelor's degree in chemistry from Marietta College and a PhD in physical chemistry from Princeton University. He is Professor of Chemistry and Co-Director of the Air Pollution Research Laboratory at the New Jersey Institute of Technology. He has published 50 papers in gas-phase chemical kinetics and air pollution analysis, and is interested in the kinetics and mechanisms of decomposition of chlorocarbons into hydrocarbons.

Joan Daisey is the head of the Chemistry Group and the Indoor Air Program of Lawrence Berkeley Laboratory in California. She was trained as a physical chemist and received her PhD from Seton Hall University. She is a member of a number of numerous professional organizations, including the American Chemical Society, the Air Pollution Control Association, Sigma Xi, the New York Academy of Sciences, the American Conference of Industrial Hygienists, and the American Association for Aerosol Research. She is currently serving on the board of directors of the American Association for Aerosol Research and is a member of the APCA Committees on Indoor Air Quality Receptor Modeling and Toxic Air Pollutants.

Dr. Daisey's research over the past decade has been directed toward assessing human exposures to toxic and carcinogenic organic pollutants in outdoor and indoor atmospheres and developing a better understanding of the nature, sources, dynamics, and atmospheric reactions of organic pollutants. She is also involved in research on the effects of complex environmental mixtures in microbial and mammalian bioassays.

Arthur Greenberg received his bachelor's degree from Fairleigh Dickinson University in chemistry and his PhD in physical organic chemistry from Princeton University. He is currently Professor of Chemistry and Co-Director of the Air Pollution Research Laboratory at the New Jersey Institute of Technology. He has published 60 papers and 5 books in the areas of

vii

strained molecules, stereochemistry, and air pollution analysis. Current interests involve reactions of polycyclic aromatic hydrocarbons and structures of unusual molecules.

Ronald Harkov is Manager of the Monitoring Development Unit in the Office of Science and Research of the New Jersey Department of Environmental Protection. Dr. Harkov's research interests include measurement techniques for noncriteria air pollutants (NCAP) in source emissions and ambient samples, exposure assessment methodologies for trace contaminants, and the evaluation of acid deposition in the environment. In addition to his work with NCAP, Dr. Harkov is an adjunct faculty member in the Department of Plant Pathology, Rutgers University, where he is assisting in the direction of research concerned with air pollution effects on plants.

Barbara Kebbekus received her undergraduate degree in chemistry from Rosemont College and her PhD from The Pennsylvania State University, in analytical chemistry. She is, at present, Professor of Chemistry, Assistant Head of the Chemistry Division, and Co-director of the Air Pollution Research Laboratory at The New Jersey Institute of Technology. She has published 15 papers in the field of air pollution analysis, predominantly dealing with the determination of trace organic vapors in ambient atmospheres.

Paul J. Lioy is an Associate Professor and Director of the Exposure Measurement and Assessment Division of the Department of Environmental and Community Medicine of Robert Wood Johnson Medical School at the University of Medicine and Dentistry of New Jersey (UMDNJ). He is also a Director in the Environmental and Occupational Health Sciences Institute of UMDNJ and Rutgers University. He received a PhD in environmental sciences at Rutgers University. He is a member of the Air Pollution Control Association, Sigma Xi, the American Conference of Governmental Industrial Hygienists (ACGIH), and the American Association for Aerosol Research, and he was named a Fellow of the New York Academy of Sciences in 1980.

Dr. Lioy is currently Chairman of the APCA Editorial Review Board, and has served as chairman or as a member of numerous committees. He is Chair of the ACGIH Air Sampling Instruments Committee, and was editor of the sixth edition of Air Sampling Instruments. He also serves as a consultant to the Science Advisory Board of the U.S. Environmental Protection Agency.

Dr. Lioy's research is directed toward understanding the dynamic process of human exposure to environmental pollutants. This includes chemical characterization and human health effects field studies. His major interests include irritant species as well as carcinogenic compounds. Recently Dr.

Lioy has initiated studies in the total exposure of humans to individual compounds, with multiple pathways to man.

Judith B. Louis received her PhD in chemistry from New York University in 1976. She is currently a Research Scientist in the Office of Science and Research of the New Jersey Department of Environmental Protection. Her research interests include the use of biological tests in the evaluation of toxicity of complex environmental samples, the development of new methods for extracting organic matter from environmental samples, and the evaluation of exposure to pesticides.

Gerard J. McGarrity is a graduate of St. Joseph's University and Thomas Jefferson University, both in Philadelphia. He is President of the Coriell Institute for Medical Research and is an adjunct professor at Thomas Jefferson University, University of Medicine and Dentistry of New Jersey, and the State University of New York. His areas of investigation are environmental mutagenesis and mycoplasmas. Doctor McGarrity is past President of the Tissue Culture Association. From 1980–1985 he was a member of the Recombinant DNA Advisory Committee of NIH, and he is still Chairman of its Working Group on Environmental Release. He is author or co-author of more than one hundred articles in his areas of interest.

Leslie J. McGeorge received her MSPH in environmental chemistry and biology from the Public Health School at the University of North Carolina in 1980. She is currently a Research Scientist in the Office of Science and Research of the New Jersey Department of Environmental Protection. Her research interests include the development and application of biological test systems to monitor the toxicity of environmental media, the evaluation of new techniques for contaminant detection in wastewaters, and the measurement and treatment of hazardous contaminants in potable water.

Maria T. Morandi is a Post-Doctoral Fellow at the University of Texas School of Public Health in Houston. After completing her primary, secondary, and preparatory education in Montevideo, Uruguay, she moved to New York City in 1972. There she received a BS in chemistry from City College of New York, and MS and PhD degrees in environmental health science from New York University's Institute of Environmental Medicine. Dr. Morandi's interdisciplinary research interests are characterization of indoor and outdoor air pollutants, air pollution source apportionment modeling, and determination of human exposures to ambient contaminants. She is an active member of the Air Pollution Control Association local chapter, and a member of the Environmental Committee of the San Jacinto Chapter of the American Lung Association.

Acknowledgments

It is difficult to creatively express thanks to all those who participated in the ATEOS project. Therefore, we give a warm thank-you to each of the individuals listed below as participants from each agency or laboratory.

New York University Medical Center

Michael Avdenko
James Butler
James Curry
Joan Daisey
John Gorczynski
Kaz Ito
Theodore J. Kneip
Paul J. Lioy
Morton Lippmann
James Miller
Maria Morandi
Frank Mukai
Steven Sherman
John Wilson

New Jersey Institute of Technology

Joseph Bozzelli
Clint Brockway
Faye Darack
Carol Eveleens
Maria Gaviero
Arthur Greenberg
James Kemp
Barbara Kebbekus
Alexander Kovalyov
Nina Kovalyov
John Laregina
Janis Racz
Hema Ramaswamy

Douglas Stout
Dale Vanyo
Robert Winkler
Jane Wu

Department of Environmental Protection of New Jersey
BAQMS of Air Quality Management and Surveillance

James Cress
John Elston
Charles Pieterinen

Department of Environmental Protection of New Jersey
Office of Science and Research

Robert Fischer
Glen Harker
Ronald Harkov
Judith Louis
Leslie McGeorge

Coriell Institute for Medical Research

Ursula Adourian
Thomas B. Atherholt
Deborah Cicero
Mary Kosciuk
Victoria Kwiatkowski
Gerard J. McGarrity
Terry Schuck

Rutgers University

Garry Baranowski
Charles Kluepful
Nathan Reiss

List of Figures

List of Tables

Contents

xx

TOXIC
AIR POLLUTION

CHAPTER 1

The Airborne Toxic Element and Organic Substances (ATEOS) Study Design

Paul J. Lioy, Joan M. Daisey, Maria T. Morandi, Ronald D. Harkov, Arthur Greenberg, Joseph Bozzelli, Barbara Kebbekus, Judith Louis, Leslie J. McGeorge

CHAPTER CONTENTS

The Airborne Toxic Element and Organic Substances (ATEOS) Study Design

INTRODUCTION

The difficulties with addressing toxic air pollutants are the sheer number of compounds present in the atmosphere and their sources. The purpose of this book is to develop an approach to understanding toxic air pollutants through synthesis of the scientific results obtained in the Airborne Toxic Element and Organic Substances (ATEOS) project. It will provide documentation on the concentration patterns of a number of toxic air pollutants, in three different urban settings and one rural area. These are examples of locations where toxic contaminants can be found in significant concentrations.

In outline form, the objectives of ATEOS were:

1. Determination of concentrations and seasonal distribution patterns of inhalable particulate matter (IPM), extractable organic matter (EOM), fine particulate matter, and various airborne toxic chemicals at one rural and three urban sites in New Jersey.
2. Examination of the relationships of IPM and its organic and inorganic components to vapor phase organic compounds and mutagenic activity of EOM as determined by the Ames Assay.
3. Extension and further development of the Factor Analysis/Multiple Regression (FA/MR) source apportionment model.
4. Use of FA/MR model results to identify and estimate contributions of major source types to IPM and EOM in three New Jersey cities.
5. Evaluation of the levels of airborne pollutants present at these sites with respect to health hazards, and recommendation of future research needs.

3

As one can readily see, these were ambitious goals which, to a large degree, were accomplished over the period from 1981 through 1985. ATEOS was the first study to focus primarily on the biologically active fraction of the atmospheric aerosol and volatile organic compounds; therefore, the variables measured and sites studied were carefully selected during the design of the program. Obviously, the techniques used were based upon state-of-the-art instrumentation and analytical procedures available at that time. This chapter includes details on the design of the study, as well as information on the analytical procedures. All variables for which data were obtained in ATEOS are shown in Table 1.1. The criteria for selection were based upon the extensive literature available on air pollutants and hazardous substances, and known emission rates and densities within the state of New Jersey. Many of the emissions data on specific contaminants were assembled after 1975. A brief description of the reasons for selection of specific compounds or compound classes are presented below.

Inhalable Particulate Matter (IPM) — Particles that are size-selectively sampled with a 15-μm inlet cut size. These can enter the tracheobronchiole and gas exchange regions of the lungs, and thus are more likely than Total Suspended Particulate to produce pollution-related health effects (National Academy of Science, 1979). The particles comprising this fraction contain some mechanically generated coarse particles, as well as primary source emissions and secondary particles (e.g., combustion, photochemistry) which are normally found in the accumulation mode (0.1 to 2.5 μm aerodynamic diameter).

Fine Particulate Matter (FPM) — The fraction of the ambient particulate matter that contains particles < 2.5 μm in aerodynamic diameter which can penetrate the conductive airways of the lower tracheobronchial tree. These can be deposited in the gas exchange region of the lung (National Academy of Sciences, 1979). Particles in the $\leq$ 2.5μm range result from both primary emissions and secondary atmospheric processes, and can remain suspended in the atmosphere for days.

Lead — A trace element primarily associated with particles in the fine particle range, and which has been shown to be present in human tissues (Bernstein et al., 1974). Children are particularly susceptible to the neurotoxic effects of lead which may occur even at concentrations measured in the ambient air (Goyer and Chisolm, 1972; Thatcher et al., 1982). A main

Table 1.1. Summary of Data Obtained During Project ATEOS

Variable	Symbol or Code	Description, if applicable (units)
Inhalable particulate matter	IPM	particles of aerodynamic size diameter $\leq 15\ \mu m$ $(\mu g/m^3)$
Fine particulate matter	FPM	particles of aerodynamic size diameter ≤ 2.5 μm $(\mu g/m^3)$
Elements		$(\mu g/m^3)$
lead	Pb	
manganese	Mn	
copper	Cu	
vanadium	V	
cadmium	Cd	
zinc	Zn	
iron	Fe	
nickel	Ni	
Sulfate	SO_4^{-2}	total sulfate concentration in IPM $(\mu g/m^3)$
Organic fractions		
cyclohexane	CX	cyclohexane-soluble or extractable organic fraction of IPM $(\mu g/m^3)$
dichloromethane	DCM	dichloromethane-soluble or extractable organic fraction of IPM $(\mu g/m^3)$
acetone	ACE	acetone-soluble or extractable organic fractio of IPM (total $\mu g/m^3$)
alkylating agents	ALK	alkylating activity of acetone-soluble fraction $(\mu g/m^3)$
Carbon monoxide	CO_{max}	maximum 1-hr daily CO concentration (parts per thousand)
Sulfur dioxide	SO_{2avg}	average daily sulfur dioxide concentration (ppm)
Ozone	O_{3max}	maximum 1-hr daily ozone concentration (ppm)
Extractable Particulate Organic Fractions	*EOM*	
Polycyclic aromatic hydrocarbons	PAHs	all PAHs measured were contained in the cyclohexane-soluble fractin (ng/m³)
cyclopenta(cd)pyrene	CcdP	
benzo(a)anthracene	BaA	
benzo(k)fluoranthene	BkF	
benzo(a)pyrene	BaP	
1,2,5,6-dibenzanthracene	DBahA	
benzo(ghi)perylene	BghiP	
indeno(1,2,3-cd)pyrene	IcdP	
1,2,4,5-dibenzpyrene	DBaePY	
coronene	Cor	
dibenzo(ac)anthracene	DBacA	
chrysene	CHRY	
anthracene	ANTH	
benzo(e)pyrene	BeP	
benzo(j)fluoranthene	BjF	
perylene	PER	
benzo(b)fluoranthene	BbF	
Volatile organic compounds	VOCs	all VOCs were measured during the first two studies (ppb)
vinyl chloride	VCL	
vinylidene chloride	VENC	

Table 1.1. Summary of Data Obtained During Project ATEOS (continued)

Variable	Symbol or Code	Description, if applicable (units)
acrylonitrile	ACN	
methylene chloride	MECL	
chloroform	CFOR	
1,2-dichloroethane	DCE	
benzene	BENZ	
carbon tetrachloride	CCL4	
trichloroethylene	TRJC or TCANE	
dioxane	DIOX	
toluene	TOL	
1,2-dibromoethane	ETBR	
tetrachloroethylene	PERC	
chlorobenzene	CLBZ	
ethylbenzene	ETBX	
m-xylene	MX	
p-xylene	PX	
styrene	STY	
o-xylene	OX	
1,1,2,2-tetra-chloroethane	TCE	
o-chlorotoluene	OCLT	
p-chlorotoluene	PCLT	
p-dichlorobenzene	PDB	
o-dichlorobenzene	ODB	
nitrobenzene	NBZ	
Meteorology:		
heating degree days	HEADD	1 degree day = 1 degree above
cooling degree days	COODD	(heating) or below (cooling) 65° during any given day
visibility	VISMD	midday visibility (miles)
precipitation	PECIP	daily precipitation (inches of water)
temperature	MAXT	maximum daily temperature (°F)
temperature	MINT	minimum daily temperature (°F)
wind direction	P1	percent of time with prevalent winds from NE on a given day (%)
	P2	percent of time with prevalent winds from SE on a given day (%)
	P3	percent of time with prevelant winds from SW on a given day (%)
	P4	percent of time with prevelant winds from NW on a given day (%)
inverse wind speed	WSPINV	inverse of the average daily wind speed (mi/hr)
Mutagenicity		
Ames Assay		TA 98 $\pm$ S9 (Revertants/m^3) TA 100 $\pm$ S9

source of lead in the urban atmosphere through the mid 1980s has been motor vehicle exhaust. However, lead is to be phased out of use as a gasoline additive by 1990. Other sources of lead are industrial operations, such as lead and nonferrous metal smelters, incineration and combustion of residual fuel oil.

Manganese—A trace element that is apparently not toxic at ambient concentrations (National Research Council, 1974). The main sources of airborne manganese in the urban atmosphere are soils and steel alloying operations. It was used from 1975 until 1978 in an antiknock additive for gasoline, methylcyclopentadienyl tricarbonyl (MMT).

Copper—An element that is toxic when inhaled in large concentrations, such as those resulting from copper processing operations (National Academy of Sciences, 1977). Concentrations in the ng/m^3 range are ubiquitous in the urban atmosphere. Known sources of copper are electroplating operations, refuse incineration, and production of a variety of metal alloys.

Vanadium—Epidemiology studies have linked increased vanadium concentrations with respiratory and hypertensive disease (Stock, 1960; Hickey et al., 1967). Ambient vanadium levels observed during these epidemiological studies were one order of magnitude larger than those existing today. The main known source of vanadium in eastern U.S. urban atmospheres is combustion of fuel oils.

Cadmium—The effects of acute and chronic exposure to cadmium have been reported by many authors (Frieberg et al., 1974). They include functional and morphological changes in several organs, including lung, kidney, and liver. Sources of cadmium in urban atmospheres will include electroplating, welding, plastic additives and smelting.

Zinc—Inhalation of zinc fumes causes metal fume fever and pneumonitis. Chronic zinc toxicity results in adverse growth, reproduction and neural health effects (Lucky and Venugopal, 1977). As in the case with most of the other metals measured during the ATEOS study, airborne ambient zinc levels are well below possible occupational exposures. Sources of zinc in the urban atmosphere are smelters, incinerators, alloy production facilities, galvanizing operations, and a large number of industrial and consumer products.

Iron — This trace element is toxic only in very high doses, which are well in excess of those observed in the atmosphere. Toxic effects are related to chronic inhalation of taconite or iron oxide ore fumes (Lucky and Venugopal, 1977). Iron is widespread in the environment. It occurs naturally in soils. Industrial uses include alloying with carbon to produce steel, as a dye and pigment component, etc.

Nickel — Nickel and nickel compounds have been found to produce lung and nasal sinus cancer in nickel refinery workers and in experimental animals (Sunderman, 1977). Sources in the urban atmosphere include fuel oil burning, electroplating, and steel production (stainless).

Sulfate — Sulfate compounds are of interest because of health effects and environmental degradation. Levels of SO_4^{-2} in the form of H_2SO_4 and at one tenth the current occupational standard (1000 $\mu g/m^3$) have been shown to produce changes in the mucociliary clearance rate of the lung (Leikauf et al., 1980). The persistence of ambient H_2SO_4 concentrations is mainly determined by factors which favor atmospheric secondary aerosol formation and accumulation, and the presence of the neutralizing gas ammonia. Levels have been observed in the atmosphere that are of the same order of magnitude as those associated with health effects. The more common forms of SO_4^{-2} are the neutralized species $(NH_4)_2SO_4$ and NH_4HSO_4. These are almost always found in urban areas.

Alkylating Agent Activity — This is a class assay used to determine the presence of a group of compounds such as epoxides and lactones (Preussman et al., 1969), many of which are carcinogens and mutagens. Sources of these compounds are primary (i.e., combustion of fuels) and secondary in nature.

Carbon Monoxide — The lethal and sublethal effects of CO poisoning have been extensively documented (National Research Council, 1977), and it is a criteria pollutant of the U.S. EPA. CO is produced during incomplete combustion of fossil fuels. The main source of CO in the urban atmosphere is vehicular traffic.

Sulfur Dioxide — It is a criteria pollutant of the U.S. EPA. Respiratory disease has been associated with elevated SO_2 concentrations in urban areas, although its effects have not been fully separated from those gaseous and particulate sulfur oxides (National Research Council, 1978). At current levels, concern about SO_2 emissions is mainly related to their role as a SO_4^{-2} precursor affecting areas far away from their point of origin. Sulfur dioxide is emitted mainly by the combustion of sulfur-containing fossil fuels.

Ozone — It is a powerful lung irritant. Recent studies have found a relationship between altered pulmonary function tests in active children and ozone levels at or below the current primary standard of 120 ppb (Lippmann et al., 1983; Lioy et al., 1985). Although ozone is produced by natural (e.g., stratosphere, lightning, and any spark traversing air) and man-made processes, its concentration in the urban atmosphere is mainly the result of photochemical reactions of anthropogenic sources of the precursors nitrogen oxide and hydrocarbons.

Extractable Particulate Organic Fractions — Also called extractable organic matter (EOM), these have the potential to cause adverse health effects. These fractions, and many compounds within them, have been shown to be mutagenic and carcinogenic in in vitro tests and laboratory animals (Hoffman and Wynder, 1977; Talcott and Wei, 1977; Pitt et al., 1977). Sources of EOM include all combustion processes and secondary formation through atmospheric reactions.

Polycyclic Aromatic Hydrocarbons — Many of these compounds have been shown to be mutagenic and carcinogenic (Hoffman and Wynder, 1976). PAHs are produced by fossil fuel combustion processes and are widespread in the urban environment. Details on the compounds measured are found in Chapter 4.

Volatile Organic Compounds — Most of the VOCs measured in this study are known or potential carcinogens, neurotoxins, etc. (Environmental Protection Agency, 1980). The main VOC sources in the urban atmosphere are combustion emissions, and evaporation of stored fuels, and direct emissions of solvents used in activities such as dry cleaning, degreasing, and painting. Details on the compounds measured in the study are found in Chapter 3.

Meteorology — Meteorological conditions will affect the levels of pollutants accumulated in the atmosphere. The calculation of heating and cooling degree days is indicative of seasonality and can be correlated to variables (e.g., ozone) which have definite seasonal relationships. When corrected for water vapor, visibility is indicative of the degree of stagnation and particulate loading in the atmosphere. Precipitation measurements can be used to examine periods when the atmosphere is suddenly "cleansed" due to a heavy or persistent rainfall. Maximum and minimum temperatures are important for identifying periods of increased overall reactivity and degradation of airborne compounds. Wind direction frequency is used to help identify location of point sources or major area sources. Wind speed gives information on the overall atmospheric mixing and dilution of pollutants.

SITE SELECTION

Because the ATEOS study has specific objectives related to the detection of the presence of toxic and carcinogenic pollutants, criteria were established for the identification and selection of each urban sampling site location used in the project. Briefly, these were:

1. location in an area of high population density
2. proximity to large centers with commercial and/or industrial activities
3. proximity to important transportation arteries
4. sites which were potentially impacted by different types of sources

Based upon these criteria, the cities of Newark, Elizabeth and Camden were chosen. Besides the basic criteria, the actual site within a city was chosen specifically because it could be expected to reflect local differences in the types, distributions and proximity of sources. The following discussion will present details on the reasoning behind the selection of each site. In addition to these urban sites, it was important to have a site which is located in an area that receives a minimal impact from local sources. Ringwood State Park, a rural area located to the north of New Jersey, was selected as the locale for a background site; this was especially true for north and west winds. The geographical locations of all the sampling sites are shown in Figure 1.1.

For a further perspective on the area surrounding the urban sites, the

ATEOS Sampling Sites

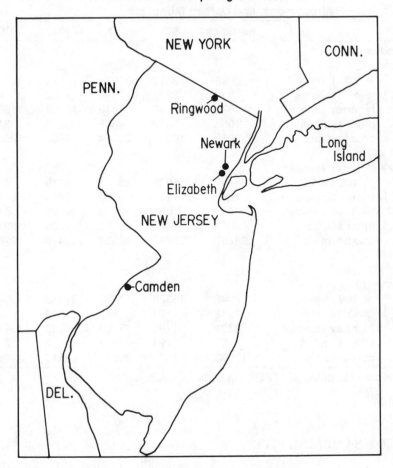

Figure 1.1.   The geographic locations of the rural site (Ringwood) and urban sites used in the ATEOS project.

countywide emissions inventories are shown in Table 1.2. The Essex County inventory was the largest for all categories except hydrocarbons, which was about 10^4 tons/yr greater in Union County. This is not surprising, since Union County has many oil refineries and petrochemical facilities. In all cases, Camden County had much lower emissions than either Essex or Union County in all categories (30–50%).

Table 1.2. Emissions Inventory for Counties in Which the ATEOS Sites Were Located—Particles, Sulfur Dioxide, Nitrogen Oxides, Hydrocarbons, and Carbon Monoxide

	Particles	SO$_2$	NO$_X$	HC	CO
Camden County					
(Camden)			Tons/yr		
$\left(\dfrac{9}{25}\right)^a$ > 100 tons/yr	2699	3617	4893	2572	0
minor facilities	1632	2232	2628	1562	494
highway vehicles	1672	850	17478	13159	116587
other sources	1055	3329	4805	9313	8442
county total	7058	10028	29804	26606	125523
Essex County (Newark)					
$\left(\dfrac{27}{40}\right)^a$ > 100 tons/yr	25461	16636	28747	15119	4347
minor facilities	1919	1111	1157	2065	409
highway vehicles	2731	1389	19940	17775	165134
other sources	2646	6479	11107	17520	22126
county totals	32757	25615	60951	52479	192016
Union County					
(Elizabeth)					
$\left(\dfrac{4}{41}\right)^a$ > 100 tons/yr	6342	15326	14452	37072	462
minor facilities	1942	723	511	1374	288
highway vehicles	2321	1180	17509	14938	136182
other sources	1458	4191	7147	9132	12753
county totals	12063	21420	39619	62516	149685

[a]Number of sources in ATEOS city/total for county.

STUDY SAMPLING SITES

The Newark air sampling station was located atop the roof of the Newark headquarters of the Salvation Army, approximately 16 m above the street level, on the corner of Clifford and Van Buren St. The building is located in an industrial-residential zone approximately 1.6 km southeast of the commercial center of Newark. The city of Elizabeth, major oil refineries, and large mineral and petrochemical plants are located to the southwest of the site. To the east and south are the New Jersey Turnpike and its major interchanges, routes 22, 1 and 9, and Newark Airport (Figure 1.2). About 10 km to the southeast are the petrochemical and oil refinery complexes of Hudson County in Bayonne. In the immediate vicinity of the site is a complex array of small to average size commercial and industrial operations. The distribution of these sources had a significant effect on the ambient levels, and will be a topic of discussion throughout the book.

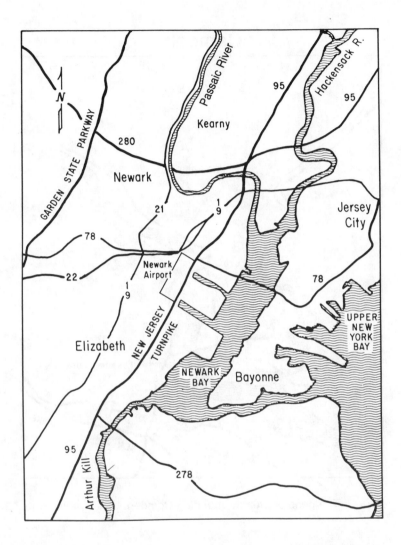

Figure 1.2. The major traffic arteries in the area surrounding the Elizabeth and Newark sites.

The Elizabeth ATEOS sampling site was situated on the roof of a two-story building, which is the headquarters of the Elizabeth Board of Education. It is located at 500 N. Broad St., about 8 km southwest from the Newark site (Figure 1.2). The samplers were placed approximately 20 m above street level. The New Jersey Turnpike and Routes 1 and 9 run in a north-south direction due east of the site. Oil refineries and oil tank farms

Camden

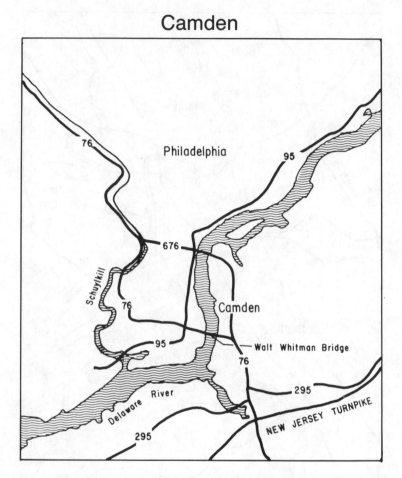

Figure 1.3.   The general area surrounding Camden.

are located approximately 2 km to the south, and Newark Airport is situated to the east-northeast. In contrast to the Newark location, there are no industrial operations in the immediate vicinity of the site. There are some commercial enterprises, and a traffic artery which services the central business district of Elizabeth.

The Camden sampling station was placed at a New Jersey Department of Environmental Protection trailer located on the grounds of the Institute for Medical Research, on Copewood and David St., and was approximately 3.3 km southeast of the city of Philadelphia, Pennsylvania (Figure 1.3). The downtown area of Camden is due north of the site. The samplers were placed approximately 7 m above ground level. The area immediately around the site is mostly residential, with no industrial operations and very few commercial activities. Major roadways in the immediate vicinity of the sampling site are Routes 676 and 31. Refineries can be found approximately 5 km southwest of the site, as well as commercial shipping warehouses and small commercial enterprises.

The Ringwood State Park station is in a rural setting located on the grounds of the New Jersey Forest Service nursery facility on an open parcel of land approximately 175 m above sea level. There are no major anthropogenic sources of airborne materials in the immediate vicinity. Impacts were anticipated from routine nursery operations during the summer studies; however, this activity did not have a major influence on the collected samples.

STUDY DESIGN

The design of the sampling study was based upon the potential for the presence of high concentrations of ambient air pollution during the summer and winter in New Jersey (Harkov, 1982; Lioy and Daisey, 1986). This is due primarily to the accumulation of secondary chemical species which result from photochemical smog reactions in the summer, and of primary chemical species from fossil fuel combustion and local automobile traffic emissions during the winter. The specific protocol involved the collection of 24-hr ambient air samples for 39 consecutive days at each site over the course of approximately six weeks. This plan was implemented four times over the span of three calendar years. The sampling schedule was as follows:

1) July 6 to August 14, 1981
2) January 18 to February 25, 1982
3) July 6 to August 14, 1982
4) January 17 to February 25, 1983

The samplers, filter types, and analytical procedures used at each sampling site are described in Table 1.3.

Continuous monitors were operated for carbon monoxide, sulfur dioxide and ozone by the New Jersey Department of Environmental Protection. The Newark CO, SO_2 and O_3 data were measured at the Public Service Electric and Gas Co. Newark substation located on Washington and Willow St., in the central business district. The substation was approximately 1.5 km due northwest of the Clifford St. sampling site, and the monitors were placed approximately 12 ft above street level. In Elizabeth, CO and SO_2 concentrations were measured at Exit 13 of the New Jersey Turnpike, approximately 2.5 km southwest of the site. Ozone values were obtained at a regional monitoring station located in Bayonne, as O_3 was not measured

Table 1.3.   Samplers, Filter Media, and Analyses Used During the Campaign of the ATEOS Project at All Sites

Type of Sample	Particle Size	Medium	Number of Samples per Site per Season	Analyses
IPM	≤ 15 μm	Gelman AE Fiberglass	39	EOM (3 fractions), PAHs, alkylating agents, mutagenic activity
IPM	≤ 15 μm	Gelman Spectro Grade	39	mass, trace metals, sulfate
FP	≤ 2.5 μm	Gelman Spectro Grade	39	mass
VOC[a]	–	Tenax, Spherocarb	39	volatile organic compounds

[a]Three urban sites only.

at any of the Elizabeth state monitoring stations. In Camden, SO_2, CO and O_3 concentrations were measured at the same site as the airborne particulate matter and volatile organic compounds. The sampling methods used for CO, SO_2 and O_3 are presented in Table 1.4. The meteorological variables were measured at the Philadelphia Airport for Camden and at Newark International Airport for the Newark and Elizabeth sampling sites.

The preceding provided information on the types of sources and distribution of sources that could provide mesoscale (1 km to 25 km) pollution impact. However, since many of the volatile organics and particulate organics can be emitted from minor source types, e.g., gas stations and dry cleaners, a qualitative microinventory was developed for the area immediately surrounding each ATEOS site. Surveys of each area were conducted with the objective of qualitatively identifying the source types that could affect the concentration of particulate mass and gaseous compounds. The information was obtained primarily by automobile and walk-through surveys. Each was supplemented by other sources of information, including the business listings in the Bell System's Telephone Directory Yellow Pages and the New Jersey Department of Environmental Protection. This type of survey could not thoroughly identify all sources and certainly not their emissions, but it was useful in qualitatively assessing the sources of many non-criteria pollutants.

MICROINVENTORY

Newark

The site is located within a very complex industrial-commercial population interface, which can be found in many cities within the midwestern and

Table 1.4. Pollutant Samples in ATEOS and Measurement Method

Parameter	Analytical Technique
inhalable particulate mass ($< 15 \, \mu m$) fine particulate mass ($< 2.5 \, \mu m$)	gravimetric
elements: Pb, V, Cd, Ni, Mn, Cu, Zn, Fe, As	Atomic absorption, spectrophotometry (arsine, generation for As)
particulate organic matter fractions	sequential Soxhlet, extraction with cyclohexane, dichloromethane, and acetone
polycyclic aromatic hydrocarbons	thin-layer chromatographic separation of PAH fraction from cyclohexane extract followed by high-pressure liquid chromatographic analysis
bacterial mutagenicity	particulate organic extracts tested in Ames assay
SO_4^{-2}	thermometric titration with $BaCl_2$
volatile organic compounds	gas chromatography and mass spectral confirmation (10%)
alkylating agents	spectrophotometric class assay
ozone[a]	chemiluminescence
sulfur dioxide	fluorescence
coefficient of haze	reflectance

[a]New Jersey Department of Environmental Protection.

northeastern U.S. The sampling station and the residential district were surrounded by a variety of large and small industrial emission sources. The sources identified within a 1-km radius of the site are shown in Figure 1.4 and the attached legends. Potential sources located 1–4 km away from the site are listed in the supplementary legend.

Several chemical manufacturing facilities are located in the northwest, west, and east. Paint, lacquer and pigment manufacturers are found to the west, southwest, and northeast. Metal fabricators and stampers are located to the east, south, northeast and west, and smelters to the west, east and south. Plating facilities can be found to the northwest, east, southwest and west. Auto body shops are located to the east, south and west. Some of these companies, particularly the metal processing operations, have more than one process. An unusual source is street side wire recovery that occurs sporadically throughout the area.

The auto body shops performed both automobile and truck repairs. Many operated with open doors during the summer, and personnel could be seen painting tractor trailers on the street. A very large truck painting facility was found to operate on side streets.

Within a 1–4 km radius of the sampling station, there are a number of

Newark

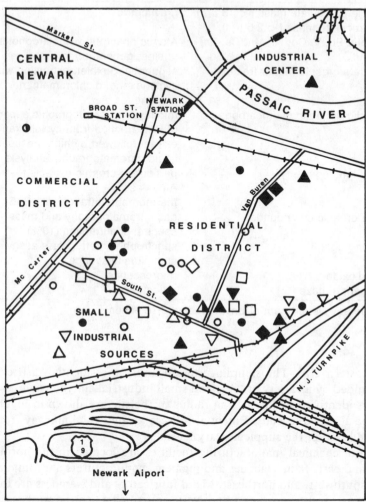

Figure 1.4. A qualitative microinventory of the area surrounding the Newark site. ▲ IPM, EOM and FPM sampling site; ◑ CO, SO$_2$ and O$_3$ monitoring site; ☐ Auto and truck body paint and repair shops; ○ Chemical manufacturers; ◆ Foundries; ● Metal fabricators (tool and die, etc.); ▲ Metal processing (smelting and refining); ▽ Metal reconditioning and finishing (alloying, plating, etc.); △ Paint spraying/paint pigment manufactures; ◇ Waste paper facility; ▼ Welding.

industrial operations similar to the ones already described (see Figure 1.4 and legend). The largest number of facilities was found south and west of the site. To the north, across the Passaic River, there were large industrial operations (i.e., smelters, foundries, chemical plants, etc.), in the Harrison-Kearny area. Port Newark is located approximately 4 km to the southeast.

In addition to the industrial activities, the area has many open, unpaved lots which are sources of windblown dust. Open areas, such as those surrounding the Conrail Railroad Lines located to the south of the site, are very large.

Besides the New Jersey Turnpike and Route 1–9 to the east and south, respectively, there are major local traffic arteries to the west (McCarter Highway), and north (Raymond Blvd., Ferry St., and Market St.) which have heavy motor vehicle traffic. Chemical, metal processing and other types of industrial facilities are also located along these major arteries. Traffic around the site is moderate, and there is a bias toward diesel trucks rather than automobiles.

The population residing in the area have mostly blue collar occupations and they live mainly in one- or two-story frame houses. There are also a few two- to three-story apartment buildings. The district is a stable population center within the City of Newark, and as can be seen from the map the population is surrounded by a variety of local sources.

Elizabeth

In contrast to the Newark site, there were no major local industrial sources within 0.5 km of the Elizabeth site; this would be indicative of the nature of source distributions associated with many commercialized urban areas. Gasoline stations were located next to and north of the building. Dry cleaners, a fast food restaurant, a car dealer and a tire store were within visual distance of the site. Auto body shops were found one to two blocks east of the site, but they were smaller than the ones in Newark and appeared to deal primarily with passenger cars. Most businesses, particularly car sales and rental dealerships, had large, blacktopped parking areas (Figure 1.5).

To the east, west and north of Westminster Avenue and N. Broad Street there were middle class residential areas with well kept, manicured lawns. Unpaved lots were almost nonexistent in the area around the site. This is an important feature of this location, and will be discussed later in the chapter on receptor modeling.

The commercial center of the city is located south of Prince and Magnolia Sts. The port of Elizabeth is found south and southeast of this area. Two kilometers northeast of the site, actually in Newark, there were a few industrial facilities: a color and dye manufacturer, a leather processor, a chemical

Elizabeth

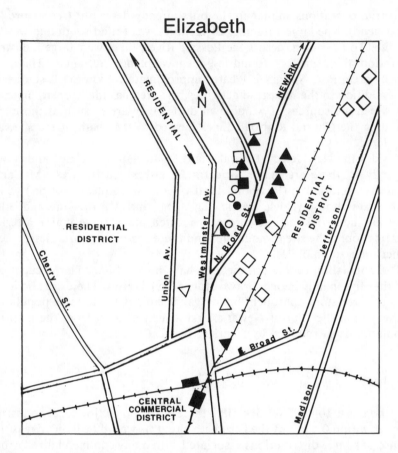

Figure 1.5.   The characteristics of the area surrounding the Elizabeth site.
▲ Sampling site; ▼ Antique dealer; ◇ Auto body paint and repair
shops; ▲ Car sales and rental dealer; □ Dry cleaning stores;
▽ Post office; △ Printing; ■ Restaurants; ○ Retail gasoline and
auto service stations.

company and a small waste oil recovery facility. To the south is an area that
includes oil refineries and oil tank farms. Traffic along Westminster Avenue
and N. Broad Street is moderately heavy, with the fleet composed mostly of
automobiles, regularly scheduled buses and some diesel trucks.

Camden

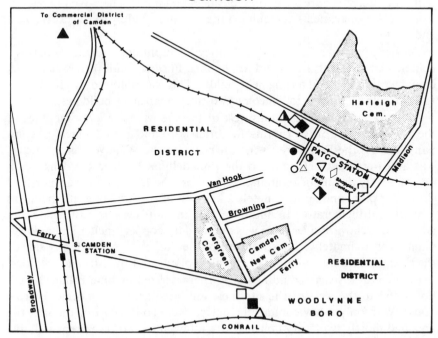

Figure 1.6. The microinventory for the area surrounding the ATEOS site in Camden. ▲ Institute for Medical Research (sampling site); ◑ R. F. Products, Inc.; ○ Thomas Nelson Book and Bible (publisher); ▽ Pioneer State Co. (shipping); □ Truck container terminal; ■ Engine rebuilder (diesel); △ American Strip Steel; ▲ Scrap metal facility; ● Channel shipping; ◇ PHC Industries; ♦ β Plastics; ◆ Community Sports field; □ Auto and truck repair shops.

Camden

The area immediately surrounding the sampling trailer in Camden was different than those observed in both Elizabeth and Newark. It was less densely populated, and the industrial and commercial enterprises were not located immediately adjacent to the population. The commercial businesses were concentrated in a shopping center, rather than spread along individual streets. There were numerous wide, grass covered, open spaces, and a Little League baseball field in the surrounding area (Figure 1.6).

Immediately to the south of the site was a shopping center with a large, paved parking lot, a train station with a very large commuter parking lot and commuter bus service. Immediately to the east and across the street from the site, there are a shipping business and a publisher. Well kept two-story garden apartments surrounded the site immediately to the north, west and south.

Further west and south of the site, along Mt. Ephraim Avenue, there was a commercial area with stores and restaurants. Further south there was a truck container terminal and an engine rebuilder. This was followed by unoccupied row housing and a few low-income two-story apartment buildings.

Approximately 1.75 km southwest of the site were the large facilities of the South Jersey Port Corporation, a train yard and a small chemical company. Across the Delaware river, just north of the Walt Whitman Bridge, was a power plant belonging to the Philadelphia Electric Co. This plant operates only during peak hours. Also across the Delaware River, north of the power plant and approximately 2 km west of the sampling site there was a municipal incinerator. In addition, 5–7 km northeast from the site and across the Delaware river there was a secondary copper smelter and a power plant. Approximately 5 km southwest of the site, on the New Jersey side of the river, there were a number of chemical plants and fuel storage facilities.

Residential districts could again be characterized as blue collar. To the north and to the west of the site there are large areas of unoccupied row houses with only a few commercial enterprises. To the east of the site, the area had mostly two-story housing with a few auto and truck repair shops.

Traffic was light to moderate around the site. The area close to the port facilities had more truck traffic. Because of the commuter parking, traffic was heavy during the rush hours.

Ringwood

As previously stated, there are no major sources affecting Ringwood with the exception of soil resuspension and natural nonanthropogenic emissions. During the summer people visit the Ringwood Mansion and use the recreational facilities in the park, which would increase local automobile traffic. Some contaminants could be expected from the nursery operations (i.e., resuspended dust and pesticides).

The microinventory surveys demonstrated that the four sampling sites have distinct characteristics which would affect the composition of the species present in the residential environment around each site. The Newark site is heavily industrialized and surrounded by traffic arteries carrying commercial and passenger vehicles. The Elizabeth site is commercial and residential in nature. The Camden site is the urban site with the fewest potential local sources, but is influenced by the Philadelphia area. Ringwood, on the other hand, is characteristically rural.

PROGRAM MANAGEMENT

In a toxic air pollution study such as ATEOS, a multidisciplinary team is necessary to facilitate the completion of various portions of the project. Programmatic structure of ATEOS is shown in Figure 1.7. The different program elements were required in order to maintain proper operation of the four sampling sites, develop efficient sample transfer protocols, conduct timely analysis of the various chemical species measured, and ultimately to have centralized management of the data.

As stated, each of the field studies was conducted for six weeks and required two weeks of preparation and approximately six weeks of followup before all samples were delivered for analyses other than mutagenic assays. Although it is difficult to put a quantitative figure on how well the different components of ATEOS functioned, the low number of lost samples ($<2\%$ for inhalable particulate matter, $<10\%$ for volatile organic compounds) and analyses would seem to be a strong indicator of the success of the ATEOS management program.

The first components in data acquisition was the field operations and the support system. The Institute of Environmental Medicine handled the coordination of the pre-campaign setup and sample preparation activities, and the day-to-day sampler performance at each site. Trained field personnel were on call each day to assist the field operators in solving minor problems over the telephone and conducting field repairs. A courier system was established as a vital link between NYU and the field sites for the transfer of spare and replacement parts and the transfer for storage of refrigerated sample filters after sampling. All filters were logged at NYU by designated personnel on the sampler transfer days and a final validity check was made on the samples.

All data management was coordinated through New York University and included a validation check for outliers, proper coding of variables and assembly of a complete data set. The data sets were eventually duplicated and a set was sent to the different program elements for their use. All pollutants sampled in ATEOS were previously shown in Table 1.1. The techniques employed for measuring each compound are shown in Table 1.4. The geometric mean and standard deviation of each pollutant measured over the course of the study are shown in Table 1.5.

The implementation of a seven-day week sampling protocol resulted in a continuous record of particulate matter and VOC air quality during New Jersey's peak pollution seasons. This type of schedule provided information on the time variation of the sampled species. Episode periods as well as nonepisode periods were sampled and the changes in air quality were documented in detail. At times, the day to day variations in air quality were dramatic. For example, in Newark, the maximum day-to-day change in

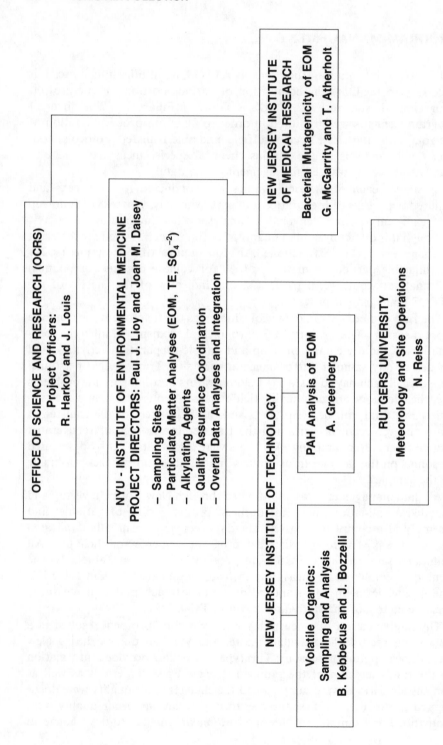

Figure 1.7. Organizational structure of the ATEOS project.

Table 1.5a. Camden Summary of Monitoring Results (Geometric Means)

Particulate-Phase pollutants	Summer 1981	Winter 1982	Summer 1982	Winter 1983	Summer Max.	Winter Max.
(μg/m^3)						
inhalable particulate matter	40.6	41.6	53.0	41.4	93.9	104.1
fine particulate matter	28.5	33.4	45.2	36.1	73.8	103.1
sulfate	10.3	11.6	15.4	10.2	31.7	23.2
CX	2.0	3.4	2.2	4.4	4.1	19.0
DCM	0.6	1.1	1.7	0.9	4.2	4.1
ACE	6.1	7.3	7.7	9.5	15.9	32.1
(ng/m^3)						
Pb	198.0	303.0	314.0	353.0	745.0	1356.0
Cd	1.0	2.0	<1.0	2.0	16.0	10.0
Ni	17.0	25.0	8.0	34.0	39.0	81.0
As	9.4	2.9	1.5	3.7	18.0	5.9
V	16.0	38.0	17.0	39.0	124.0	205.0
Fe	578.0	496.0	474.0	509.0	1142.0	3219.0
Cu	18.0	17.0	16.0	21.0	100.0	231.0
Mn	15.0	16.0	11.0	17.0	77.0	97.0
Zn	111.0	157.0	68.0	269.0	941.0	897.0
benzo(a)pyrene	0.20	0.87	0.11	0.94	2.00	4.22
benzo(e)pyrene	0.14	2.55	0.03	1.35	0.88	29.25
benzo(j)fluoranthene	0.13	0.58	0.10	0.86	1.40	4.87
benzo(b)fluoranthene	0.27	1.07	0.17	1.03	1.37	4.69
benzo(k)fluoranthene	0.15	0.53	0.09	0.55	0.73	1.82
benzo(ghi)perylene	0.35	1.88	0.24	1.13	2.10	8.82
coronene	0.29	0.92	0.14	0.56	1.21	2.65
Indeno(cd)pyrene	0.34	1.66	0.20	0.94	1.70	13.95
dibenzo(ah)anthrene	0.02	0.46	0.15	–	0.98	1.29
benz(a)anthracene	0.14	1.08	0.07	0.68	2.26	5.44
cyclopenta(cd)pyrene	–	–	0.03	0.43	1.61	2.64
dibenz(ac)anthracene	0.03	0.13	0.02	–	0.24	0.51
dibenz(aj)anthracene	–	–	0.14	0.22	1.23	0.75
chrysene	–	2.66	0.22	0.62	0.71	14.73
benzo(ghi)fluoranthene	–	–	0.12	1.29	2.75	4.97
perylene	0.06	0.01	0.01	0.15	0.43	0.51
pyrene	–	–	0.15	1.90	3.30	7.75
dibenzo(al)pyrene	–	–	0.35	0.24	1.31	1.09
benz(a)aceanthrylene	–	–	0.03	0.38	0.79	1.89
benzo(b)chrysene	–	–	0.07	–	10.84	–
benzo(a)phenanthrene	–	–	0.07	0.05	0.21	0.37
dibenzo(ak)fluoranthene	–	–	–	–	–	–
dibenzo(bk)fluoranthene	–	–	–	0.20	–	0.44
dibenzo(ae)pyrene	0.64	1.18	0.08	0.51	1.35	6.84

Table 1.5a.   (Continued)

Volatile Organic Compounds (ppbv)	Summer 1981		Winter 1982	
	Gm[a]	24-hr Max.	Gm[a]	24-hr Max.
Aromatics				
benzene	1.11	2.65	2.82	12.5
toluene	1.82	6.80	3.38	20.7
ethylbenzene	0.17	0.59	0.23	1.63
m,p-xylene	0.49	1.78	0.90	5.25
o-xylene	0.15	0.57	0.23	1.53
styrene	0.07	0.29	0.15	0.99
Chlorinated HC				
vinyl chloride	0.00	0.00	0.00	0.00
vinylidene chloride	0.39	3.82	1.02	4.52
methlyene chloride	0.72	10.2	1.19	20.2
chloroform	0.04	0.23	0.26	77.4
ethylene dichloride	0.00	0.00	0.01	1.01
ethylene dibromide	1.11	0.10	0.00	0.17
carbon tetrachloride	0.01	0.16	0.02	0.23
trichloroethylene	0.21	8.20	0.32	1.46
perchloroethylene	0.26	1.10	0.29	1.38
1,1,2-trichloroethane	0.07	0.67	0.02	16.0
1,1,2,2-tetrachloroethane	0.00	0.05	0.00	0.07
chlorobenzene	0.07	0.42	0.18	2.80
o-dichlorobenzene	0.01	0.12	0.03	0.22
p-dichlorobenzene	0.04	0.20	0.02	0.20
o-chlorotoluene	0.01	0.08	0.01	0.56
p-chlorotoluene	0.22	1.24	0.07	0.79
Miscellaneous				
nitrobenzene	0.07	1.99	0.00	0.15
1,4-dioxane	0.02	0.13	0.01	0.84

[a]Geometric mean.

Table 1.5b.   Elizabeth: Summary of Monitoring Results (Geometric Means)

Particulate-Phase pollutants	Summer 1981	Winter 1982	Summer 1982	Winter 1983	Summer Max.	Winter Max.
$(\mu g/m^3)$						
inhalable particulate matter	34.8	46.3	51.1	37.4	97.0	117.1
fine particulate matter	20.1	–	–	32.3	67.1	103.0
sulfate	11.3	10.5	13.3	9.7	30.7	18.8
CX	2.2	5.6	3.0	5.5	5.1	21.7
DCM	0.6	1.3	1.5	0.9	2.9	4.7
ACE	4.8	8.3	6.2	7.6	16.1	37.9
(ng/m^3)						
Pb	243.0	432.0	386.0	389.0	785.0	1870.0
Cd	2.0	3.0	<1.0	2.0	15.0	23.0
Ni	5.0	18.0	8.0	28.0	24.0	96.0
As	6.7	4.2	1.5	3.4	13.0	10.9
V	7.0	53.0	15.0	43.0	101.0	279.0
Fe	514.0	449.0	659.0	444.0	1570	2010
Cu	29.0	28.0	21.0	36.0	120.0	493.0
Mn	10.0	14.0	13.0	12.0	42.0	34.0
Zn	83.0	162.0	87.0	286.0	310.0	3390.0
benzo(a)pyrene	0.14	1.01	0.14	0.69	2.12	4.37
benzo(e)pyrene	0.13	11.2	0.08	1.09	1.31	236
benzo(j)fluoranthene	0.09	0.92	0.10	0.70	1.61	5.55
benzo(b)fluoranthene	0.20	1.71	0.24	0.78	3.95	10.3
benzo(k)fluoranthene	0.14	0.61	0.11	0.40	1.53	3.85
benzo(ghi)perylene	0.41	2.25	0.35	1.28	1.51	9.78
coronene	0.47	1.62	0.23	0.59	7.47	11.2
indeno(cd)pyrene	0.35	2.46	0.25	0.94	1.10	13.95
dibenzo(ah)anthracene	0.03	1.32	0.61	0.28	2.93	33.91
benz(a)anthracene	0.07	1.38	0.11	0.56	0.64	11.3
cyclopenta(cd)pyrene	–	–	0.03	0.54	1.18	10.23
dibenz(ac)anthracene	0.03	0.17	0.05	0.06	0.16	0.93
dibenz(aj)anthracene	–	–	0.23	0.33	–	2.2
chrysene	–	5.33	0.31	1.01	3.29	47.92
benzo(ghi)fluoranthene	–	–	0.12	0.99	–	13.64
perylene	0.04	0.01	0.01	0.08	0.24	2.17
pyrene	–	–	0.12	1.79	0.63	10.4
dibenzo(al)pyrene	–	–	0.05	–	1.78	1.95
benz(a)aceanthrylene	–	–	0.03	0.42	1.79	4.56
benzo(b)chrysene	–	–	0.12	–	4.44	–
benzo(a)phenanthrene	–	–	0.13	0.13	4.06	1.10
dibenzo(ak)fluoranthene	–	–	–	–	–	
dibenzo(bk)fluoranthene	–	–	–	0.19	–	–
dibenzo(ae)pyrene	0.16	2.67	0.21	0.55	27.1	16.7

Table 1.5b. (Continued)

Volatile Organic Compounds (ppbv)	Summer 1981		Winter 1982	
	Gm[a]	24-hr Max.	Gm[a]	24-hr Max.
Aromatics				
benzene	1.05	4.32	3.11	7.50
toluene	2.89	13.60	4.09	18.4
ethylbenzene	0.26	1.41	0.32	2.40
m,p-xylene	0.75	4.14	1.10	16.21
o-xylene	0.22	1.24	0.28	2.20
styrene	0.11	1.25	0.14	1.00
Chlorinated HC				
vinyl chloride	0.00	0.24	0.00	0.00
vinylidene chloride	0.35	4.20	0.52	4.4
methylene chloride	0.23	1.67	0.87	21.0
chloroform	0.10	1.06	0.29	10.1
ethylene dichloride	0.00	0.00	0.01	1.90
ethylene dibromide	0.00	0.11	0.00	0.11
carbon tetrachloride	0.01	0.18	0.03	0.36
trichloroethylene	0.27	1.82	0.46	4.70
perchloroethylene	0.39	1.43	0.44	2.80
1,1,2-trichloroethane	0.01	0.59	0.05	18.0
1,1,2,2-tetrachloroethane	0.01	0.21	0.00	0.49
chlorobenzene	0.08	0.40	0.21	1.42
o-dichlorobenzene	0.02	0.65	0.05	0.80
p-dichlorobenzene	0.07	0.46	0.02	0.26
o-chlorotoluene	0.02	0.47	0.02	0.64
p-chlorotoluene	0.25	1.76	0.14	1.02
Miscellaneous				
nitrobenzene	0.10	4.79	0.00	0.07
1,4-dioxane	0.34	1.35	0.00	4.70

[a]Geometric mean.

Table 1.5c.   Newark: Summary of Monitoring Results (Geometric Means)

Particulate-Phase pollutants	Summer 1981	Winter 1982	Summer 1982	Winter 1983	Summer Max.	Winter Max.
($\mu g/m^3$)						
inhalable particulate matter	46.3	47.8	61.4	45.7	124	202
fine particulate matter	25.6	31.7	45.5	32.3	86.7	163
sulfate	10.2	10.7	13.4	9.3	30.8	28.0
CX	3.2	5.4	3.8	5.2	9.3	30.0
DCM	0.9	1.5	1.9	1.0	3.2	7.3
ACE	6.3	10.5	7.7	8.7	21.9	43.7
(ng/m^3)						
Pb	318.0	433.0	343.0	503.0	842.0	2180.0
Cd	4.0	4.0	3.0	4.0	82.0	108.0
Ni	10.0	19.0	10.0	27.0	33.0	112.0
As	4.8	3.2	2.0	3.0	11.0	6.5
V	14.0	42.0	21.0	53.0	127.0	472.0
Fe	929.0	587.0	895.0	631.0	1850.0	2020.0
Cu	33.0	21.0	25.0	27.0	131.0	380.0
Mn	20.0	15.0	15.0	18.0	53.0	57.0
Zn	132.0	404.0	155.0	590.0	1970.0	26,500
benzo(a)pyrene	0.23	1.63	0.21	1.06	8.74	7.85
benzo(e)pyrene	0.18	2.38	0.20	1.83	6.12	27.9
benzo(j)fluoranthene	0.16	1.06	0.21	1.04	6.50	10.3
benzo(b)fluoranthene	0.27	1.35	0.34	1.09	11.2	10.0
benzo(k)fluoranthene	0.20	0.97	0.15	0.63	7.97	3.70
benzo(ghi)perylene	0.56	2.74	0.62	1.44	9.52	28.1
coronene	0.47	1.62	0.37	0.52	2.21	12.1
indeno(cd)pyrene	0.46	2.90	0.37	0.98	16.4	17.2
dibenzo(ah)anthracene	0.01	0.14	1.05	–	3.58	1.61
benz(a)anthracene	0.18	1.36	0.15	0.88	1.18	8.8
cyclopenta(cd)pyrene	–	–	0.05	0.66	0.56	6.08
dibenz(ac)anthracene	0.03	0.05	0.06	0.13	1.90	0.47
dibenz(aj)anthracene	–	–	0.28	0.37	2.46	1.37
chrysene	–	4.94	0.52	2.42	2.57	23.1
benzo(ghi)fluoranthene	–	–	0.20	1.31	12.5	9.52
perylene	0.10	0.01	0.01	0.09	3.3	12.1
pyrene	–	–	0.35	2.77	1.17	13.1
dibenzo(al)pyrene	–	–	0.14	–	0.14	2.18
benz(a)aceanthrylene	–	–	0.04	0.42	0.93	2.93
benzo(b)chrysene	–	–	1.19	–	16.3	–
benzo(a)phenanthrene	–	–	0.19	0.08	2.00	0.46
dibenzo(ak)fluoranthene	–	–	–	0.00	–	0.00
dibenzo(bk)fluoranthene	–	–	–	0.20	–	0.78
dibenzo(ae)pyrene	0.38	1.21	0.06	0.83	2.27	17.4

Table 1.5c.   (Continued)

Volatile Organic Compounds (ppbv)	Summer 1981		Winter 1982	
	Gm[a]	24-hr Max.	Gm[a]	24-hr Max.
Aromatics				
benzene	1.03	6.53	2.61	12.70
toluene	4.65	137.00	4.93	33.8
ethylbenzene	0.33	2.16	0.51	2.10
m,p-xylene	0.99	4.98	1.79	18.0
o-xylene	0.26	1.39	0.44	1.70
styrene	0.13	1.12	0.24	1.09
Chlorinated HC				
vinyl chloride	0.00	0.59	0.00	0.00
vinylidene chloride	0.38	3.09	0.31	13.3
methylene chloride	0.35	3.56	0.68	7.96
chloroform	0.06	0.40	0.21	36.0
ethylene dichloride	0.00	0.00	0.01	1.65
ethylene dibromide	0.01	0.17	0.00	0.00
carbon tetrachloride	0.01	0.21	0.02	0.19
trichloroethylene	0.50	5.21	0.59	5.13
perchloroethylene	0.45	3.40	0.42	2.33
1,1,2-trichloroethane	0.01	1.72	0.04	12.0
1,1,2,2-tetrachloroethane	0.01	0.25	0.00	0.00
chlorobenzene	0.11	0.78	0.22	0.68
o-dichlorobenzene	0.03	0.90	0.02	9.61
p-dichlorobenzene	0.05	0.73	0.06	0.12
o-chlorotoluene	0.02	0.63	0.03	0.18
p-chlorotoluene	0.21	1.07	0.17	0.77
Miscellaneous				
nitrobenzene	0.11	7.46	0.00	0.25
1,4-dioxane	0.03	0.17	0.01	1.45

[a]Geometric mean.

Table 1.5d.   Ringwood Summary of Monitoring Results (Geometric Means)

Particulate-Phase pollutants	Summer 1981	Winter 1982	Summer 1982	Winter 1983	Summer Max.	Winter Max.
(μg/m^3)						
inhalable particulate matter	23.2	25.7	33.4	21.8	63.7	43.0
fine particulate matter	9.7	25.1	22.3	20.4	34.4	43.0
sulfate	10.7	9.5	5.8	9.7	18.5	14.8
	0.8	1.4	0.9	1.2	2.2	3.2
	0.4	0.9	0.6	0.7	1.2	4.7
	3.2	4.6	3.7	3.9	7.5	10.6
(ng/m^3)						
Pb	65.0	96.0	242.0	81.0	522.0	178.0
Cd	1.0	1.0	<1.0	<1.0	3.0	2.0
Ni	5.0	5.0	10.0	13.0	22.0	32.0
As	6.0	3.7	1.3	4.5	9.0	6.6
V	6.0	20.0	29.0	30.0	164.0	175.0
Fe	326.0	138.0	426.0	150.0	831.0	421.0
Cu	13.0	6.0	63.0	18.0	77.0	29.0
Mn	7.0	6.0	14.0	4.0	24.0	10.0
Zn	42.0	23.0	61.0	38.0	158.0	83.0
benzo(a)pyrene	0.06	0.32	0.04	0.17	0.19	1.52
benzo(e)pyrene	0.03	0.35	0.03	0.32	0.43	9.36
benzo(j)fluoranthene	0.06	0.24	0.01	0.17	0.13	0.81
benzo(b)fluoranthene	0.06	0.46	0.07	0.29	0.23	0.85
benzo(k)fluoranthene	0.03	0.28	0.04	0.08	0.12	1.84
benzo(ghi)perylene	0.09	0.59	0.02	0.26	0.18	1.28
coronene	0.08	0.34	0.07	0.19	1.02	1.07
indeno(cd)pyrene	0.79	0.79	0.10	0.21	0.22	1.57
dibenzo(ah)anthracene	0.01	0.17	0.04	0.05	0.04	0.46
benz(a)anthracene	0.03	0.42	0.02	0.12	0.34	0.96
cyclopenta(cd)pyrene	–	–	0.01	0.07	0.05	0.19
dibenz(ac)anthracene	0.02	0.10	0.01	0.03	0.22	0.20
dibenz(aj)anthracene	–	–	0.08	0.08	0.34	0.32
chrysene	–	1.32	0.12	0.29	1.07	2.69
benzo(ghi)fluoranthene	–	–	0.07	0.20	3.17	1.43
perylene	0.03	0.09	0.01	0.02	0.12	0.18
pyrene	–	–	0.08	0.43	0.94	1.57
dibenzo(al)pyrene	–	–	0.04	0.03	0.01	0.08
benz(a)aceanthrylene	–	–	0.02	0.12	0.13	0.10
benzo(b)chrysene	–	–	0.01	–	2.32	–
benzo(a)phenanthrene	–	–	0.01	0.05	0.01	0.43
dibenzo(ak)fluoranthene	–	–	–	–	–	–
dibenzo(bk)fluoranthene	–	–	–	0.05	–	–
dibenzo(ae)pyrene	0.10	0.47	0.19	0.14	2.77	0.52

IPM mass was $> 100 \, \mu g/m^3$, and in Elizabeth it was $> 80 \, \mu g/m^3$ (Lioy et al., 1985).

SIZE-SELECTIVE PARTICLE SAMPLERS

Although particulate matter has been sampled by many agencies and other organizations for well over thirty years, it has usually been collected by high-volume samplers. This sampler collects particulate matter on a filter contained in a housing that is dependent on wind speed and direction and has imprecise particle cut size (average $d_{50} = 30 \, \mu m$; range from 20 to 50 μm). In addition, in any given sampling period, the sampling flow rate could vary by approximately 10% and may or may not have affected the inlet cut size. Conversely, the samplers used in the ATEOS were size-selective samplers and were required to operate at a predetermined flow in order to maintain the preselected particle cut size ($d_{50} = 15 \, \mu m$ or $d_{50} = 2.5 \, \mu m$). From Table 1.3, two IPM samplers (General Metal Works, SSI) and one fine particle sampler were located at each site. To establish a constant flow a pressure-sensitive flow controller was used on each sampler. The operation of the flow controller was quite satisfactory for both the summer and the winter study, and each sampler was calibrated before, during and after a study. A second generation of controllers was eventually used in the second and third year, and these were much better designed for durability; however, both maintained the 40-cubic feet per minute (CFM) flow to within $\pm$ 1.5%. The actual inlet characteristics for the 15-μm sampler have been shown to be affected by higher wind speeds, which caused 15 μm to be an imprecise cut size.

The fine particle samplers employed the base of a General Metal Works high-volume sampler with a 2-in. Aerotech cyclone as the sampling inlet. It was operated at 25 CFM to achieve a 2.5-μm cut size. In the winter of 1982 some of the filters were spotted or soaked by rain. The fine particle sampler moisture problem was solved by the construction of a louvered canopy (plenum) over the cyclone inlet. The plenum also helped to reduce the directionality of sampling. As a result of the improved inlet design the number of lost fine particle measurement (FPM) samples was reduced from 41 (Summer 1981 + Winter 1982) to 7 (Summer 1982 + Winter 1983).

SAMPLE TRANSFER AND STORAGE

The IPM #1 sampler was used for inorganic pollutant analysis. Storage of these filters prior to analysis required only ordinary care. This consisted of maintaining proper records, not disturbing the particulate matter on the filter, and keeping the filters in plastic bags and manila folders until the samples were analyzed. For the FPM sampler, similar procedures were used to store the filters. Transport of these samples from the field was done simultaneously with the IPM #2 organic samplers. The organic samples, however, did require special handling procedures to minimize the potential for alteration of the chemical composition. One of the first studies conducted in the ATEOS was an IPM #2 Gelman AE glass fiber filter storage experiment in 1981. The major findings for the Gelman AE glass fiber filters were 1) the different EOM fractions were stable when stored at 30°C for between 1 and 30 days, and 2) variations in the polycyclic aromatic hydrocarbons due to storage were inconclusive, due in part to the extremely low levels encountered during the ministudy. In any case, during subsequent studies filters were stored a maximum of 3 to 4 days prior to extraction.

The cold storage of the filters commenced immediately after sampling. This required a field operator to have a dry ice chest onsite and transport the filters to a designated freezer until sample pickup and delivery was made to the Institute of Environmental Medicine.

VAPOR-PHASE SAMPLER

At the time of the inception of ATEOS, the sampling protocol for measuring hazardous volatile organic compounds was unique since it involved collection of 24-hr samples on Tenax® cartridges each day for a six-week period. Of the available 78 sampling days for Newark, Elizabeth and Camden (summer of 1981, winter of 1982), analyses were made on 68, 73, and 73 samples, respectively. Quality assurance procedures were implemented throughout the study, using compound standards, and mass spectrometric verification of observed species for at least 10% (25% maximum) of the samples. Table 1.6 shows the standard recovery from the Tenax absorbant; eighteen of these compounds had recoveries >90% (Harkov et al., 1982). Thirty-eight duplicate samples were collected and analyzed during the summer and winter. The overall relative standard deviation for the duplicate samples was 48%. This was fairly consistent for each compound, and is similar to that observed in previous ambient studies. The highest deviations observed were for the lowest concentrations. The flow of the vapor-phase sampler was checked each day of sampling, and calibrated periodically throughout the campaign. A schematic drawing of the sampler used in the field is shown in Figure 1.8. During any given 24-hr period a sampler loaded with a Tenax cartridge held its flow to within 10% throughout the interval. Not all compounds obtained from the analysis were considered to be useful for quantitative determination of ambient air concentrations. Unreported compounds, such as benzaldehyde, were found to be artifacts caused by reactions on the Tenax media.

Table 1.6.   Data from Paired Samples Taken for the Volatile Organic Compound Sampler

Compound	Number[a]	Average Conc (ppb)	% Relative Standard Deviation Summer 81	Winter 82	Overall
vinyl chloride	0	–	–	–	–
vinylidene chloride	20	0.88	54	59	58
methylene chloride	22	0.60	40	29	36
chloroform	30	0.12	33	6	25
benzene	32	1.69	40	66	50
carbon tetrachloride	6	0.02	25	67	50
trichloroethylene	30	0.39	50	38	47
toluene	30	3.39	52	31	49
tetrachloroethylene	30	0.37	47	25	46
chlorobenzene	32	0.14	54	93	76
ethylbenzene	30	0.30	61	40	60
p&m-xylene	32	0.89	60	38	57
styrene	32	0.37	27	21	26
o-xylene	32	1.62	9	42	10
p-chlorotoluene	30	0.43	67	82	67
o-chlorotoluene	18	0.07	22	38	29
p-dichlorobenzene	26	0.09	56	80	53
o-dichlorobenzene	18	0.48	20	96	21
nitrobenzene	22	0.26	96	–	96
		Averages	45	50	48

[a]Number of samples in which observed.

ORGANIC EXTRACTION PROCEDURES

Details on the Soxhlet method used to sequentially extract the separate fractions of organic particulate matter are available in work by Daisey et al. (1979). The purpose is to separate organic compound fractions into nonpolar, semipolar, and polar fractions. The extraction solvents used were cyclohexane (CX) dichloromethane (DCM), and acetone (ACE), which removed nonpolar, semipolar, and polar compounds, respectively (Daisey et al., 1979). The cyclohexane fraction is found to contain most (>95%) of the polycyclic aromatic hydrocarbons, alkanes and alkenes. The other fractions contain more oxidized compounds which are either directly emitted into the atmosphere or are produced by chemical reactions. A wide variety of compound classes have been detected in particulate organic matter by various investigations. These include acids, aldehydes, ketones, phenols and quinones.

The sample duration was adequate for the detection of all fractions extracted, although there was some variability in the blank values from study to study (Table 1.7), and the DCM values had a higher degree of

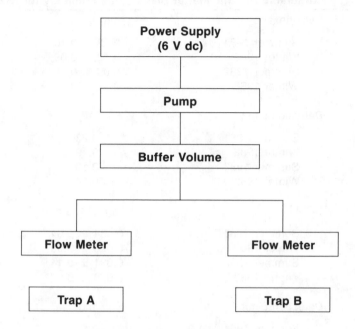

Figure 1.8.   Sampling pump assembly schematic.

uncertainty at lower concentrations. All concentrations were corrected for filter solvent blanks. Sample size is of extreme importance, and in future studies considerable care must be exercised when defining the sampling duration. If shorter time intervals of sampling are desired, some consideration should be given toward the selection of a higher-volume air sampler.

Of considerable concern in the ATEOS study was the presence of inorganic compounds in the polar extractable portion of the EOM, i.e., the acetone-soluble fraction, which would result in artifactually high mass concentration for the ACE fractions. Since nitric acid and sulfuric acid can be produced during a photochemical smog episode, it was necessary to determine if in fact the inorganic mass was the cause of the increase in ACE mass increase during such periods. Analyses of Summer 1981 episode and nonepisode ACE extract composites were completed to address the question. The results indicated that there were no significant percentage increases of inorganic nitrate or sulfate for the episode samples. A summary of these results is presented in Table 1.8, which in fact shows that the percentage of NO_3^- actually decreased. Therefore, the actual ACE results can be examined with a high degree of confidence that the observed changes were real. In

Table 1.7.   Extractable Organic Matter Blank Value Summary for ATEOS[a]

Cyclohexane	mg ± 1 s.d.
Summer 1981	0.13 ± 0.10
Winter 1982	0.10 ± 0.09
Summer 1982	0.05 ± 0.05
Winter 1983	0.11 ± 0.06
Detection Limit	mg
Summer 1981	0.23
Winter 1982	0.19
Summer 1982	0.10
Winter 1983	0.18
DCM	mg ± 1. s.d.
Summer 1981	0.084 ± 0.04
Winter 1982	0.023 ± 0.09
Summer 1982	0.031 ± 0.14
Winter 1983	0.028 ± 0.27
Detection Limit	mg
Summer 1981	0.12
Winter 1982	0.31
Summer 1982	0.44
Winter 1983	0.64
Acetone	mg + 1 s.d.
Summer 1981	0.30 ± 0.16
Winter 1982	0.37 ± 0.09
Summer 1982	0.47 ± 0.19
Winter 1983	0.69 ± 0.39
Detection Limit	mg
Summer 1981	0.46
Winter 1982	0.46
Summer 1982	0.66
Winter 1983	1.13

[a]n = 20. Blank is for 8″ × 10″ filter extracted with 200 mL of solvent

Table 1.8.   Concentrations of Inorganic Ions in Composites of ACE
Extracts from Samples Collected in Newark

Period	n/n[a]	ACE	NH_4^+	NO_3^-	SO_4^{-2}	% Inorganic Ions in ACE
			$\mu g/m^3$			
7/6–7/12/81	0/6	6.7	0.08	1.10	0.07	18.7
7/18–1/24/81	2/6	7.9	0.07	1.37	0.58	25.6
7/28–8/1/81	0/4	4.0	0.01	0.80	0.02	20.8
8/1–8/5/81	3/4	10.9	0.10	1.60	0.05	16.1
8/5–8/9/81	2/4	6.6	0.07	0.43	0.08	8.8
8/9–8/14/81	5/5	13.4	0.14	1.67	0.06	14.0

[a]Ratio of number of episode day ACE extracts in composite to total number of ACE extracts in composites.

future investigations of this sort care must be taken to separate inorganic materials extracts in the more polar-extractable fraction.

MUTAGENICITY

The persistent question of what species are directly related to the mutagenic activity of the atmospheric particulate mass, and which will therefore be of concern for potential health effects in man, could not be answered in this study. Although this was never the intent of the analyses conducted in the ATEOS study, it is an issue which requires much further investigation. The purpose of conducting the Ames Assay (Ames et al., 1975) on the ATEOS samples was to obtain some insight on the levels (# revertant/m^3) and the activity (# revertant/μg) of the EOM, as a function of season and urban setting. Composite samples were bioassayed with five Ames strains with and without S9 activation. The TA98 strain was generally found to be the most positive.

Initially, the assays were completed on six-week composites of the air samples for each location and each of the three extracts. This approach provided valuable information on intersite variability and seasonal differences in the mutagenic activity of a number of strains, with and without S9 microsomal activation. However, the association with other variables, such as PAH, was difficult to establish. Noting this problem, the Summer 1982 and Winter 1983 samples were handled somewhat differently. In these cases an attempt was made to modify the compositing procedures to obtain more detail on the variability in the mutagenic activity in photochemical smog episodes during the summer and local stagnation episodes during the winter. The basic six-week composite protocol was still used for the intersite and seasonal trends.

TRACE ELEMENTS

Because of design considerations a selected number of toxic elements and elemental tracers were analyzed in each sample by the standard technique of atomic absorption spectrophotometry (AAS). The materials for analysis were obtained by extracting the filters using a $HClO_4/HNO_3$ digestion procedure. The trace elements selected were Ni, Fe, Cd, V, Pb, Cu, As, Mn, and Zn. Quality control of the analytical procedure was derived from the NBS Standard #1648, urban particulate matter.

In the course of the study it became apparent that data on a number of other elements were necessary in order to make more detailed estimates of the sources contributing to the particulate mass at each site. In part, this was a result of the lack of a good tracer for diesels at the time the proposal was written, and the lack of information on the potential significance of wood burning emissions in the New Jersey areas. Archived samples were subsequently analyzed for Ba and K, which are potential tracers for diesels and woodburning, respectively (Pierson and Brachaczek, 1983, and Cooper and Watson, 1980).

The elements detected in ATEOS were usually found in quantifiable levels; however, in some samples, especially for Ringwood, the levels were below the detection limit. The detection limits determined for ATEOS are found in Table 1.9. In addition, the number of values below the statistical detection limit are listed as a percentage of the total number of samples for each site. However, it should be noted that the detection limits are low, and the reason for the levels being below these limits is the presence of very low concentrations in the ambient atmosphere, and not high blank values.

PAH ANALYTICAL PROCEDURES

Collection Procedure

The technique of high-volume sampling on glass fiber filters is perhaps the one most widely employed, giving ATEOS an advantage of comparability with other investigations. There is no question that <4-membered ring compounds suffer volatility losses, which were not compensated for through backup adsorption media such as Tenax or polyurethane plugs. The high winter/summer ratios observed for benz(a)anthracene, benzo(ghi)fluoranthene, cyclopenta(cd)pyrene, pyrene and chrysene are testimony to this problem. However, the >5-membered ring compounds, which include benzo(a)pyrene and most of the carcinogenic PAHs, suffer negligible volatility losses. The detection limits for the sampled compounds are found in Table 1.10. It is probable that low-volume sampling could significantly reduce these volatility losses, but at the price of sensitivity. Another

Table 1.9. Calculated AA Detection Limits

Element	Average Blank Total $\mu g \pm 1$ s.d.	Detection Limit μg	Detection Limit[a] $\mu g/m^3$	% Samples[b] Below Detection Limit
Pb	6.72 ± 8.59	15	0.021	0
Cd	0.232 ± 0.218	0.44	0.0006	11
Mn	1.72 ± 0.689	2.4	0.0033	0.2
Fe	58.0 ± 14.3	72	0.10	0.6
Zn	39.2 ± 21.2	60	0.083	19.6
Cu	5.84 ± 4.08	9.8	0.011	21.6
Ni	3.34 ± 1.01	5.2	0.007	13.3
V	1.79 ± 1.57	3.3	0.0046	4.5
As	0.006 ± 0.005	0.014	6×10^{-6}	(assuming 2154.9 m^3 for 3-day composite)
As	0.010 ± 0.007	0.021	4×10^{-6}	(assuming 5028 m^3 for 7-day composite)

$$\text{Detection Limit} = \text{mean value of blank} + \left[\text{one s.d.} \times \sqrt{2/n}(t_{0.10,n-1} + t_{0.20,n-1}) \right]$$

$$\text{for } n = 19, \sqrt{2/n}(t_{0.10,n-1} + t_{0.20,n-1}) = 0.97$$

$$n = 18, \sqrt{2/n}(t_{0.10,n-1} + t_{0.20,n-1}) = 0.99$$

[a]Assuming 718.3 m^3 volume for analyzed portion of filter.
[b]All campaigns included in this analysis: Winter 1982, 1983; Summer 1981, 1982.

Table 1.10.   Detection Limits for PAH Analyses in ATEOS[a]

PAHs	Quantitation Limits ng/m³	PAHs	Quantitation Limits ng/m³	PAHs	Quantitation Limits ng/m³
PYR	0.12	BkF	0.08	3-Me-chlor	0.04
			0.01		0.04
BaA	<0.03				
		DBacA	0.1	IcdP	0.03
					0.05
CHRY	<0.07				0.03
		BaP	0.01		
BjF	0.08			DBaePy	0.04
		DBajA	0.48		
			1.1		
BaF	<0.03			BBCHRY	0.08
		DBalPy	0.03		
BeP	0.01			DBaePy	0.04
					0.14
		DBahA	0.01		
BjF	0.08				
		DBalPy	0.03		
BeP	0.10		0.04		
				Anth	0.03
					0.03
BaF	<0.16	DBahA	0.01		
				Cor	0.01
BbF	0.02	BghiP	0.01		
			0.05		
				CcdP	<0.04
PER	0.06				
				BghiF	1.12
BkF	0.08				1.65
					0.01
DBacA	0.10				

[a]The detection limits are subject to constraints due to co-elutors and the use of different detectors.

problem was reactivity of PAH. Very little quantitative information is available, and the vast majority of ambient studies have the same problem. Sample preservation and integrity were judged to be as good as or better than that attained by the vast majority of researchers. Soxhlet extraction is time consuming, but a well employed technique. The extraction efficiency of cyclohexane is generally lower for PAH than benzene, toluene, and even methylene chloride. However, relatively little (<10%) PAH was extracted by methylene chloride following cyclohexane extraction. The advantage of cyclohexane extraction is that certain other organics which interfere with PAH analyses are not extracted by this solvent. Isolation of the PAH class was accomplished through thin-layer chromatography (TLC) on silica gel. This is somewhat time consuming (ca. 1 hr/sample) and PAHs are known to be photochemically active on silica gel. Despite this reactivity and the fact that normal fluorescent lights were in use in the labs (TLC plates were protected from light during the chromatographic process), PAH recoveries from samples applied to glass fiber filters generally exceed 90%, with the most reactive parent PAH being recovered to the extent of 80% (the recovery of 3-methylcholanthrene was 55%). A quicker PAH separation technique would involve solvent extraction and back extraction. However, the TLC technique offers the ability to separate many compound classes. Individual PAH compounds were separated by high-performance liquid chromatography (HPLC) and quantitated by ultraviolet (UV) absorbance and fluorescence. The advantages of HPLC over gas chromatography (GC) are speed and sensitivity of analysis (smaller sample size), the use of multiple detectors, and the applicability of UV and fluorescence techniques.

A Vydac 201 column was used; this column is widely used currently for PAH work (it is the column employed by the National Bureau of Standards). Detection was by absorbance at two UV wavelengths (280 nm and 365 nm) and fluorescence (350 nm excit., > 440 nm emiss.). A strength of the multiple detector technique was the ability to quantitate up to three co-eluters. It must be recognized, however, that quantitation of three co-elutors offered no checks of compound identity other than retention time. On the other hand, quantitation of two co-elutors allowed such independent checks through comparison of peak height ratios for two detectors.

A problem with the HPLC technique employed was the variability of retention times and compound resolution on some occasions. The reasons for this variability were threefold: a) variability in HPLC columns yielding anywhere between 17,000 and 22,000 theoretical plates, b) variability in column temperature, and c) variation in sample matrix. Standards were run each day that samples were run to keep a check on these conditions.

The different absorbance/fluorescence characteristics of the PAH require unique quantitation criteria for each. In some cases, two co-elutors would not exhibit all three spectroscopic signals. Thus, one was quantitated alone using its unique response, and the number was applied iteratively to the other simultaneous equations. Under certain circumstances, it was found that benzo(a)pyrene, dibenzo(aj)anthracene, and naphthacene (or tetracene) co-eluted. Since naphthacene has not been reported in ambient air and the major losses were observed during workup of naphthacene standards, it was assumed that none was present. We found excellent quantitative results using this assumption. Benzo(e)pyrene, benzo(j)fluoranthene and benzo(a)fluoranthene also co-elute occasionally. This posed a problem since no independent confirmation of compound identities was then available. Columns were changed when this occurred since it usually was an early signal of column deterioration.

REFERENCES

Ames, B. N., McCann, J., and Yamasaki, E. (1975) *Mut. Res*, 113, 347–364.

Bernstein, D. M., Kneip, T. J., Kleinman, M. T., Riddick, R., and Eisenbud, M. (1974). In: *Trace Substance in Environmental Health VIII*. A Symposium, Hempshill, D. D., Ed., University of Missouri, Columbus, MO.

Cooper, J. A., and Watson, G. J. (1980), *JAPCA* 30, 1116–1125.

Daisey, J. M., Leyko, M. A., Kleinman, M. T., and Hoffman, E. (1979), *Ann NY Acad. Sci.*, 322: 125–141.

Environmental Protection Agency (1980), Potential Atmospheric Carcinogens – Phase 1. Identification and Classification. U.S. EPA, Research Triangle Park, NC.

Frieberg, L., Piscator, M., Nordberg, G. F., and Kjellstrom, T. (1974), Cadmium in the Environment, 2nd ed., CRC Press, Cleveland, OH.

Goyer, R. A., and Chisolm, J. J. (1972), Lead. In: *Metallic Contamination and Human Health*, 57–86. D. H. Lee, Ed., Academic Press, Inc., New York.

Harkov, R., Kebbekus, B., Bozzelli, J., Lioy, P. J., and Daisey, J. M. (1984), *Sci. Total Environ.* 38, 259–274.

Harkov, R. (1982) *Sci. Total Environ.* 26, 67–85.

Hickey, R. J., Schaff, E. P., and Clelland, R. C. (1967), Relationship Between Air Pollution and Certain Chronic Disease Death Rates. *Arch. Environ. Health*, 15, 728–738.

Hoffman, D., and Wynder, E. L. (1977), Organic Particulate Pollutants: Chemical Analysis and Bioassays for Carcinogenicity. In: *Air Pollution*. A. C. Stern, Ed., 3rd Ed. 2: 361–455, Academic Press, Inc., New York.

Hoffman, D., and Wynder, E. L. (1976), Environmental Respiratory Carcinogenesis. In: *Chemical Carcinogens*, Ch. 7, S. E. Searle, Ed., American Chemical Society, Washington, DC.

Leikauf, G., Yeates, D. B., Wales, K. A., Spektor, D., Albert R. E., and Lippmann, M. (1981), *J. Amer. Indust. Hyg. Assoc.*, 41,273–282.

Lioy, P. J., Samson, P. J., Tanner, R. L., Leaderer, B. P., Minnich, T., and Lyons, W. (1980), *Atmos. Environ.*, 14, 1391–1407.

Lioy, P. J., Daisey, J. M., Greenberg, A., and Harkov, R. (1985), *Atmos. Environ.*, 19, 429–436.

Lioy, P. J., Vollmuth, T., Lippmann, M. (1985), *JAPCA*, 35, 1068–1071.

Lioy, P. J., and Daisey, J. M. (1986), *Environ. Sci Technol.* 20, 8–14.

Lippmann, M., Leikauf, G., Spektor, D., Schlesinger, R.B., and Albert, R.E. (1981), *CHEST*, 80: 873S–876S.

Lippmann, M., Lioy, P. J., Leikauf, G., Green, K. B., Baxter, D., Morandi, M., Pasternack, B. S., Fife, D., and Speizer, F. E. (1983), Effects of Ozone on the Pulmonary Function of Children. *Advances in Modern Environmental Toxicology*, 423–446.

Lucky, T. D., and Venugopal, B. (1977), Metal Toxicity in Mammals. I., 129–188, Plenum Press, New York.

National Academy of Sciences. (1979), Airborne Particles, University Park Press, Baltimore, MD.

National Academy of Sciences. (1977), Medical and Biological Effects of Environmental Pollutants—Copper, National Academy of Sciences, Washington, DC.

National Research Council. (1977), Medical and Biological Effects of Environmental Pollutants—Carbon Monoxide, National Academy of Sciences, Washington, DC.

National Research Council. (1978), Sulfur Oxides. Committee on Sulfur Oxides. Board of Toxicology and Environmental Health Hazards, Assembly of Life Sciences, National Academy of Sciences, Washington, DC.

National Research Council. (1974), Manganese. Committee on Biological Effects of Atmospheric Pollutants, National Academy of Sciences, Washington, DC.

Pierson, W. R., and Brachaczek, W. W. (1983). *Aerosol Sci. Technol.* 16, 1–40

Pitts, J. N., Jr., Grosjean, D., and Mischke, T. M. (1977), Mutagenic Activity of Airborne Particulate Organic Pollutants, Toxicol. Lett., 1, 65–70.

Preussman, V. R., Schneider, H., and Epple, F. (1969), *Arzneinei Hed-Forschung*, 19, 1059–1073.

Stock, P. (1960), *Brit. J. Cancer*, 14, 397–410.

Sunderman, F. W. The Metabolism and Toxicology of Nickel (1977), In: *Clinical Chemistry and Chemical Toxicology of Metals*, 231–259, S. S. Brown, Ed. Elsevier Biomedical Press, New York.

Talcott, R., and Wei, E. (1977), *J. Nat. Cancer Inst.*, 58, 449–451.

Thatcher, R. W. Lester, M. L., McAlaster, R., and Horst, R. (1982), *Arch. Environ. Health* 37, 159–166.

Chemical Composition of Inhalable Particulate Matter—Seasonal and Intersite Comparisons

Joan M. Daisey

CHAPTER CONTENTS

Chemical Composition of Inhalable Particulate Matter—Seasonal and Intersite Comparisons

INTRODUCTION

The ATEOS study provided an extensive and unique set of aerosol composition measurements. The purpose of this chapter is to present an overview of the composition of inhalable (D_{50} = μm) particulate matter (IPM) at the four ATEOS sites in both absolute ($\mu g/m^3$) and relative terms, their intersite and seasonal variability, and relationships to the nature of the sources and meteorology at these sites.

MAJOR ORGANIC AND INORGANIC AEROSOL COMPONENTS

The major organic and inorganic components of IPM which are discussed in this chapter are the extractable organic fractions, sulfate, resuspended soil, and certain trace elements (Pb, Fe, V, Zn, As). In some instances, measurements of elemental and organic carbon were made and are included. It should be kept in mind that these are bulk aerosol measurements and that IPM is a mixture of individual particles which can range in composition from totally inorganic to totally carbonaceous.

Extractable organic matter (EOM) is defined here as the sum of three fractions extracted sequentially with increasingly polar solvents. The nonpolar cyclohexane-soluble fraction (CX), which is extracted first, contains polycyclic aromatic hydrocarbons (PAHs), aliphatic hydrocarbons, nitro-PAH and other unidentified nonpolar compounds (Daisey et al., 1981; Schwartz et al., 1981; Harkov et al., 1984; Butler et al., 1985 in press, Daisey et al., 1986). Both anthropogenic and natural sources can contribute to the CX fraction. Analyses of ambient samples (Schuetzle et al., 1975;

Appel et al., 1979), and of emissions from combustion and industrial sources (Graedel, 1978) indicate that many of the compounds in this fraction are primary in nature, i.e., they are directly emitted from sources. Natural sources of nonpolar organics include waxes from plants (aliphatic hydrocarbons) and forest fires (PAHs and other hydrocarbons) (Simoneit and Mazurek, 1981).

The moderately polar dichloromethane-soluble (DCM) fraction has been shown by infrared spectroscopy and chemical class analyses (Daisey et al., 1982; Butler et al., in press) to contain carbonyl compounds (aldehydes, ketones, quinones), phenols, and carboxylic acids. Such compounds can originate from both anthropogenic and natural sources and may be primary or secondary (i.e., formed in the atmosphere via chemical reactions and gas-to-particle conversion). Carboxylic acids, such as palmitic and stearic acid, for example, can originate from plant waxes and pollen (Simoneit and Mazurek, 1981). The dicarboxylic acids, e.g., succinic acid, are believed to be produced by photochemical oxidation (Grosjean et al., 1978). Phenols, which are toxic to both mammalian and bacterial cells, have been found in motor vehicle exhaust (Graedel, 1978; Schuetzle et al., 1981). Aldehydes, ketones and quinones have been identified in emissions from combustion sources (Graedel, 1978; Schuetzle et al., 1981), in smog chambers (Grosjean, 1982), and in aerosols collected during photochemical pollution episodes (Grosjean, 1982).

The polar acetone-soluble fraction (ACE), which is extracted last, contains both organic and inorganic components (Daisey et al., 1984; Butler, 1985). Infrared spectra indicate the presence of carbonyl-containing compounds (Daisey et al., 1982; 1984); chemical class analyses have indicated the presence of carboxylic acids, aza-arenes and alkylating/acylating agents (Butler et al., in press) in this fraction. The term alkylating agents includes a number of chemical classes, such as epoxides and aziridines, which react with p-(nitrobenzyl)pyridine or other reagents which detect compounds which can transfer an alkyl group. The reagent p-(nitrobenzyl) pyridine was used in a class assay to detect alkylating/acylating agents. Levels of this class in the ACE fraction are reported as equivalents of styrene epoxide, a positive control used in the assay. Many alkylating agents are direct-acting (require no metabolic activation) mutagens and/or carcinogens. The ACE fraction has also been shown to contain varying amounts of inorganic species, chiefly NH_4^+ and NO_3^- (Daisey et al., 1984). Inorganic ions constituted 9–26% of this fraction in IPM samples collected in Newark during the summer of 1981 (Daisey et al., 1984). The percentage of these inorganic ions in the ACE fraction was lower during the photochemical smog episodes than during other periods. Both primary emissions and secondary atmospheric reactions can contribute to ambient levels of the ACE fraction (Daisey et al., 1984; Daisey and Hopke, 1984; Morandi, 1985).

The sulfate component of the aerosol can be present as H_2SO_4,

NH_4HSO_4, $(NH_4)_2SO_4$, or other sulfate salts. Measurements made in the United States during summer periods suggest that aerosol sulfate in urban areas is at least partially neutralized by NH_3 (Lioy et al., 1980c; Appel et al., 1982; Cobourn and Husar, 1982). As H^+ and NH_4^+ were not measured during ATEOS, for some composition comparisons it has been assumed that sulfate was present as NH_4HSO_4.

Resuspended soil constitutes a significant fraction of airborne particles, particularly of the coarse fraction, i.e., particles greater than about 2 μm mass mean aerodynamic diameter (MMAD). Estimates of the contributions of resuspended soil to IPM at the ATEOS urban sites were based on the receptor source apportionment models developed for those sites by Morandi (1985). At the rural Ringwood site, levels of resuspended soil were estimated based on concentrations of Fe and Mn, assuming that Fe and Mn were 5.4% and 0.20% of the resuspended soil, respectively.

Although there were a limited number of measurements of elemental carbon, they are included in the discussion. For Elizabeth, 10 and 36 samples were analyzed for organic carbon (OC) and elemental carbon (EC) from the Summer 1982 and Winter 1983 campaigns, respectively. For Camden, OC and EC were measured in 12 samples from Summer 1982 and 5 samples from Winter 1982; for Ringwood, there were 34 and 38 samples from Summer 1981 and Winter 1983, respectively.

INTERSITE COMPARISONS

Tables 2.1 and 2.2 summarize the geometric mean concentrations of inhalable particulate matter (IPM), its major components, and selected trace elements for each season at each site. Average concentrations of fine particulate matter (FPM) (D_{50} = 2.5 μm) and of alkylating agents in the ACE fraction are also presented.

Average concentrations of IPM and FPM were highest at the Newark site, followed by Camden and Elizabeth, which had similar levels. Lowest concentrations were observed at Ringwood. Fine particles constituted varying percentages of IPM at these sites, ranging from 94% in Ringwood during winter to 58%, on average, at Elizabeth during summer 1981.

Sulfate was a major component of IPM at all sites in all seasons (Tables 2.1 and 2.2). Average concentrations of sulfate were generally quite similar at all sites ($\sim$ 10 μg/m^3) for both winter and summer. Daily variations in sulfate concentrations showed high intersite correlations (Lioy et al., 1980a); this is consistent with the secondary nature of sulfate aerosol and regional influences on the distribution of sulfate aerosol during both summer and winter.

Concentrations of extractable organic particulate matter (EOM) showed more intersite variation than did sulfate, ranging from 13.8 μg/m^3 (4-season

Table 2.1. Geometric Mean Concentrations[a] of IPM, Its Major
Components, Selected Trace Elements and Alkylating Agents
in Newark and Elizabeth, N.J., $\mu g/m^3$

Species	Summer 1981	Winter 1982	Summer 1982	Winter 1983
		NEWARK		
IPM	43.3(1.6)	47.3(1.5)	61.4(1.4)	45.7(1.8)
FPM	25.6(2.9)	36.9(1.5)	45.5(1.4)	34.3(1.8)
SO_4^{-2}	10.2(2.1)	10.4(1.4)	13.4(1.6)	9.3(2.4)
CX	3.2(1.4)	5.4(1.6)	3.8(1.3)	5.2(2.0)
DCM	0.85(1.4)	1.46(1.7)	1.90(1.4)	1.00(1.8)
ACE	6.3(1.8)	10.4(1.5)	7.8(1.5)	8.7(2.0)
Pb	0.318(1.6)	0.433(1.8)	0.343(1.6)	0.503(1.9)
Fe	0.929(1.6)	0.587(1.7)	0.895(1.6)	0.631(2.0)
Zn	0.132(2.1)	0.404(2.3)	0.155(2.7)	0.590(5.1)
V	0.014(2.3)	0.042(2.1)	0.021(2.5)	0.053(2.3)
As	0.005(2.7)	0.003(1.4)	0.002(1.8)	0.003(1.7)
Alk. Agents[b]	0.045(3.4)	0.094(2.1)	0.034(2.2)	0.036(2.4)
EC	–	3.3(1.5)[c]	3.0(1.2)[c]	–
OC	–	5.9(1.7)[c]	4.1(1.4)[c]	–
		ELIZABETH		
IPM	34.8(1.7)	46.2(1.5)	51.1(1.4)	37.1(1.9)
FPM	20.1(2.9)	44.1(1.4)	–	32.2(2.0)
SO_4^{-2}	11.3(1.9)	10.5(1.4)	13.3(1.6)	9.7(1.6)
CX	2.2(1.5)	5.6(1.9)	3.0(1.3)	5.5(2.1)
DCM	0.60(1.6)	1.28(1.7)	1.5(1.5)	0.85(2.0)
ACE	4.8(1.7)	8.4(1.5)	6.2(1.5)	7.6(2.1)
Pb	0.243(1.9)	0.432(1.8)	0.386(1.4)	0.389(2.3)
Fe	0.514(1.8)	0.449(1.9)	0.659(1.5)	0.444(2.7)
Zn	0.083(2.2)	0.162(2.0)	0.087(1.9)	0.286(2.7)
V	0.007(3.4)	0.053(2.3)	0.015(2.0)	0.043(3.4)
As	0.006(1.6)	0.004(1.7)	0.002(1.9)	0.003(1.5)
Alk. Agents[b]	0.015(4.8)	0.091(2.6)	0.040(2.0)	0.044(2.1)
EC	–	2.3(1.6)[c]	1.7(1.4)[c]	3.8(2.2)
OC	–	7.1(2.2)[c]	2.1(1.8)[c]	6.3(2.4)

[a]Geometric deviation presented in parentheses; 39 samples per season, for
first three seasons, 38 samples for winter, 1983.
[b]Alkylating agents reported as equivalents of styrene epoxide.
[c]Six samples from Winter, 1982 and 12 samples from Summer, 1982 analyzed
for EC and OC.

Table 2.2. Geometric Mean Concentrations[a] of IPM, Its Major Components, Selected Trace Elements and Alkylating Agents in Camden and Ringwood, N.J., $\mu g/m^3$

Species	Summer 1981	Winter 1982	Summer 1982	Winter 1983
		CAMDEN		
IPM	40.6(1.6)	41.6(1.4)	53.0(1.3)	41.4(1.6)
FPM	28.5(2.3)	33.4(1.5)	45.1(1.4)	36.1(1.7)
SO_4^{-2}	10.3(2.3)	11.6(1.3)	15.4(1.5)	10.2(1.6)
CX	2.1(1.3)	3.4(1.5)	2.1(1.4)	4.4(1.9)
DCM	0.67(1.5)	1.12(1.7)	1.67(1.6)	0.85(2.1)
ACE	6.1(1.6)	7.3(1.8)	7.7(1.5)	9.5(1.8)
Pb	0.198(1.7)	0.303(1.5)	0.262(1.5)	0.353(2.0)
Fe	0.578(1.5)	0.496(1.7)	0.474(1.6)	0.509(1.8)
Zn	0.111(2.2)	0.157(1.6)	0.068(2.2)	0.269(1.8)
V	0.016(2.4)	0.038(1.4)	0.017(2.0)	0.039(2.4)
As	0.009(1.6)	0.003(1.7)	0.002(1.3)	0.004(1.3)
Alk. Agents[b]	0.024(3.1)	0.062(1.6)	0.027(1.9)	0.057(1.6)
EC	–	2.0(1.2)[c]	1.3(1.6)[c]	–
OC	–	5.2(1.6)[c]	2.2(1.8)[c]	–
		RINGWOOD[d]		
IPM	23.2(1.7)	25.7(1.4)	33.4(1.4)	21.8(1.5)
FPM	–	25.1(1.4)	22.3(1.7)	20.4(1.6)
SO_4^{-2}	10.7(1.7)	9.3(1.3)	5.8(1.6)	9.7(1.2)
CX	0.8(1.4)	1.4(1.6)	0.9(1.6)	1.2(1.7)
DCM	0.45(2.0)	0.92(1.6)	0.58(1.7)	0.75(2.4)
ACE	3.2(1.6)	4.6(1.7)	3.7(1.6)	3.9(1.6)
Pb	0.065(2.4)	0.096(1.6)	0.242(1.6)	0.081(1.7)
Fe	0.326(1.6)	0.138(1.8)	0.426(1.5)	0.150(1.6)
Zn	0.042(1.5)	0.023(2.2)	0.061(1.6)	0.038(1.6)
V	0.006(2.7)	0.020(2.0)	0.029(2.6)	0.030(4.0)
As	0.002(1.4)	0.004(1.3)	0.001(1.7)	0.005(1.2)
Alk. Agents[b]	0.008(1.4)	0.051(1.6)	0.028(2.7)	0.082(1.3)
EC	0.35(1.5)	0.86(2.2)[c]	–	0.60(1.5)
OC	1.9(1.9)	2.9(1.9)[c]	–	1.52(2.6)

[a]Geometric deviations given in parentheses; 39 samples per season for first three seasons and 38 samples for Winter 1983.
[b]Alkylating agents reported as equivalents of styrene epoxide.
[c]Five samples from Winter 1982 and 12 samples from Summer 1982 analyzed for EC and OC.
[d]For Ringwood, 13 3-day composites analyzed except for EC and OC.

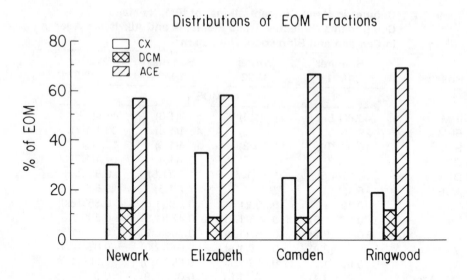

Figure 2.1   Distributions of EOM fractions.

average) at Newark, to 11.4 μg/m^3 at Elizabeth, 11.6 μg/m^3 at Camden, and only 5.5 μg/m^3 at Ringwood. The average distributions of the three EOM fractions also differed among the three sites (Figure 2.1). The differences between Ringwood and the three urban sites, and between Camden and Newark, and Camden and Elizabeth, were statistically significant (p = 0.05). The differences were tested for statistical significant using a t-test for pairwise (2 sites at a time) comparisons of the means of the percentage of a given fraction in the total EOM. It should be noted that the percentages of the three fractions are not statistically independent, i.e., if the percentage of CX is higher at one site, then the percentage of another fraction must be lower at that site. Nonpolar (CX-soluble) organics were 32% and 34% of EOM at the Newark and Elizabeth sites, respectively, but only 25% at the Camden site and 20% at Ringwood. The moderately polar (DCM) fraction was about 9% of EOM at the three urban sites, but only 12.5% at the Ringwood site. Polar organics (ACE) were 58% of EOM at Newark and Elizabeth, but averaged 65% and 67% at Camden and Ringwood. The greater percentage of ACE at the latter sites is probably related to fewer local sources and "aging" of the aerosol, i.e., the aerosol contains greater proportions of secondary organics produced by oxidation of gaseous organics and gas-to-particle conversion. There is evidence of this from the greater proportions of ACE observed during periods of photochemical smog during the summers (Daisey et al., 1984) and from measurements made at a very remote site in the Arctic (Daisey et al., 1981). At the latter site, ACE constituted 71% to 85% of EOM during periods in which the Arctic site was influenced by long-range transport of polluted air masses form the mid-latitudes. The Camden site is influenced by emissions from both local sources and from Philadelphia, which is frequently upwind of this site. Pollutants emitted in Philadelphia would be expected to undergo some reactions during transport. Greater proportions of secondary particulate organics would also be expected at the Ringwood site, which has few local sources but is influenced by the eastern U.S. regional background aerosol.

Average concentrations of alkylating agents also showed intersite variations. The highest average concentration was observed for the Newark site, followed closely by Elizabeth. Levels of the alkylating agents at Camden and Ringwood were similar and about half of those seen at the other two urban sites. Individual compounds within this class have not been identified and may differ significantly among the ATEOS sites. Butler (1985; Butler et al., in press) has reported evidence of intersite differences in the alkylating agents in ACE extracts from a number of U.S. and overseas cities.

In this study, trace elements in the ambient aerosol were of interest chiefly as tracers of sources of particulate matter. Lead, however, is a toxic metal which can have adverse health effects at sufficiently high levels. Concentrations of Pb measured at the ATEOS sites were always well below the annual average standard of 1.5 $\mu g/m^3$. The highest average concentrations of Pb were observed in Newark and Elizabeth; levels in Camden were about 75% of those at the other urban sites, while the average concentrations at the Ringwood site were about half those measured at the urban sites. Concentrations of Pb at the urban sites were much lower than those measured at these sites during the previous decade (U.S. DHEW, 1968; U.S. EPA, 1971; 1972), due principally to increased use of unleaded fuels for motor vehicles. At current levels, sources of Pb other than motor vehicles have become proportionately more significant. Morandi (1985) has reported evidence of contributions to airborne Pb from resuspended soil, oil burning and small-scale smelting at the Newark site which taken together accounted for more than half of the airborne lead.

Intersite variation in V paralleled those observed for Pb, i.e., levels were highest in Newark and Elizabeth and somewhat lower in Camden. Vanadium concentrations at the Ringwood site were about half those observed in Camden. Oil burning for space heating and power production is the principal source of V in this part of the United States and the intersite variations in concentrations are what would be expected, i.e., higher levels at urban than rural sites.

Average concentrations of Fe and Zn showed a different intersite pattern than that seen for Pb and V. The highest average concentrations of Fe and Zn were observed in Newark, while concentrations were similar in Elizabeth and Camden. Resuspended soil is the major source of Fe in most urban areas, but certain industries in the Newark area probably contributed to the higher concentration of Fe at this site. The higher concentrations of Zn are also attributable to industrial sources in Newark. A zinc smelter, located to the north, frequently impacted the Newark site. In one instance, the 24-hr average concentration of Zn reached 26 $\mu g/m^3$!

Average concentrations of As have also been included in Tables 2.1 and 2.2, as this element is not generally measured but can provide evidence of coal-burning contributions to the aerosol (Tuncel et al., 1985). Concentrations of As were generally low and were similar at the urban and rural sites, suggesting that the chief sources of this element are resuspended soil and/or regional sources to the west (Sheffield and Gordon, 1985; Tuncel et al., 1985) where coal is burned in power plants.

SEASONAL VARIATIONS

Seasonal differences in the atmospheric concentrations of IPM and its components reflect seasonal differences in the sources of aerosols, atmospheric chemistry and meteorology. During the winter, there is a large increase in the amount of fuel burned for space heating in the eastern United States. No. 2 fuel oil and gas are the major fuels used for this purpose, but there has been increased wood burning in recent years (Harkov and Greenberg, 1985). There are also seasonal differences in the statewide distributions and levels of emissions from motor vehicle and industrial sources due to summer vacations for both adults and school children.

Seasonal differences in atmospheric chemistry are strongly influenced by meteorology. During the summer, the east coast is often impacted by synoptic-scale photochemical oxidant episodes characterized by high temperatures, atmospheric stagnation, and high levels of ozone and sulfate aerosol (Lioy and Samson, 1979; Lioy et al., 1980a; Wolff and Lioy, 1980; Parekh and Husain, 1981). Lioy et al. (1980a) have shown that these episodes are frequently associated with slow-moving high pressure systems and long-range transport from the Midwest. During wintertime, with lower temperatures and sunlight intensity and a greater preponderance of winds from the less populated Northwest, there is much less photochemistry and aerosol transport from other regions of the United States. In wintertime, local (< 10 km) emissions from space heating, traffic, and mesoscale meteorology become more significant.

Seasonal differences in aerosol composition at the ATEOS sites were quite striking for certain components. Figure 2.2 presents the average compositions of IPM for the two summers combined and two winters combined (based on arithmetic averages for additivity); geometric mean concentrations of IPM and FPM are given below each figure.

In general, for IPM there was no consistent pattern of summer-winter seasonal difference in concentrations (Tables 2.1 and 2.2). There was, how-

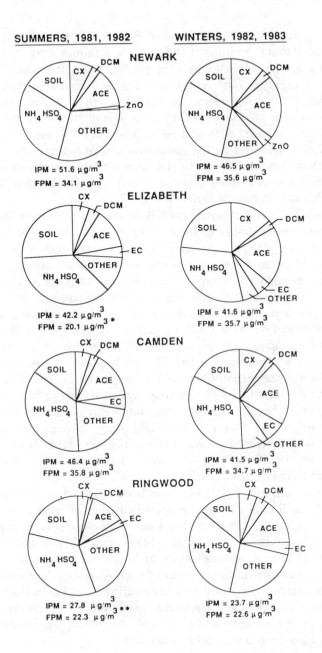

SUMMERS, 1981, 1982   WINTERS, 1982, 1983

NEWARK

IPM = 51.6 μg/m^3
FPM = 34.1 μg/m^3

IPM = 46.5 μg/m^3
FPM = 35.6 μg/m^3

ELIZABETH

IPM = 42.2 μg/m^3 *
FPM = 20.1 μg/m^3 *

IPM = 41.6 μg/m^3
FPM = 35.7 μg/m^3

CAMDEN

IPM = 46.4 μg/m^3
FPM = 35.8 μg/m^3

IPM = 41.5 μg/m^3
FPM = 34.7 μg/m^3

RINGWOOD

IPM = 27.8 μg/m^3 **
FPM = 22.3 μg/m^3

IPM = 23.7 μg/m^3
FPM = 22.6 μg/m^3

Figure 2.2 Average composition of inhalable particulate matter during two summers and two winters.

ever, an increase in the proportion of FPM in IPM for the winter aerosol compared to that of summer at all four sites, although it was a much smaller difference at the Newark site. Fine particulate matter was 75% of IPM (arithmetic average of individual days) for the Newark site during the summers and 77% during winter. At the Elizabeth, Camden and Ringwood sites, FPM as a percentage of IPM, for the summer and winter seasons, respectively, averaged 60% and 90%,82% and 86%, and 77% and 90%. This reflects decreases in the concentrations of resuspended soil (coarse particles) during winter due to the frozen ground and increases in fuel combustion for space heating during winter. Fuel combustion tends to generate fine particle aerosol (Friedlander, 1977).

Figure 2.2 shows that sulfate (as NH_4HSO_4) was the largest component of IPM, constituting about one-third of the mass at all sites for both summer and winter sampling periods. Average sulfate concentrations were generally similar at 10 $\mu g/m^3$ for the winter and summer at all four sites (Tables 2.1 and 2.2), although the average concentration at Ringwood was only 5.8 $\mu g/m^3$ for the summer 1982 campaign. While the average levels of sulfate showed few seasonal differences, the ranges of the sulfate measurements for summer and winter did differ significantly. For the two summers combined, sulfate levels were greater than 20 $\mu g/m^3$ for 15 or more sampling days out of 78 days at each urban site. For the two winters, sulfate concentrations were greater than 20 $\mu g/m^3$ for only 2 days in Newark and 4 days in Camden out of a total of 77 sampling days. A similar pattern was observed for Ringwood, but the extremes were not as obvious due to the analysis of 3-day composites. Summertime peaks were strongly associated with synoptic-scale meteorology and movements of air masses from the Midwest (Lioy et al., 1980a). In between such episodes, levels of sulfate generally decreased to only a few $\mu g/m^3$.

Peak concentrations of H_2SO_4 have been observed in rural areas of New York (Morandi et al., 1983), Pennsylvania (Pierson et al., 1980) and New Jersey (Lioy et al., 1980a) during summertime episodes of high levels of ozone and sulfate. Tanner et al. (1981), and Lioy et al. (1980c) have reported evidence of neutralization of H_2SO_4 aerosols as air parcels with H_2SO_4 are transported through urban areas. Although the chemical form of the sulfate aerosol was not determined during the ATEOS study, Tanner et al. (1981) have concluded that during the summer aerosols are likely to be more acidic in rural areas and more neutral in urban regions, although acid episodes have been reported in urban areas.

Resuspended soil was one of the major components of IPM at all of the ATEOS sites. At the three urban sites, there were no significant seasonal differences in the concentrations of resuspended soil nor in the percentage of this component in IPM. A significant seasonal difference was observed for the Ringwood site; resuspended soil was estimated to have contributed

6.5 $\mu g/m^3$ (21% of IPM) during the two summer seasons, but only 2.8 $\mu g/m^3$ (11% of IPM) during the winter seasons.

The carbonaceous components of the aerosol showed the greatest seasonal differences, both in concentration and as a percentage of IPM. During the summertime, total EOM averaged about 23% of IPM at the urban sites and 17% at the Ringwood site. During wintertime, EOM increased to about 35% of IPM at the urban sites and 25% of IPM at Ringwood. Wintertime concentrations of EOM averaged 16.0 $\mu g/m^3$, 14.6 $\mu g/m^3$ and 13.2 $\mu g/m^3$ at the Newark, Elizabeth and Camden sites, and 6.4 $\mu g/m^3$ at Ringwood. The greatest wintertime increase in total EOM concentrations, 62%, was observed at the Elizabeth site; increases at the other sites were about 33%, relative to summertime. The concentrations of both the CX and ACE fraction of EOM were significantly greater during the winter than the summer sampling periods. The CX concentrations increased 52% to 116% on average, while those of ACE increased by 22% to 46% during the winter. The DCM fraction did not show any seasonal pattern of variation.

The distribution of particulate organic matter among nonpolar and polar fractions also showed seasonal differences which were statistically significant ($p < 0.05$) for the CX and ACE fractions in most instances. The nonpolar CX fraction, as a percentage of EOM, increased during the winter at all sites. Nonpolar organics increased from about 29% to 38% at the Elizabeth site and from 21% to 29% at the Camden site for the winter relative to summer. More modest average increases of 2% to 3% were observed for the other sites, but these were also statistically significant. The ACE fraction was a smaller percentage of EOM in the winter than in the summer at the Elizabeth, Camden and Ringwood sites, but not at the Newark site. Concentrations of polycyclic aromatic hydrocarbons, a significant component of the CX fraction, were also higher during the winters than the summers (Harkov et al., 1984; Harkov and Greenberg, 1985) as discussed in Chapter 4. Concentrations of elemental and organic carbon were higher for the winter than the summer sampling periods. Although these measurements are generally fewer in number than those of EOM, the seasonal pattern is consistent with that observed for EOM.

Alkylating agents, found in the polar ACE fractions, were also higher during the winter than the summer at both the urban and nonurban sites. We suspect that the nature of these alkylating agents as well as their levels vary with season, based on the work of Butler (Butler, 1985; Butler et al., 1985b). The chemical identities of these alkylating agents, however, remain to be elucidated.

The wintertime increases in concentrations of EOM and related carbonaceous species are probably due principally to increased emissions from space heating. This is supported by parallel increases in the average concentrations of V at all four ATEOS sites. Concentrations of Pb were also generally higher in the winter than the summer, suggesting a greater winter-

Table 2.3. Long-term Trends in the Concentrations of Sulfate and
Particulate Organics at Two Sites in New Jersey[a]

Site	Year	SO_4^{-2}	BSO
		μg/m³	
Newark	1964	16.3	9.7
	1968	13.2	7.1
	1981–83[b]	10.7	5.6
Camden	1964	19.4	9.7
	1968	19.8	5.9
	1981–83[b]	11.7	4.0

[a]NASN data for TSP samples; annual geometric means reported.
[b]ATEOS averages are geometric means for four seasons (153 days).

time contribution to EOM from motor vehicles as well. Lower wintertime temperatures, however, can also contribute to increased particulate organic matter through a shift in the distribution of organics between vapor and particulate phases. Evidence of this has been reported for the polycyclic aromatic hydrocarbons (Yamasaki et al., 1982).

LONG-TERM TRENDS

The average concentrations of sulfate and the sum of the CX plus DCM fractions measured during the ATEOS study have been compared to NASN data for total suspended particulate matter (TSP) in Table 2.3. Since these species are concentrated in the accumulation mode of the aerosol, differences in the particle sizes of the samples should have a minimal effect on the averages. For the purposes of the comparison, it has been assumed that the sum of the organic matter extracted with CX and DCM is comparable to that extracted with benzene (BSO) in the NASN data; this is a reasonable approximation based on the extraction efficiencies reported by Grosjean (1975). Differences in sampling protocols and exact locations of sampling sites may also contribute to any differences seen. However, if the differences are large and consistent with other data, the direction if not the absolute magnitude of the differences is likely to be real.

Average concentrations of sulfate appear to have declined by 30% to 40% in both Newark and Camden over the past two decades. Altshuller (1980) has reported evidence of declines in SO_4^{-2} concentrations for urban sites in the northeastern United States between 1963 and 1977 for three out of four quarters of the year. The third quarter (summer) trend, however, was an increase during the late 1960s and early 1970s, with a subsequent

Table 2.4.   Long-term Trends in Concentrations of Lead at Two Sites in New Jersey[a]

Year	$\mu g/m^3$	
	Newark	Camden
1964	0.9	–
1966	0.9	0.8
1978	0.9	0.8
1979	0.6	–
1980	0.3	–
1981	0.4	0.2
1981–83[b]	0.4	0.3
1984	–	0.3

[a]Annual geometric means reported; NASN data for TSP samples for 1964, 1966; data for later years from E. Finfer, U.S. Environmental Protection Agency, New York, N.Y.
[b]Geometric means for four seasons from the ATEOS study (153 days).

decline. The overall decrease between 1963–65 and 1976–78 was about 6 $\mu g/m^3$ and was similar to that suggested by the data in Table 2.3.

The concentrations of nonpolar particulate organic matter also appear to have declined significantly since the 1960s in Newark and Camden. The direction and magnitude of the decrease are consistent with declines in BSO reported by Faoro (1975) for 32 U.S. urban stations between 1960 and 1970, from an average of 10.6 $\mu g/m^3$ to 4.8 $\mu g/m^3$. This decrease is believed to be due largely to a decrease in the use of coal for home space heating (Faoro, 1975). The current levels of CX plus DCM observed in the ATEOS study (4.0–5.6 $\mu g/m^3$) for the three urban sites suggest smaller changes between 1970 and the early 1980s. During this period emissions per kilometer from automobiles declined due to the increased percentage of autos equipped with catalytic converters. Emissions from space heating have increased in the past decade due to the greater use of wood as a fuel (Harkov and Greenberg, 1985).

Table 2.4 presents annual average concentrations of Pb at Newark and Camden for years between 1964 and 1984 for which data are available. The levels of Pb appear to have decreased by half at these sites. Such a decline is consistent with the reduced use of leaded gasoline. Declines in airborne Pb in recent years have been noted in other cities (Lioy et al., 1980b; Saltzman et al., 1985).

COMPARISONS WITH OTHER CITIES

Table 2.5 presents a comparison of the average concentrations of IPM, SO_4^{-2} and EOM for the ATEOS urban sites to those measured at several non-U.S. cities and New York City during wintertime sampling periods. The concentrations of IPM, SO_4^{-2} and EOM were comparable for all four U.S. cities, and were generally lower than those observed overseas. In Beijing, where coal is used for space heating, cooking, and power production, concentrations of SO_4^{-2} and EOM were approximately three and two times greater, respectively, than those observed in the U.S. cities where No. 2 oil and gas (New Jersey) or low-sulfur residual oil (New York City) are used. Concentrations of particulate matter (TSP) were also much higher in Beijing than in the U.S. cities, even when allowances are made for differences in the particle size of the samples.

In Mexico City, motor vehicles are a major area source, and leaded gasoline is used (Lioy et al., 1983). Petroleum refineries, and petrochemical and metallurgical industries also contribute to air pollution. Although winter space heating is not generally required, during colder periods tires are sometimes burned in the poorer areas to provide heat. Levels of SO_4^{-2} were similar to those measured in the United States, but the concentrations of EOM were among the highest ever seen in our laboratory, and four times greater on average than in the U.S. cities.

In Rio de Janeiro, although levels of IPM were about 70% higher than those observed in the eastern U.S. cities, the concentrations of EOM were comparable, and sulfate concentrations were approximately half those observed in the United States (Daisey and Miguel, in press). Motor vehicles fueled by gasohol and hydrated ethanol and diesel buses are major sources of inhalable particulate matter and EOM. Due to the tropical climate, no space heating is required in winter. Oil is used for power production and is probably the major source of sulfate aerosol.

It is clear from these comparisons that air quality at the ATEOS urban sites during the early 1980s is generally better than that observed in cities which have not instituted controls on emissions from motor vehicles or on SO_2 sources.

SIGNIFICANCE FOR HUMAN HEALTH

Concentrations of ambient particulate matter, as well as its sulfate, organic, and lead components, were significantly lower at the urban ATEOS sites during the early 1980s than during the 1960s. Current levels of airborne particulate matter measured at the ATEOS sites would generally be regarded as posing little health risk. Recent results from the Harvard Six

Table 2.5. Comparisons of Atmospheric Concentrations of Particulate Pollutants at the ATEOS Urban Sites and Other Cities, $\mu g/m^3$

City	Period	Particle Size	Particulate Matter	SO_4^{-2}	EOM	Reference
Newark	Winter, 1982, 1983	IPM	46.5	9.8	16.0	This work
Elizabeth	Winter, 1982, 1983	IPM	41.6	10.1	14.6	This work
Camden	Winter, 1982, 1983	IPM	41.5	10.9	13.2	This work
New York City	Winter, 1979–80	RSP	29.4	5.1	11.9	This work
Beijing, China	Mar., Apr., 1981	TSP	267	~30	23.9	Daisey et al., 1983
Mexico City, Mexico	Feb., 1982	TSP	268	12.6	44.9	Lioy et al., 1983
Rio de Janeiro, Brazil	Aug., Sept., 1984[a]	IPM	68.8	4.4	17.2	Daisey and Miguel, in press

[a]Wintertime in the southern hemisphere.

Cities Study, however, indicate that exposures to moderately elevated levels of particulate matter increase the risk of bronchitis and lower respiratory illnesses in preadolescent children (Ferris et al., 1985; Ware et al., 1985).

Concentrations of particulate matter and its major components were also substantially lower at the ATEOS urban sites than in the cities of Beijing and Mexico City, where emissions controls have not yet been instituted. Although the consequences of lower exposures at these New Jersey sites were likely to be a reduced risk of adverse health effects, the risk reduction may not be directly proportional to the differences in the concentrations of these pollutants. Both the particle size distribution and chemical composition can significantly influence the health impact of airborne particulate matter. A 50% reduction in TSP may have little influence on the health impact of airborne particles if only the very coarse, nonrespirable particles are reduced. The influence of particle size on the health effects of airborne particles has been recognized by the regulatory community through the proposed PM-10 standard.

Chemical composition can be equally significant with respect to the health impact of airborne particles. For example, sulfate aerosol, in the form of sulfuric acid, is more damaging to lung function than is ammonium sulfate (Lippmann et al., 1982; Leikauf et al., 1984; Schlesinger, 1984).

The ATEOS study has shown that the chemical compositions of urban aerosols can differ significantly between seasons, even when levels of IPM vary little. Wintertime increases in the concentrations of extractable organic matter did not reflect changes in IPM levels or in the mutagenic activity of the urban aerosols (Chapter 5). The relative proportions of the three organic fractions and levels of alkylating agents and polycyclic aromatic hydrocarbons (Chapter 4) showed significant seasonal variations which are likely to affect the biological activity of the aerosols. Relationships between chemical composition and mutagenic activity are not well understood at present. Even less is known about the human health consequences of such compositional differences in airborne aerosols. It would be prudent in future epidemiological studies to give some considerations to the chemical compositions of the particulate matter to which populations are exposed and their relationships to the health outcomes under investigation.

ACKNOWLEDGMENTS

Special thanks to Dr. George Wolff of General Motors Research Laboratories and Dr. Roger Tanner of Brookhaven National Laboratory for the carbon analyses done on the ATEOS samples.

REFERENCES

Altshuller, A. P. (1980), *Environ. Sci. Technol. 14*: 1337–1249.

Appel, B. R., Hoffer, E. M., Kothny, E. L., Wall, S. M., Haile, M., and Knights, R. (1979), *Environ. Sci. Technol. 13*: 98–104.

Appel, B. R., Hoffer, E. M., Tokiwa, Y. and Kothny, E. L. (1982), *Atmos. Environ. 16*: 589–593.

Butler, J. P. (1985), *Separation and Characterization of Biologically Significant Chemical Classes in Airborne Particulate Organic Matter*. Doctoral dissertation, New York University.

Butler, J. P., Kneip, T. J., Mukai, F., and Daisey, J. M. (1985), In: *Short-Term Bioassays in the Analysis of Complex Environmental Mixtures*. IV. M. Waters et al., Eds., Plenum Publishing Corp., New York, NY, pp. 322–246.

Butler, J. P., Kneip, T. J., and Daisey, J. M. In press.

Cobourn, W. G., and Husar, R. B., (1982), *Atmos. Environ. 16*: 1441–1450.

Daisey, J. M., Hershman, R. J., and Kneip, T. J. (1982), *Atmos. Environ. 16*: 2162–2168.

Daisey, J. M., and Hopke, P. K. (1984), Paper No. 84-16.4, Proceedings of the 77th Annual Meeting of the Air Pollution Control Association, San Francisco, CA, June 24–29.

Daisey, J. M., Miguel, A. H. In press. *J. Air Poll. Control Assoc.*

Daisey, J. M., McCaffrey, R. J., and Gallagher, R. A. (1981), *Atmos. Environ. 15*: 1353–1363.

Daisey, J. M., Kneip, T. J., Wang, M.-X., Ren, L.-X. and Lu, W.-X. (1983), *Aerosol Sci. Technol. 2*: 407–415.

Daisey, J. M., Morandi, M., Wolff, G. T., and Lioy, P. J. (1984), *Atmos. Environ. 18*: 1411–1419.

Daisey, J. M., Allen, C. F., McGarrity, G., Atherhold, T., Louis, J., McGeorge, L., and Lioy, P. J. (1986), *Aerosol Sci. Technol. 5*: 69–80.

Faoro, R. B. (1975), *J. Air Pollut. Control. Assoc. 25*: 638–640.

Ferris, Jr., B. G., Spiezer, F. E., Ware, J. H., Spengler, J. D., and Dockery, D. W. (1986), In: *Aerosols: Research, Risk Assessment and Control Strategies*, S. D. Lee et al., Eds., Lewis Publishers, Chelsea, MI.

Friedlander, S. K. (1977), *Smoke, Dust and Haze: Fundamentals of Aerosol Behavior*. John Wiley and Sons, Inc., New York.

Graedel, T. E. (1978), *Chemical Compounds in the Atmosphere*. Academic Press, New York.

Grosjean, D. (1975), *Anal. Chem. 47*: 797–805.

Grosjean, D. (1982), *Environ. Sci. Technol. 16*: 254–262.

Grosjean, D., Van Cauwenberghe, K., Schmid, J. P., Kelley, P. E., and Pitts, J. N., Jr. (1978), *Environ. Sci. Technol. 12*: 313–316.

Harkov, R., and Greenberg, A. (1985), *J. Air Pollut. Control Assoc. 35*: 238–243.

Harkov, R., Greenberg, A., Darack, F., Daisey, J. M., and Lioy, P. J. (1984), *Environ. Sci. Technol. 18*: 287–291.

Leikauf, G. D., Spektor, D. M., Albert, R. E., and Lippmann, M. (1984), *Am. Ind. Hyg. Assoc. J. 54*: 285–292.

Lioy, P. J., and Samson, P. J. (1979), *Environ. Int. 2*: 77–83.

Lioy, P. J., Daisey, J. M., Reiss, N. M., and Harkov, R. (1980a), *Atmos. Environ. 17*: 2321–2330.

Lioy, P. J., Mallon, P., and Kneip, T. J. (1980b), *J. Air Pollut. Control Assoc. 30*: 153–156.

Lioy, P. J., Samson, P. J., Tanner, R. L., Leaderer, B. P., Minnich, T., and Lyons, W. (1980c), *Atmos. Environ. 14*: 1391–1407.

Lioy, P. J., Falcon, Y., Morandi, M. T., and Daisey, J. M. (1983), *Aerosol Sci. Technol. 2*: 166.

Lippmann, M., Schlesinger, R. B., Leikauf, R. B., Spektor, D., and Albert, R. E. (1982), *Ann. Occup. Hyg. 26*: 677–690.

Morandi, M. (1985), *Development of Source Apportionment Models for Inhalable Particulate Matter and its Extractable Organic Fractions in Urban Areas of New Jersey*. Doctoral dissertation, New York University.

Morandi, M., Kneip, T. J., Cobourn, W. G., Husar, R. B., and Lioy, P. J. (1983), *Atmos. Environ. 17*: 843–848.

Parekh, P. P., and Husain, L. (1981), *Atmos. Environ. 15*: 1717–1725.

Pierson, W. R., Brachaczek, W. W., Truex, T. J., Butler, J. W., and Korniski, T. J. (1980), *Ann. N.Y. Acad. Sci. 338*: 145–173.

Saltzman, B. E., Cholak, J., Schaefer, L. J., Yeager, D. W., Meiners, B. G., and Svetlik, J. (1985), *Environ. Sci. Technol. 19*: 328–333.

Schlesinger, R. B. (1984), *Environ. Res. 34*: 268–279.

Schuetzle, D., Cronn, D., Crittenden, A. L., and Charlson, R. J. (1975), *Environ. Sci. Technol. 9*: 838–845.

Schuetzle, D., Lee, F. S.-C., Prater, T. J., and Tejada, S. B. (1981), *Intern. J. Environ. Anal. Chem. 9*: 93–144.

Schwartz, G. P., Daisey, J. M., and Lioy, P. J. (1981), *Am. Ind. Hyg. Assoc. J. 42*: 258–263.

Sheffield, A., and Gordon, G. E. (1986), In: TR-5, *Transactions, Receptor Methods for Source Apportionment, Real World Issues and Applications*, T. G. Pace, Ed., Air Pollution Control Association, Pittsburgh, PA, pp. 9–22.

Simoneit, B. R. T., and Mazurek, M. A. (1981), *CRC Critical Rev. Environ. Control 11*: 219–276.

Tanner, R. L., Leaderer, B. P., and Spengler, J. D. (1981), *Environ. Sci. Technol. 15*: 1150–1153.

Tuncel, S. G., Olmez, I., Parrington, J. R., Gordon, G. E., and Stevens, R. L. (1986), In: TR-5, *Transactions, Receptor Methods for Source*

Apportionment, Real World Issues and Applications, T. G. Pace, Ed., Air Pollution Control Association, Pittsburgh, PA, pp. 116–126.

U.S. Department of Health, Education and Welfare. (1968), *Air Quality Data from the National Air Sampling Networks and Contributing State and Local Networks*. 1966 Edition.

U.S. Environmental Protection Agency. (1971), *Air Quality Data for 1967 from the National Air Surveillance Networks and Contributing State and Local Networks*.

U.S. Environmental Protection Agency. (1972), *Air Quality Data for 1968 from the National Air Surveillance Networks and Contributing State and Local Networks*.

Ware, J. H., Ferris, B. G., Jr., Dockery, D. W., Spengler, J. D., Stram, D. O., and Speizer, F. E. (1986), *Amer. Rev. Resp. Diseases 133:* 834–842.

Wolff, G. T., and Lioy, P. J. (1980), *Environ. Sci. Technol. 14:* 1257–1260.

Yamasaki, H., Kuwata, H., and Miyamoto, H. (1982), *Environ. Sci. Technol. 16:* 189–194.

CHAPTER 3

Volatile Organic Compounds
at Urban Sites in New Jersey

Ronald Harkov, Barbara Kebbekus, Joseph W. Bozzelli

CHAPTER CONTENTS

Volatile Organic Compounds at Urban Sites in New Jersey

INTRODUCTION

Many of the modern industrial and commercial processes utilized by our society involve the application of organic solvents (Verschueren, 1983). Through the transport, storage, transfer, and use of these materials, releases can occur to the atmosphere. In addition, the use of liquid fuels by motor vehicles can also result in evaporative and tailpipe losses of organic substances to the air environment (NAS, 1981). A significant quantity of the organic materials emitted into the atmosphere as solvents or through the use of liquid fuels can be classified as volatile organic compounds (VOCs). In the present context, VOCs are defined as organic substances with a vapor pressure greater than or equal to 0.02 psi.

A significant number of VOCs have been shown to be associated with chronic health problems in the workplace, including various forms of cancer (IARC, 1982). In addition, long-term animal bioassays have identified many VOCs as carcinogens (Haseman et al., 1984). Since VOCs have been shown to have direct health impact potential and play an important role in the formation of ozone and smog aerosols (NAS, 1977), these pollutants were incorporated as part of the New Jersey Project on Airborne Toxic Elements and Organic Substances (ATEOS).

METHODS

Although many VOCs are used widely in industrial and commercial operations, a selection process was established for the ATEOS project to allow inclusion of only those substances which were used in significant quantities in New Jersey and which could have some relationship to human health in the state (Table 3.1). Since information pertaining to usage of a particular VOC was often difficult to obtain, we relied heavily on national assessments conducted for the U.S. EPA which tended to focus on large (> 10,000 tons/yr emissions) facilities (SAI, 1981a,b; Mara and Lee, 1978a,b; Suta, 1979; Mara et al., 1979) and *Chemical and Engineering News* reports (CEN, 1981) on national organic chemical production. Carcinogenicity data were primarily obtained from NCI reports (HEW, 1976–1980) and IARC monographs (1972–1978), with supplementary information coming from review articles in the technical literature (Fishbein, 1979a,b). Ten of the eleven VOCs regulated under New Jersey Administrative Code 7:27–17 – "Control and prohibition of air pollution by toxic substances" – were included in the study, as were projections on increased coal, municipal solid waste, and sewage sludge combustion emissions in the state (Harkov et al., 1982). Monitoring and analytical technology for VOCs were evaluated for reproducibility and application to more long-term monitoring efforts in complex environmental situations.

Sampling

Collection of VOC samples occurred during Summer 1981 and Winter 1982 and at only the three urban locales: Newark, Elizabeth, and Camden. The VOC aspect of the ATEOS project was limited in scope compared to the inhalable particulate matter studies as a result of cost constraints and due to our previous experience of sampling for this class of contaminant in rural areas (Harkov et al., 1981). All samples were collected as previously described (Harkov et al., 1983; 1984) utilizing low-volume diaphragm pumps and tandem cartridges packed with either Tenax-GC or Spherocarb. A sodium thiosulfate-treated glass fiber prefilter was used to reduce any ozone reactions on the adsorbent and was placed in front of the two stainless steel adsorbent cartridges. Ambient air was pumped through the cartridges at 10 to 15 ml/min for 24 hr.

Analysis

All cartridges were analyzed by thermal desorption and gas chromatography (GC). For the Tenax-GC cartridges, samples were separated on a fused-silica SP2100 column with 90% of the effluent being sent to a flame ionization detector (FID) for quantitation and 10% to an electron capture detector (ECD) for qualitative confirmation of the halogenated hydrocarbons. The Spherocarb samples were separated on a carbosieve B 60/80 mesh column and quantified by FID. Since identification of organic compounds by GC is primarily accomplished by retention times, mass spectrom-

Table 3.1.   Production (U.S.) Sources and Health Impacts of Selected VOCs

Pollutant	Production (lb/yr)	Major Emission Sources[a,b,c]	Mutagenic or Carcinogenic Potential
vinyl chloride	7.5×10^9/1980[a]	monomer production pvc production and use	Animal and human carcinogen[d]
vinylidene chloride	–	copolymer production of Sarans	Animal and human carcinogen[e]
methylene chloride	6.6×10^8/1978[b]	paint remover solvent degreasing	animal carcinogen[f]
chloroform	3.3×10^8/1978[c]	fluorocarbon production	animal carcinogen[d]
ethylene dichloride	11.8×10^9/1980[a]	vinyl chloride monomer production automobiles	animal carcinogen[e]
carbon tetrachloride	7.5×10^8/1978[c]	fluorocarbon production	animal and human carciniogen[d]
trichloroethylene	2.9×10^8/1978[c]	metal degreasing	animal carcinogen[e]
tetrachloroethylene	7.3×10^8/1978[b]	dry cleaning metal degreasing	animal carcinogen[b]
1,1,2-trichloroethane	–	solvent applications	animal carcinogen[b]
1,1,2,2-tetrachloroethane	–	solvent applications	animal carcinogen[b]
chlorobenzene	3.6×10^8/1978[c]	solvent applications	animal carcinogen[e]
o-dichlorobenzene	5.9×10^7/1978[c]	solvent applications	suspected carcinogen[e]
p-dichlorobenzene	5.5×10^7/1978[c]	deodorizing	suspected carcinogen[e]
o-chlorobenzene	–	solvent applications	suspected carcinogen[e]
p-chlorobenzene	–	solvent applications	suspected carcinogen[e]
ethylene dibromide	2.2×10^8/1976[b]	automobiles	animal carcinogen[d]
benzene	12.7×10^9/1980[a]	automobiles	human and animal carcinogen[d]
toluene	11.9×10^9/1980[a]	solvent applications automobiles	–
ethylbenzene	8.5×10^9/1980[a]	solvent applications automobiles	–
o-xylene			
p-xylene	11.1×10^9/1980[a]	solvent applications	–
m-xylene		automobiles	
styrene	7.5×10^9/1980[a]	copolymer formation	suspected carcinogen[4]
1,4 dioxane	–	paint production	animal carcinogen[4]
nitrobenzene	8.5×10^8/1978[c]	aniline production	–

[a]*Chemical Eng. News* (1981).
[b]Singh et al. (1981).
[c]SAI (1981).
[d]IARC (1982).
[e]Fishbein (1979a,b).
[f]NTP (1985).
[g]Haseman et al. (1984).

etry (MS) was utilized as an additional confirmation step in compound identification and quantitation. Approximately 10% and 25% of the Tenax-GC cartridges were also analyzed by a Varian MAT44 quadrapole mass spectrometry equipped with a fused-silica SP2100 column for the summer of 1981 and winter of 1982, respectively. A full description of the method can be found in Kebbekus and Bozzelli (1983).

Data Assurance

A summary of the sampling and analysis quality assurance/quality control (QA/QC) results for the ATEOS project has recently been presented (Harkov et al., 1985). The QA/QC plan for the VOCs included calibration of the samplers, training personnel to use the samplers, checking daily flow rates and flow stability studies. The laboratory plan included analysis of spiked samples, sample trap blanks, use of quantitative and qualitative standards, trap cleaning, recovery and breakthrough studies. Based on 30 side-by-side duplicate samples, the overall precision of the VOC method was ±48% for an average VOC concentration of 0.67 parts per billion by volume (PPBV).

VOC CONCENTRATION PATTERNS

The geometric mean concentrations for twenty-five selected VOCs in New Jersey during the summer and winter seasons are shown in Tables 3.2 and 3.3, respectively. The lower limit of detection for all compounds was 0.005 ppbv, while the quantitation limits were 0.05 ppbv for aromatics and 0.10 ppbv for the chlorinated VOCs. Five to six compounds were generally found in unquantifiable amounts during the two monitoring campaigns, while two to five pollutants were quantified in 20% to 75% of the samples, and fifteen to seventeen substances were quantified in 75% of the samples. The mass spectrometric analysis verified the presence of the selected pollutants detected by GC in virtually 100% of the samples subjected to this analytical measure.

Carbon tetrachloride and ethylene dibromide proved to be particularly troublesome during this study. Laboratory recovery studies indicated that these compounds had a recovery of only about 40% from Tenax-GC cartridges, as opposed to 80% to 110% for the remaining compounds. The levels reported here for carbon tetrachloride and ethylene dibromide are likely to be underestimates of the actual concentrations in New Jersey. Due to breakthrough problems it is also known that Tenax-GC is not the ideal adsorbent for lightweight halogenated hydrocarbons (Brown and Purnell, 1979; Cox, 1983). Thus the methylene chloride results are probably deflated

Table 3.2. Geometric Means of VOC Concentrations[a] July 6 to August 16, 1981

	Newark			Elizabeth			Camden		
	Mean	Number of Samples	Number Present	Mean	Number of Samples	Number Present	Mean	Number of Samples	Number Present
vinyl chloride	0.00	38	2	0.00	37	0	0.00	38	1
vinylidene chloride	0.38	35	33	0.35	34	33	0.36	30	28
methylene chloride	0.35	35	33	0.23	35	34	0.72	32	28
chloroform	0.06	39	35	0.10	38	31	0.04	35	33
ethylene dichloride	0.00	38	0	0.00	38	0	0.00	35	0
benzene	1.03	38	38	1.05	38	38	1.11	35	34
carbon tetrachloride	0.01	38	17	0.01	38	16	0.01	35	20
trichloroethylene	0.50	38	37	0.27	38	37	0.21	35	32
dioxane	0.01	38	21	0.02	38	15	0.01	35	21
1,1,2-trichloroethane	0.01	38	11	0.01	38	6	0.01	35	13
toluene	4.65	38	38	2.89	38	38	1.82	35	35
ethylene dibromide	0.00	38	5	0.00	38	4	0.00	35	3
tetrachloroethylene	0.45	38	38	0.31	37	36	0.24	35	33
chlorobenzene	0.11	38	35	0.08	37	36	0.07	35	32
ethylbenzene	0.33	38	38	0.26	37	36	0.17	35	33
m, p-xylene	0.99	38	38	0.75	37	37	0.49	35	34
styrene	0.13	38	36	0.11	37	35	0.07	35	33
o-xylene	0.26	38	38	0.22	37	37	0.15	35	33
1,1,2,2 tetrachloroethane	0.01	38	9	0.01	37	1	0.00	35	4
o-chlorotoluene	0.02	38	29	0.02	37	18	0.01	35	31
p-chlorotoluene	0.21	38	36	0.25	37	36	0.22	35	34
p-dichlorobenzene	0.05	38	32	0.07	37	30	0.04	35	34
o-dichlorobenzene	0.03	38	29	0.02	37	24	0.01	35	27
nitrobenzene	0.07	37	30	0.10	36	31	0.07	35	32

[a]Concentrations in parts per billion. Undetected quantities set to 0.0025 ppb, which is one half the detection limit. Quantitation limits are set at three times signal-to-noise ratios, or 0.05 ppb for aromatic VOCs and 0.10 for chlorinated VOCs.

Table 3.3.   Geometric Means of VOC Concentrations[a] January 18 to February 26, 1982

	Newark			Elizabeth			Camden		
	Mean	Number of Samples	Number Present	Mean	Number of Samples	Number Present	Mean	Number of Samples	Number Present
vinyl chloride	0.00	32	0	0.00	36	0	0.00	37	0
vinylidene chloride	0.31	23	17	0.52	29	24	1.02	33	31
methylene chloride	0.68	24	22	0.87	30	29	1.19	34	33
chloroform	0.21	27	24	0.29	36	32	0.26	36	32
ethylene dichloride	0.01	30	8	0.01	38	10	0.01	37	10
benzene	2.61	30	30	3.11	38	38	2.82	37	37
carbon tetrachloride	0.02	29	23	0.03	36	29	0.02	33	25
trichloroethylene	0.59	30	29	0.46	38	38	0.32	37	36
dioxane	0.01	30	7	0.00	38	6	0.01	37	8
toluene	4.93	30	30	4.09	38	38	3.38	37	37
1,1,2-trichloroethane	0.04	29	13	0.05	36	16	0.02	33	11
ethylene dibromide	0.00	30	3	0.00	38	3	0.00	37	5
tetrachloroethylene	0.46	30	30	0.44	38	38	0.29	37	37
chlorobenzene	0.22	30	30	0.21	38	38	0.18	37	36
ethylbenzene	0.51	30	30	0.32	38	38	0.23	37	36
m,p-xylene	1.79	30	30	1.10	38	38	0.90	37	37
styrene	0.24	30	30	0.14	38	37	0.15	37	36
o-xylene	0.44	30	30	0.28	38	38	0.23	37	36
1,1,2,2 tetrachloroethane	0.00	30	1	0.00	38	2	0.00	37	1
o-chlorotoluene	0.03	28	25	0.02	38	29	0.01	37	23
p-chlorotoluene	0.17	28	27	0.14	38	35	0.07	37	29
p-dichlorobenzene	0.02	27	25	0.02	38	29	0.02	36	27
o-dichlorobenzene	0.06	27	26	0.05	38	37	0.03	36	30
nitrobenzene	0.00	28	4	0.00	36	3	0.00	33	2

[a]Concentrations in parts per billion. Undetected quantities set to 0.0025 ppb, which is one-half the detection limit. Quantitation limits are set at three times signal-to-noise ratios, or 0.05 ppb for aromatic VOCs and 0.10 ppb for chlorinated VOCs.

from the actual ambient concentrations due to breakthrough, which is estimated to be on the order of 10% to 25%.

Generally, VOC levels were highest in Newark, followed by Elizabeth and Camden. However, each site was influenced by particular VOCs, as evidenced by the frequent high concentrations recorded in these locales. Newark had the highest levels of toluene and trichloroethylene, Camden the highest of methylene chloride and vinylidene chloride, and Elizabeth the highest of benzene. The aromatic VOCs (benzene, toluene, o,p,m-xylenes, ethylbenzene, and styrene) were generally found to have the highest concentrations and frequency of occurrence. Of the chlorinated VOCs measured, vinylidene chloride, methylene chloride, trichloroethylene, perchloroethylene, and chlorobenzene were found to have the highest concentrations. During the winter season, chloroform could be included in the group of chlorinated organics found in high concentrations.

SEASONAL VARIATIONS

For illustrative purposes, the day-to-day variations of toluene and methylene chloride for all sites during both seasons are shown in Figures 3.1a,b and 3.2a,b. Significant increases in the target substances were thought to reflect either prevailing meteorology or industrial/commercial emissions or a combination of the two. Repeated occurrences of peak concentrations, irrespective of prevailing meteorology, were thought to be indicative of industrial/commercial contributions. This conclusion is illustrated by toluene at Newark and methylene chloride at Camden (Figures 3.1 through 3.4). Generally, the aromatic compounds had similar day-to-day trends within a site. This pattern of covariation among the selected aromatic VOCs occurred during both seasons and at all sites. Spearman-rank correlation matrices (Table 3.4) show that these pollutants were highly correlated at each site during both seasons. Additional similarities were noted for day-to-day trends in aromatic VOC between the three urban areas, particularly between the Newark and Elizabeth sites. These observations contrast with the chlorinated VOCs, which were poorly correlated among themselves; Spearman-rank correlation coefficients were ≤ 0.40 at all sites during both seasons.

During the summer, the meteorological conditions associated with peak concentrations of VOCs also corresponded to high levels of O_3, SO_4^{-2} and extractable particulate organic matter. For the periods of stagnation (7/19-21, 8/10-13) and with the presence of a Bermuda high pressure system (8/3-5) (Lioy et al., 1983a), peak VOCs were as much as 2 to 20 times the seasonal averages. In addition, the average concentrations of six selected VOCs at Newark and Elizabeth sites increased by as much as 155% during

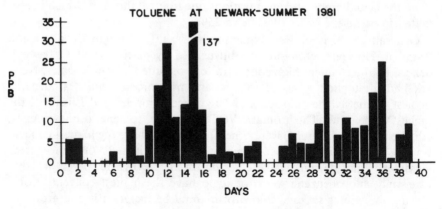

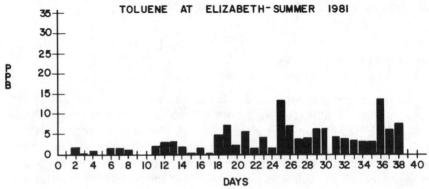

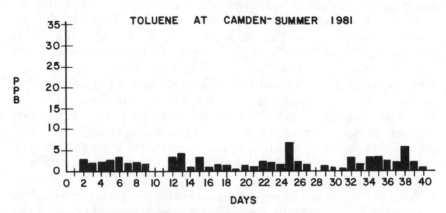

Figure 3.1.   Daily comparisons of toluene at three urban sites in New Jersey during the summer of 1981.

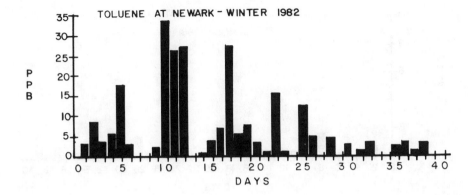

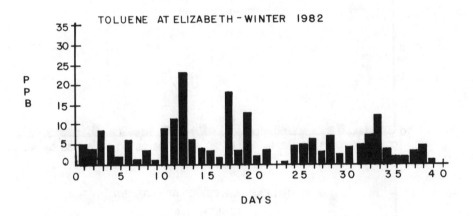

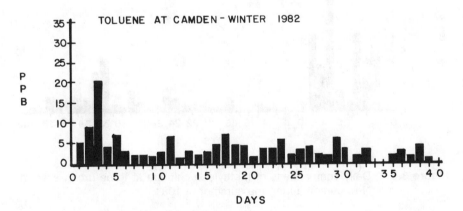

Figure 3.2.   Daily comparisons of toluene at three urban sites in New Jersey during the winter of 1982.

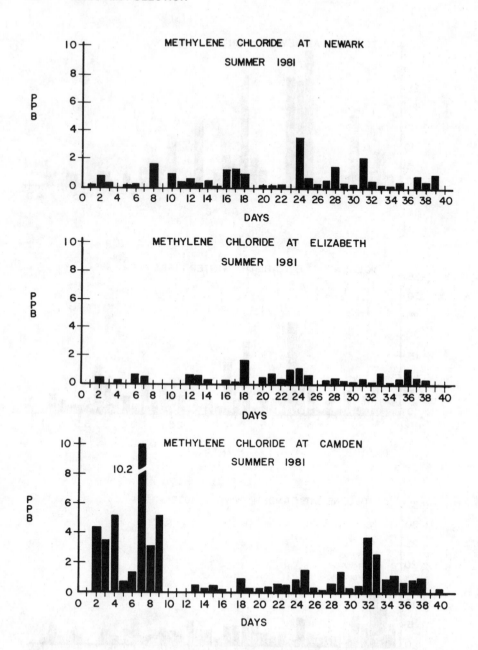

Figure 3.3.   Daily comparisons of methylene chloride at three urban sites in New Jersey during the summer of 1981.

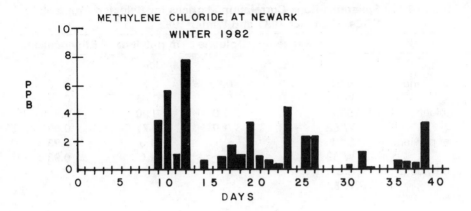

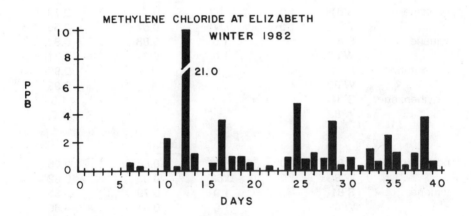

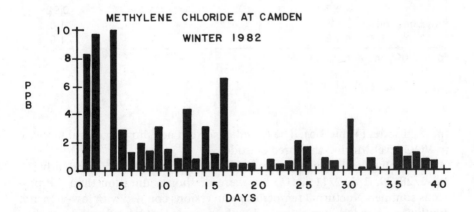

Figure 3.4.   Daily comparisons of methylene chloride at three urban sites in New Jersey during the winter of 1982.

Table 3.4. Spearman-Rank Correlation Matrices for Selected Aromatic VOCs—Summer 1981 and Winter 1982

		Benzene	Toluene	m,p-Xylene	Ethylbenzene
			Camden		
benzene	S'81	1.0	0.83	0.72	0.73
	W'82	1.0	0.50	0.66	0.57
toluene	S'81		1.0	0.90	0.86
	W'82		1.0	0.71	0.69
m,p-xylene	S'81			1.0	0.95
	W'82			1.0	0.93
ethylbenzene	S'81				1.0
	W'82				1.0
			Elizabeth		
benzene	S'81	1.0	0.89	0.79	0.79
	W'82	1.0	0.50[a]	0.57	0.55
toluene	S'81		1.0	0.88	0.88
	W'82		1.0	0.71	0.71
m,p-xylene	S'81			1.0	0.99
	W'82			1.0	0.99
ethylbenzene	S'81				1.0
	W'82				1.0
			Newark		
benzene	S'81	1.0	0.78	0.66	0.66
	W'82	1.0	0.62	0.65	0.62
toluene	S'81		1.0	0.79	0.81
	W'82		1.0	0.61	0.66
m,p-xylene	S'81			1.0	0.99
	W'82			1.0	0.92
ethylbenzene	S'81				1.0
	W'82				1.0

[a]$p > 0.001$. $n = 30$ to 38.

these episodes (Table 3.5). The Camden site did not show a general increase in VOC levels during the three episodes.

Pollution episodes during the winter season occurred more frequently (1/ 19, 1/28–29, 2/5, 2/11, 2/15) but were of shorter duration than the previous summer. Nocturnal temperature inversions coupled with low-velocity, southwesterly winds can account for the general buildup of pollutants during the winter in New Jersey (Lioy et al. 1983b). In addition, fossil fuel combustion is at a peak during the winter season, and has a substantial

Table 3.5.   Locally Accumulated VOCs During Summer Regional Oxidant Episodes (ppbv)

	Newark		Elizabeth		Camden	
	EP[a]	SWG[b]	EP	SWG	EP	SWG
methylene chloride	0.56	0.35	0.27	0.23	0.48	0.72
trichloroethylene	0.69	0.50	0.70	0.27	0.23	0.21
perchloroethylene	0.56	0.45	0.70	0.31	0.26	0.24
benzene	1.57	1.03	1.84	1.05	2.82	1.11
toluene	11.89	4.65	6.47	2.89	1.80	1.82
m,p-xylene	1.86	0.99	1.51	0.75	0.43	0.49

[a]EP = episode periods associated with regional oxidant (7/10–21, 8/3–5, 8/10–13; geometric mean n = 10).
[b]SWG = six week geometric means (n = 22–28).

Table 3.6.   Locally Accumulated VOCs During Winter Pollution Episodes (ppbv)

	Newark		Elizabeth		Camden	
	EP[a]	SWG[b]	EP	SWG	EP	SWG
methylene chloride	0.27	0.68	1.18	0.87	2.0	1.19
trichloroethylene	0.85	0.59	0.82	0.46	0.59	0.32
perchloroethylene	0.87	0.46	0.77	0.44	0.47	0.29
benzene	3.65	2.61	5.23	3.11	4.83	2.82
toluene	14.04	4.93	7.40	4.09	4.51	3.38
m,p-xylene	3.17	1.79	2.71	1.10	1.89	0.90

[a]EP = episode periods during nocturnal temperature inversions (1/19, 1/28–29, 2/5, 2/11, 2/15; geometric mean n = 6).
[b]SWG = six week geometric mean (n = 15–28).

influence on the levels of many pollutants in New Jersey. While peak VOC levels increased by as much as five times, the mean episodic levels of selected VOCs increased from 1.33 to 4 times the geometric mean winter levels (Table 3.6). The selected VOC accumulated in the atmosphere at all three sites during the winter, as opposed to increases observed only at Newark and Elizabeth in the summer. The largest winter episodic increase in selected VOCs occurred at the Newark site.

INTRA/INTERSITE ASSESSMENTS

Aromatic VOCs

The levels of aromatic VOCs reported here are consistent with those reported in the recent air pollution literature for urban air (Table 3.7). Motor vehicles and gasoline loading and unloading are the major sources of hydrocarbon emissions in urban areas, and aromatic hydrocarbons represent a significant fraction of the tailpipe and evaporative emissions from these sources (Table 3.8). Comparison of the proportions of toluene, benzene, m,p-xylene, and ethylbenzene indicates that motor vehicle exhaust and evaporative emissions made a major contribution to ambient levels of these pollutants at the Newark and Elizabeth sites during the 1981 summer.

At the Camden site, it was hypothesized that urban plume transport from the Philadelphia airshed coupled with photochemical reactions were the most important determinants of the atmospheric concentrations of the selected aromatic VOCs (Harkov et al., 1983). The evidence to support this hypothesis is 1) on 78% of the days during the summer of 1981 campaign prevailing winds were from the westerly direction for at least 12 hr/day at the Camden site, 2) published atmospheric reaction rate estimates suggest that these aromatic compounds are preferentially degraded in the following order: m, p-xylene > ethylbenzene > toluene > benzene, although actual atmospheric half-lives are uncertain (Singh et al., 1981a; NAS, 1981; Korte and Klein, 1982), and 3) a survey of industries in the Camden area did not identify any major benzene users or manufacturers within a 4-km radius from the monitoring site. Thus the greater proportion of benzene at this site does not appear to be related to localized point sources. It should be noted that a number of oil refineries are located southwest of the Camden site; however, the closest facility is more than 15 km away. Also, the Elizabeth site is within 3 km of the largest refinery in New Jersey, yet the results from this locale do not appear to reveal the influence of this source category on the relative proportions of these aromatic VOCs during the summer season.

A comparison of the ratio of selected aromatic VOCs in automobile exhaust, combined exhaust, and evaporative emissions and tunnel atmospheres indicates that additional source contributions influence the levels of these pollutants at the three sites during the winter (Table 3.8). The most pronounced shift is the increased proportion of benzene found during this season. An initial hypothesis developed from this data assessment is that combustion of residential oil, which is a major fuel used in New Jersey during the heating season, contributes to the shift in the ratio of the various aromatic VOC species. Additional evidence exists in support of this hypothesis, in that oil combustion in stationary boilers produced a 2:1 ratio of benzene to toluene in the flue gases (Bucone et al., 1978). As shown in Table 3.9, toluene, benzene, p-xylene, and ethylbenzene are significantly correl-

Table 3.7. Comparison of Selected Aromatic VOC Concentrations (ppbv) in Urban Atmospheres[a]

Site	Benzene	Toluene	m,p-Xylene	o-Xylene	Ethylbenzene	Sample Number	Reference
Sydney, Australia (9/79–6/80)	2.6	8.9	3.9	1.5	1.3	140	Nelson and Quigley (1982)
Los Angeles, California (4/79)	6.0	11.7	4.6	1.9	2.3	12	Singh et al. (1981a)
Oakland, California (6/79)	1.6	3.1	1.5	0.8	0.6	12	Singh et al. (1981a)
Houston, Texas (5/80)	5.7	10.3	3.8	1.3	1.4	11	Singh et al. (1981b)
Denver, Colorado (6/80)	4.4	6.2	2.9	1.3	2.2	13	Singh et al. (1981b)
Lincoln-Holland Tunnel (NY/NJ) (11/81)	40	72	33	11	16	8	Kebbekus et al. (1983)

[a]Arithmetic means.

Table 3.8. Comparison of Ratios of Selected Aromatic VOCs from Automotive Exhaust, Exhaust and Evaporation, and Tunnel Atmosphere With Those Reported For Three Urban New Jersey Locations

Site	Toluene		Benzene		m,p-Xylene		Ethylbenzene	Reference
automotive exhaust	4	:	3	:	4	:	1	Jackson (1978)
automotive exhaust and evaporation	13	:	4	:	3	:	1	Black and High (1980)
tunnel	5	:	3	:	3	:	1	Kebbekus et al.(1983)
Summer 1981								
Newark	14	:	3	:	4	:	1	ATEOS
Elizabeth	11	:	4	:	3	:	1	ATEOS
Camden	11	:	7	:	3	:	1	ATEOS
Winter 1982								
Newark	9	:	5	:	4	:	1	ATEOS
Elizabeth	13	:	10	:	3	:	1	ATEOS
Camden	15	:	13	:	4	:	1	ATEOS

Table 3.9. Spearman-Rank Correlation Matrices for Selected Aromatic VOCs and Two Trace Elements for Winter 1982 Campaign

Sites	Toluene	Benzene	m,p-xylene	Ethylbenzene
		Newark		
Pb	0.65	0.63	0.68	0.81
Ni	0.65	0.68	0.60	0.67
		Elizabeth		
Pb	0.56	0.69	0.71	0.72
Ni	0.48[a]	0.51	0.53	0.54
		Camden		
Pb	0.67	0.42[a]	0.52	0.43[a]
Ni	0.47[a]	0.59	0.39[a]	0.26[a]

[a]$p < 0.001$.

ated with both Pb and Ni tracers for motor vehicle and residential oil combustion, respectively. The poorest relationship occurs at the Camden site and may be a result of different atmospheric loss mechanisms operating to remove particulate-phase pollutants, i.e. Pb and Ni, as opposed to vapor-phase pollutants, i.e. m,p-xylenes, as the urban plume from the Philadelphia airshed passes the receptor site. The prevailing winds at the Camden site were from the westerly direction for 67% of the days for at least 12 hr/day during the winter of 1982. The Camden site is also the furthest from major roadways, thus the poor Pb correlation may reflect different fates of Pb and aromatic VOCs as they are transported to the monitoring locale.

Many aromatic compounds are utilized in solvent applications, and a thorough review of the data for Newark indicates that such a source for toluene exists near this site. Recently, Morandi (1985) identified paint spraying operations as an important source of PM-15 at the Newark site. Most coating operations utilize a solvent, and motor vehicle paints often contain significant quantities of toluene (Sexton and Westburg, 1980). Thus we attribute the frequent peaks of toluene at the Newark site to the large number of truck and autobody painting operations located near this monitoring site. Localized industrial and/or commercial impacts on aromatic VOCs at Elizabeth and Camden were not evident from this data analysis.

Chlorinated VOCs

The chlorinated VOCs appear to be minor components of the air quality at the urban sites included in the ATEOS program. This observation is consistent with the results of Singh et al. (1982) and Pellizzari et al. (1982). While each of the monitoring sites was influenced by chlorinated VOCs, the daily variation of these pollutants was poorly coupled with the other contaminants measured in this study, indicating the likelihood that localized point sources are the primary contributors to the ambient levels of these pollutants. In addition, these chlorinated compounds are poorly correlated with each other at a given site ($R_{sp} \leq 0.40$). This result is not entirely unexpected since chlorinated VOCs are used widely in a variety of industrial/commercial processes. Only those compounds which are used extensively by a large number of industrial/commercial enterprises were found in relatively high frequencies and concentrations. These compounds are vinylidene chloride, methylene chloride, trichloroethylene and perchloroethylene. Vinylidene chloride is primarily used in production of various copolymers known commonly as "Sarans" (Fishbein, 1979a). Methylene chloride is used as a solvent in paint remover, aerosol sprays, metal degreasing, and plastics production (Fishbein, 1979b). Ninety percent of the trichloroethylene is used for degreasing and cleaning metals, while most of the perchloroethylene is used in textile cleaning (Fishbein, 1979a).

The vinylidene chloride results from this study are somewhat of a surprise. Singh et al. (1981a,b; 1982) have identified vinylidene chloride in a number of urban areas throughout the U.S. in the 1 to 50 ppt range, which is lower than reported here. In the present study, mass spectrometry positively identified vinylidene chloride in all samples in which gas chromatography detection was also noted. A statewide survey of industries in New Jersey has only been successful in locating three small to intermediate users of vinylidene chloride. Thus we have no satisfactory explanation for the presence, in relatively high concentrations, of vinylidene chloride in the New Jersey urban atmosphere. Vinylidene chloride is formed commercially from the dehydrochlorination of 1,1,1-trichloroethane or 1,1,2-trichloroethane. Both of these substances are high-use compounds in New Jersey, with 1,1,1-trichloroethane occurring in the 1 to 5 ppb range, in ambient air (J. Bozzelli, unpublished). There thus remains the possibility that vinylidene chloride is formed either in the atmosphere or on Tenax-GC, as an artifact, from 1,1,1-trichloroethane dehydrochlorination. However, 1,1,1-trichloroethane is thought to be recalcitrant in the atmosphere (Singh et al., 1981a), thus leaving the vinylidene chloride issue uncertain. Obviously, additional studies are needed to resolve this problem as it relates to vinylidene chloride sources and sampling utilizing Tenax-GC cartridges.

While the remaining chlorinated compounds are generally minor components of urban air quality at the three ATEOS sites, they occasionally become a major fraction of the selected VOC measurements. Some examples of peak winter concentrations of selected chlorinated VOCs are shown in Table 3.10. These peak concentrations were generally poorly correlated (rsp ≤ 0.40) with the meteorological variables and the other air pollutants measured during the ATEOS project.

The Camden site appears to be the most affected by local emissions of

Table 3.10. **Peak Levels of Selected Chlorinated VOCs Found at Three Urban New Jersey Sites During the Winter (1982) Season (ppbv)**

Pollutant	Newark	Elizabeth	Camden
ethylene dichloride	1.7 (1/19)[a]	1.9 (1/18)	5.3 (1/26)
chloroform	36.0 (1/29)	10.1 (1/30)	77.4 (2/2)
1,1,2-trichloroethane	12.0 (2/14)	18.1 (2/28)	16.0 (2/2)
chlorobenzene	0.7 (2/3)	1.4 (1/28)	2.8 (2/16)

[a]Date of peak value.

chlorinated VOCs. This is best illustrated by the large number of peaks of methylene chloride found at this site. Many small commercial and industrial operations, such as machine shops and a rivet manufacturer, in addition to a medical and a food science research laboratory, are adjacent to the Camden monitoring site and could be contributing to the excess methylene chloride present at this locale.

IMPLICATIONS FOR HUMAN HEALTH

The data collected on ambient VOC levels at the three urban sites in New Jersey have a number of important implications for studying the effects of this compound class on human health. Seasonal differences in the concentration of selected VOCs indicate that human exposures to these pollutants can be significantly altered by the prevailing meteorology and shifting source categories such as space heating with #2 fuel oil. In this regard, air pollution episodes can significantly raise ambient levels of specific VOCs, and hence increase human exposure to these substances. Although general human activities such as motor vehicle use seem to have a major impact on ambient VOC levels, relatively small, local sources of specific VOCs, such as autobody shops, can have a significant impact on exposures in a nearby population.

Since small, localized sources of VOCs can have significant impacts on a population's exposure to these substances, monitoring at background locations will not be an adequate means of determining the air quality situation for this class of pollutants. Traditional monitoring approaches for air pollutants tend to reflect the area source nature of most of the criteria pollutants and are an attempt to understand average population exposures. In the case of VOCs, air monitoring studies need to be focused near sources, since the impacted populations are primarily found in close vicinity to VOC emitters. As a result of this situation, monitoring strategies for VOCs near emission sources must be associated with a more concentrated effort focusing on sample collection approaches and documentation of micrometeorological conditions. Studies are being carried out in New Jersey at Publicly Owned Treatment Works (POTWs), sanitary landfills, and industrial sites utilizing this type of monitoring strategy.

Trace amounts of a number of VOCs which are human and/or animal carcinogens were found to be ubiquitous in urban New Jersey. Whether long-term exposures to these materials in ambient air will have any adverse health effects is unknown. However, the VOC levels are sufficiently low in New Jersey to disregard the notion that a statewide problem exists for this class of ambient air pollutant. Monitoring efforts adjacent to VOC source categories, such as abandoned hazardous waste sites (Harkov et al., 1985), can be compared to VOC levels recorded in urban areas in New Jersey. Thus by having a data base on background levels of VOCs in urban/industrial areas of New Jersey, it is now feasible to do site-specific studies so that comparative assessments may be made.

CONCLUSIONS

The measurement of 25 selected VOCs at three urban locations in New Jersey revealed that most substances occur at concentrations less than 1.00 ppbv with the exception of toluene (2 to 5 ppbv) and benzene (1 to 3 ppbv). Prevailing meteorology caused levels of selected VOCs to rise two- to tenfold at Elizabeth and Newark during summer oxidant episodes and two- to threefold during wintertime nocturnal temperature inversions. Motor vehicles have a significant impact on aromatic VOCs during the summer, but additional sources contribute to ambient levels during the winter season. Finally, small, local sources can cause levels of selected VOCs to be significantly elevated above background concentrations typical of urban New Jersey.

REFERENCES

Black, F., and High, L. (1980), Passenger car hydrocarbon emission speciation. EPA-600/2-80-085.

Bozzelli, J., and Kebbekus, B. (1982), Collection and Analysis of Selected Volatile Organic Compounds in Ambient Air. Proceedings of 75th Annual APCA meeting in New Orleans, LA. 82-65.2.

Brown, R. H., and Purnell, C. J., (1979), *J. Chromatog.* 17:79.

Bucone, H. W., Macko, J. F., and Tabeck, H. J. (1978), Volatile Organic Compound Species Data Manual. EPA-450/3-78-119.

CEN. (1981), *Chem. Eng. News* 59:35.

Cox, R. D. (1983), Sample Collection for Volatile Organics in Air. In: *Measurement and Monitoring of Non-criteria (Toxic) Contaminants in Air*, SP-50. APCA, Pittsburgh, PA.

Fishbein, L. (1979a), *STOTEN* 11:113.

Fishbein, L. (1979b), *STOTEN* 11:163.

Harkov, R., et al. (1986), *JAPCA* 36:388.

Harkov, R., et al. (1985), *J. Env. Sci. Health* 20:491.

Harkov, R., et al. (1984), *STOTEN* 38:259–274.

Harkov, R., Kebbekus, B., Bozzelli, J. W., and Lioy, P. J. (1983), *JAPCA* 33:1177–1183.

Harkov, R., and Fischer, R. (1982), Development and Initiation of an Integrated Monitoring Program for Toxic Air Pollutants. Proceedings of 75th Annual APCA meeting in New Orleans, LA. 81-1.1

Harkov, R., Katz, R., Bozzelli, J., and Kebbekus, B. (1981), Toxic and carcinogenic air pollutants in New Jersey-volatile organic substances. MASAPCA Proceedings Toxic Air Contaminant; 245 pp.

Haseman, J. K., et. al. (1984), *J. Tox. Env. Health* 14:621.

HEW. (1976–1980), NCI Carcinogenesis Technical Report Series No. 1-190. USDHEW, PHS Washington, DC.

IARC. (1982), Chemicals, Industrial Processes and Industries Associated with Cancer. Int. Agency. Research on Cancer, Lyons France Suppl 4, 292 pp.

IARC. (1972–1978), IARC Monograph on the Evaluation of the Carcinogen Risk of Chemicals to Man. Vol. 1–18. IARC, Lyon France.

Jackson, N. W. (1978), Effect of Catalytic Emission Control on Exhaust Hydrocarbon Composition and Reactivity. Presented at SAE Passenger Car Meeting, Troy, Michigan No. 780624.

Kebbekus, G., Greenberg, A., Hogan, L., Bozzelli, J., Darack, F., Eveleens, L., and Stangeland, L. (1983), *JAPCA* 33:328.

Korte, F., and Klein, W. (1982), *Eco. Env. Safety* 6:311.

Lioy, P. J., Daisey, J. M., Reiss, N. M., and Harkov, R. (1983), *Atmos. Env.* 17:2321.

Lioy, P. J., et al. (1983), The Second Annual Report from the Project ATEOS. Submitted to N.J. DEP.

Mara, S. J., et al. (1979), Assessment of Human Exposure to Atmospheric Perchloroethylene. EPA Contract No. 68-01-2835.

Mara S. J., and Lee, S. S. (1978a), Assessment of Human Exposure to Atmospheric Benzene. EPA Contract No. 68-02-2835.

Mara, S. J., and Lee, S. S. (1978b) Atmospheric Ethylene Dibromide a Source Specific Assessment. EPA Contract No. 68-02-2835.

Morandi, M. T. (1985), Development of Some Apportionment Models for Inhalable Particulate Matter and Its Extractable Organic Fractions in Urban Areas of New Jersey. Doctoral Thesis, NYU Medical Center, NY, NY.

NAS. (1985), *The alkylbenzenes.* National Academy Press, Washington, DC; 284 pp.

NAS. (1977), *Ozone and Other Photochemical Oxidants*. National Academy of Sciences, Washington, DC; 719 pp.

Nelson, P. F., and Quigley, S. M. (1982). *Env. Sci. Tech*. 16:650.

NTP. (1985), Technical Report on the Toxicology and Carcinogenicity Studies of Dichloromethane, NTP 306, RTP, NC 94.

Pellizarri, E. D. (1982), *Env. Sci. Tech*. 16:781.

SAI. (1981), Human Exposure to Atmospheric Contaminants. U.S. EPA OAQPS, RTP, NC.

Singh, H. B., Salas, L. J., and Stiles, R. E. (1982), *Env. Sci. Tech*. 16:572.

Singh, H. B., Salas, L. J. Smith, A. J., and Shigeishi, H. (1982), *Atmos. Env*. 15:601.

Singh, H. B., Salas, L. J. Smith, A., Stiles, R., and Shigeishi, H. (1981b), Atmospheric Measurements of Selected Hazardous Organic Chemicals. EPA-600/3-81-032.

Suta, B. E. (1979), Assessment of Human Exposures to Atmospheric Acrylonitrile. EPA Contract No. 68-02-2835.

Verschueren, K. (1983), Handbook of Environmental Data on Organic Chemicals. Van Nostrand Reinhold Comp. NY, NY; 1310 pp.

CHAPTER 4

Analyses of Polycyclic Aromatic Hydrocarbons

Arthur Greenberg

CHAPTER CONTENTS

Analyses of Polycyclic Aromatic Hydrocarbons

RATIONALE FOR STUDY OF NONVOLATILE AND SEMIVOLATILE ORGANIC POLLUTANTS

The ATEOS study, which is the basis of this monograph, focused on the measurement of pollutants and biological activity thought to be associated with chronic diseases, notably cancer. New Jersey is known to have high overall and lung cancer mortality rates relative to other states (Greenberg, 1979; New Jersey Department of Health, 1981). However, the difficulties in making correlations between mortality and air pollution have been reviewed recently (Lipfert, 1985; Greenberg, 1986). While there is reasonable convergence between different studies of acute health effects of air pollution [measured by total suspended particulates (TSP), coefficient of haze (COH), or sulfate], there remains considerable divergence in analogous studies of chronic health effects. Attempts to understand the relationship of cancer risk to air pollution are confounded by the subtlety of the effects themselves, colinearity of independent variables and ambiguities in diagnoses and case histories. A recent U.S. EPA study (Haemisegger et al., 1985) based upon consideration of three epidemiological studies (NESHAP Study, 35-County Study, and Ambient Air Quality Study), concluded that the estimated cancer risk in the United States due to air pollution was between 5 and 7.5 cases per million per year. The total estimated annual cases from air pollution, 1300 to 1700, is small compared to the total estimate of cancer cases (440,000 in 1983). Nonetheless, the number is still sizable and the rate of occurrence should be higher in industrialized and densely populated regions; this is in line with the findings of the earlier cited New Jersey study.

The EPA study estimated that roughly half of the cancer incidence assigned to air pollution is attributable to products of incomplete combustion (PIC). PIC consists of organic compounds, including polycyclic aromatic hydrocarbons (PAHs), as well as numerous PAH derivatives (nitro compounds, quinones, hydroxy and hydroxynitro compounds), PAH degradation products (aldehydes, carboxylic acids, and anhydrides), and heteroanalogs (notably containing nitrogen and sulfur), as well as numerous as yet unknown classes. The EPA study employed benzo(a)pyrene (BaP) as a surrogate for PIC. This reflects the EPA's own longtime survey of this pollutant (Faoro and Manning, 1981), as well as other studies (Clement Associates, 1983). In the EPA study the average potency rate for BaP (0.6 × 10^{-5} deaths per ng/m^3 per year, or 0.42 deaths per 70 years per μg/m^3) was used as representative for the entire PIC class.

Although the Faoro and Manning study reveals a steady decline in airborne PAH levels, interest in continuing such studies hinges on at least two factors. First, it is worthwhile to attempt to relate present and future studies to earlier data. Second, the past decade has witnessed a diversification in fuel use. Thus, an increasing fraction of automobile traffic is diesel powered, more homes burn wood for heating purposes, and incineration is an inviting alternative to the use of landfills for disposal of municipal and industrial waste. Polycyclic aromatic hydrocarbons are by-products of these combustion processes.

POLYCYCLIC AROMATIC HYDROCARBONS: SOURCES AND PROPERTIES

Polycyclic aromatic hydrocarbons (PAHs) are by-products of the combustion of organic matter (Bjorseth, 1983; Grimmer, 1983a; Lee et al., 1981; National Academy of Sciences, 1972, 1983). Many of these compounds are potent carcinogens (Santodonato et al., 1981) which must be activated metabolically before gaining the ability to attack DNA (Jerina et al., 1981; Harvey, 1981, 1982). For example, benzo(a)pyrene (1) is metabolized to its ultimate carcinogen, the 7,8-diol-9,10-epoxide (2).

1   2

This is the reason why PAHs do not exhibit direct (unactivated) Ames mutagenicity and can only manifest such biological activity when mammalian liver enzyme extract is added to the Salmonella culture (Ames et al., 1975).

Most of the PAHs are associated with the fine particulate matter (2.5 μm in aerodynamic diameter) present in air and originate during the combustion process (Miguel and Friedlander, 1978). Unfortunately, these particles penetrate deeply into the lung and can remain suspended in air for many days, allowing for the possibility of long-range transport (National Academy of Sciences, 1983). Indeed, long-range transport has been demonstrated for PAHs (Lunde and Bjorseth, 1977) and is consistent with the existence of trace levels in remote areas of the Swiss Alps (Blumer, 1975, 1977).

Sources of atmospheric PAHs are mostly anthropogenic (fossil fuel combustion from point and area sources, wood combustion, smoking, and smelting) although forest fires and geothermal processes play a role. A widely cited inventory of emission rates (Hangebrauck et al., 1967) is almost twenty years old at this writing. A more current survey of BaP emission rates (Harkov and Greenberg, 1985) is displayed in Table 4.1. The range of data reflects differences in results obtained by respected laboratories, each of which employs different combustion, sample collection, and analytical protocols. The choice of values represents the authors' most judicious choice of reasonable numbers in the middle of reported ranges. Emission controls have significantly lowered the emission rates since the 1967 survey; this is especially apparent for motor vehicles. The efficiencies of scale are also obvious, for example, for comparison of residential and utilities emission rates for coal combustion. Residential wood combustion appears to produce BaP at rates between 500 to 1 million times that for residential oil-based heating, and there are virtually no mandated controls on such emissions in most areas of the United States.

Annual fuel use in New Jersey is summarized in Table 4.2. The largest uncertainty in this data is for wood combustion although Harkov and Greenberg (1985) cite consistency between two independent studies. Little use of coal for domestic heating is reported in the state. Most coal is burned by power generating stations in New Jersey which emit little particulate organic matter. Peak loading periods and, thus, coal combustion, occur during summer when air conditioner use is greatest. The Btu's produced from residential wood combustion represent a total of roughly five percent of that due to residential heating using oil and gas. Nevertheless, the very high BaP emission rate from wood combustion would appear to make this a very significant and perhaps even dominant contributor during the heating season. Table 4.3 lists estimates of the total contributions of BaP to the air from the major New Jersey sources on an annual basis as well as from the

Table 4.1. BaP Emission Rates (ng/Btu) for Combustion Sources (Harkov and Greenberg, 1985)

Fuel	User	Rate reported	Rate per Btu
Solid fuels			
Coal	Utilities	58 $\mu g/10^6$ Btu	5.8×10^{-2} ng/Btu
		2.0 $\mu g/kg$	7.0×10^{-2} ng/Btu
			5.6×10^{-2} ng/Btu
			range = $5.6–7.0 \times 10^{-2}$ ng/Btu
Coal	Residential	11×10^{-5} ng/J	0.12 ng/Btu
		1,500 $\mu g/g$	52 ng/Btu
		61,000 $\mu g/10^6$Btu	61 ng/Btu
			range = 0.12–61 ng/Btu
Wood	Residential	0.1–6 ng/J	105–6300 ng/Btu
		500–700 $\mu g/kg$	27 ng/Btu
		45–134 $ng/10^6$Btu	45–135 ng/Btu
		1.8 ng/J	1900 ng/Btu
		5×10^6 ng/kg	227 ng/Btu
			range = 27–6300 ng/Btu
Oil			
Heating	Residential	≤0.1 mg/kg	$\leq 2.6 \times 10^{-3}$ ng/Btu
Misc. distillate	Commercial/industrial	≤ 40–60 $\mu g/10^6$Btu	$\leq 4–5 \times 10^{-2}$ ng/Btu
Residual oil	Utility/commercial/ industrial	≤ 20–47 $\mu g/10^6$Btu	$\leq 2–4.7 \times 10^{-2}$ ng/Btu
			4.3×10^{-4} ng/Btu
Natural gas			
Heating	Residential	≤ 20 $\mu g/10^6$Btu	$\leq 2 \times 10^{-2}$ ng/Btu
Motor fuels			
Gasoline	Auto/trucks	73 $\mu g/gal$ (0.1–1µg/km)	0.6 ng/Btu
Diesel	Trucks/buses	321 $\mu g/gal$ (1–11 µg/km)	2.3 ng/Btu

Table 4.2.   Fuel Use Information, 1981, New Jersey (Harkov and Greenberg, 1985)

Fuel	User	Mass consumption (Kg)	Energy consumption (Btu)
Solid fuels			
Coal	Utilities	2.6×10^9	7.34×10^{13}
Coal	Residential	3.6×10^7	$1 \quad \times 10^{12}$
Wood	Residential	$1 \quad \times 10^6$cords	2.7×10^{13}
Oil			
Heating oil	Residential	4.1×10^9	1.6×10^{14}
Misc. distillate	Commercial/industrial	2.5×10^9	9.8×10^{13}
Residual oil	Utility/commercial/industrial	5.0×10^9	2.0×10^{14}
Natural gas			
Heating	Residential	7.4×10^9	4.0×10^{14}
Motor fuel			
Gasoline	Auto/trucks	8.5×10^9	3.8×10^{14}
Diesel	Trucks/buses	8.2×10^8	3.7×10^{13}
Misc.			
Refuse	Incinerators	Unknown	Unknown

heating and nonheating seasons. The BaP emissions rates are middle-range values taken from Table 4.1 which are then multiplied by Btu production data from Table 4.2. Not surprisingly, motor vehicle emissions account for roughly 98% of airborne BaP during the summer season, reflecting New Jersey's high population and motor vehicle traffic density. The total BaP load in the winter would be predicted to be over thirty times that during the summer, with wood combustion accounting for about 98% of the total. If one were to use the lowest domestic wood combustion emission rate in Table 4.1, then wood combustion would still account for about 85% of the winter BaP, and the winter/summer BaP ratio would be about five. The issue of actual differences in summer and winter PAH levels will be discussed later in this chapter.

There are a number of other points related to PAH levels that will be discussed in this chapter. One is the possibility of using PAH profiles to establish the nature of the dominant sources of these pollutants at various sites. A PAH profile is a catalog of the relative amounts of different PAH relative to an index compound. This raises the issue of PAH reactivity. Many of these compounds are potentially reactive under ambient conditions in the presence of ultraviolet light, oxides of nitrogen, acid aerosols, ozone, singlet oxygen and hydroxyl radical. If the ambient environment is a reaction vessel for PAH, then they might "lose the memory of their sources," and PAH profiles will merely represent the conditions of the "ambient reaction vessel." On the other hand, differential PAH reactivity

Table 4.3. Estimated Annual Heating Season (Nov.-Mar.) and Non-Heating Season BaP Emission Rates for New Jersey (Harkov and Greenberg, 1985)

Fuel	User	BaP Estimated rate (ng/Btu)	Annual (kg)	Heating season (kg)	Non-heating season (kg)
Solid fuels					
Coal	Utilities	6.1×10^{-2}	4.5	1.9	2.6
Coal	Residential	37.7	3.8	3.8	
Wood	Residential	227	6129	6129	2.6
Total			6137	6135	
Oil					
Heating	Residential	2.6×10^{-3}	0.4	0.4	0.1
Misc. distillate	Commercial/industrial	2×10^{-4}	0.2	0.1	
Residual	Utility/commercial/industrial	4.3×10^{-4}	<0.1	0.5	0.1
Total			0.6		
Natural gas					
Heating	Residential	2.0×10^{-4}	0.1	0.1	
Motor fuels					
Gasoline	Autos/trucks	0.6	228	95	133
Diesel	Trucks/buses	2.3	85	35	50
Total			313	130	183
Grand Total			6451	6266	186

(i.e., a reactive PAH such as cyclopenta(cd)pyrene versus an unreactive one such as benzo(j)fluoranthene) may help in the understanding of long-range transport. It is possible that ambient reactivity may explain some of the winter/summer concentration differences that will be described later. Perhaps the most important aspect of PAH reactivity is the formation of derivatives that are also mutagenic. Thus, while the PAH pyrene is noncarcinogenic and nonmutagenic, 1-nitropyrene, which is found in quantities comparable to BaP, is a carcinogen in animals and a direct mutagen in bacterial bioassay (Rosenkranz, 1982, 1984). Some of these derivatives, for example the dinitropyrenes, are such strong carcinogens that even very tiny conversions to these compounds are cause for concern. The potential formation of PAH derivatives will be discussed later in this chapter.

SAMPLE COLLECTION AND ANALYSIS

The procedures for sample collection and storage are discussed in Chapter 1. Twenty-four-hour samples of inhalable particulate matter (IPM, 15 μm) were collected on prefired Gelman-AE fiberglass filters using high-volume samplers (General Metal Works). This method of collection is not useful for the analysis of smaller, more volatile PAHs such as anthracene and phenanthrene which are lost during the collection process, unless gas-phase pollutants are subsequently trapped cryogenically or on adsorption media, including charcoal, Tenax®, or polyurethane foam (PUF). None of these techniques were employed during the ATEOS program. It is known that volatility losses of pentacyclic PAHs, including BaP and larger compounds, are negligible (Yamaski et al., 1982; Galasyn et al., 1984; You and Bidleman, 1984). These studies indicate that losses of tetracyclic PAHs, including pyrene, chrysene, triphenylene and benzo(a)anthracene, vary seasonally. Of these four compounds, only the last one is carcinogenic. Most of the known carcinogenic PAHs have from four to six rings, and thus the loss of the more volatile PAHs, which tend to be far more abundant than the larger compounds, will not entail very much loss of carcinogenic compounds.

The process of collection itself may produce artifacts arising from exposure of particulate matter to a continuous stream of air containing reactive substances (Pitts, 1979). There has been concern over the ability of glass fiber filters to catalyze chemical reactions during the collection process, and at least one group of researchers recommends sample collection on Teflon®*-coated surfaces (Lee et al., 1980). However, Grosjean et al. (1983)

---

*Registered trademark of E.I. du Pont de Nemours and Company, Inc., Wilmington, Delaware.

found no measurable reaction of even the reactive PAHs perylene and BaP when collected on glass fiber filters and exposed to realistic ambient collection conditions. Our own studies prior to the formal commencement of ATEOS sampling were indecisive on the comparison between glass fiber and Teflon filters. It is worthwhile to mention that if only very minute quantities of PAHs react to form very potent mutagens or carcinogens, studies of biological activity could manifest a significant artifactual component even as the chemical analyses are not affected.

Specific details of the analysis of PAHs, as well as techniques of quality assurance and quality control, are described in the literature (Greenberg and Darack, 1984) and in Chapter 1 of this volume. The samples were analyzed using gradient high-performance liquid chromatography (HPLC) employing ultraviolet and fluorescence detectors. Although capillary column gas chromatography (GC) is usually capable of better resolution of compounds than HPLC, the latter method has been spectacularly successful for the PAH class (Wise and Sander, 1985). Furthermore, the most powerful GC detector, the mass spectrometer (MS), is not very informative for the PAHs. The overwhelming abundance of the parent peak and absence of large numbers and quantities of fragment peaks allows ready determination of the molecular mass of a PAH but does not facilitate easy discrimination between isomers. In contrast, the ultraviolet (UV) and fluorescence detectors commonly employed with HPLC are highly sensitive to small differences in PAH structure as well as to very minute amounts (e.g., picograms) of this class of compound. In the ATEOS study, gradient HPLC was performed initially using Perkin-Elmer PAH/10 columns and subsequently with Separations Group Vydac® 201TP54 columns using aqueous acetonitrile solutions for elution, as described in Chapter 1. Solutions of National Bureau of Standards (NBS) Standard Reference Material (SRM) 1647 as well as extracts of NBS SRM 1649 urban dust were run regularly for calibration purposes. A more complete discussion of these procedures can be found in the literature (Harkov et al., 1985). The ATEOS extraction scheme involved following cyclohexane extraction of airborne particulate matter with subsequent extractions by dichloromethane (DCM) and acetone (ACE). The amount of PAH in the subsequent DCM extract was generally less than 10% of that in the cyclohexane extract (Greenberg and Darack, 1984; Greenberg et al., 1985a). The results of comparisons and recoveries using NBS SRMs 1647 and 1649 have been summarized elsewhere (Greenberg et al., 1985a).

Although they were not part of the ATEOS campaign, we will also discuss in this chapter the results of our study of benzo(a)pyrene levels in suspended particulate matter collected at 27 New Jersey locations (Harkov and Greenberg, 1985). There is an interesting point to note here in the philosophy of environmental measurements. The ATEOS sampling scheme involved collection once each day for 39 consecutive 24-hr periods at each of four sites during a campaign. There were four such campaigns. Such a sampling scheme is particularly useful for following the course of weather patterns which may, for example, produce inversions accompanied by high-pollution episodes lasting several days. Practical limitations in the cost of sampling and the time needed for analysis limited the number of sites to four. The choice of the sampling months in advance of the campaign guaranteed measurements of high and low PAH periods, but not necessarily the maximum and minimum, and also voided the possibility of observing continuous variation during the intervening seasons. The number of PAHs analyzed per sample during the ATEOS project was as high as 25. Thus, the analyses were complex, time consuming, and expensive. However, the advantages of such analyses include not having to be completely dependent upon a single PAH surrogate, e.g., BaP, having the potential for comparison of PAH profiles at sites with those of sources for the purpose of source apportionment, and having the ability to compare seasonal changes in PAH profiles to gain insight into losses due to reactivity and volatility.

The 27-site study involved measurement of BaP only and exactly duplicated the U.S. EPA measurement for this compound (Swanson et al., 1981; Swanson and Walling, 1981). It employed ultrasonic extraction of the filter using cyclohexane at 78–80°C, development on acetylated cellulose TLC plates using ethanol/dichloromethane, and plate scanning spectrofluorometry using 383-nm excitation and 428-nm emission. Satisfactory agreement with the U.S. EPA laboratory was obtained for duplicate analyses of the same samples. Suspended particulate matter was collected at 27 New Jersey sites following 24-hr sampling once every six days. This task, beyond the capability of our own staff, was accomplished as part of the activities of the Office of Air Quality of the New Jersey Department of Environmental Protection. The analysis is easier than and about one-tenth as expensive as the ATEOS PAH analysis. While providing no data on profiles and relying specifically on BaP as a PAH surrogate, the analysis allowed continuous sampling throughout the year, thus identifying transition periods as well as maximum and minimum periods and providing data for a sizable collection of sites around the state.

RESULTS AND DISCUSSION OF PAH MEASUREMENTS

ATEOS Results

The results of the Summer 1981 campaign (Harkov et al., 1984) as well as all four campaigns (Greenberg et al., 1985) have been published. Tables 4.4 through 4.7 list PAH data for each of the four campaigns. The steady increase in the number of PAHs monitored and reported chronologically represents acquisition of additional standards as well as improvement in

Table 4.4. Geometric Mean Concentrations of Selected PAHs at Four Sites in New Jersey during the Summer 1981 ATEOS Program (Greenberg et al., 1985)

Compound (Rel. Carc.)[a]	Newark N[b]	NBDL[c]	M_G[d] (ng/m³)	Elizabeth N	NBDL	M_G (ng/m³)	Camden N	NBDL	M_G (ng/m³)	Ringwood[e] N	NBDL	M_G (ng/m³)
Benzo(a)pyrene (+ + +)	33	0	0.23	28	0	0.14	29	0	0.20	11	0	0.06
Benzo(b)fluoranthene (+ +)	30	0	0.27	23	1	0.20	30	1	0.27	10	1	0.06
Benzo(j)fluoranthene (+ +)	37	0	0.16	33	0	0.09	37	0	0.13	10	0	0.06
Dibenzo(ac)anthracene (+)	36	0	0.03	29	1	0.03	32	0	0.03	9	0	0.02
Indeno(1,2,3-cd)pyrene (+)	29	0	0.46	27	0	0.46	27	0	0.34	12	0	0.09
Benzo(k)fluoranthene (–)	28	1	0.20	22	0	0.14	33	0	0.15	8	1	0.03
Benzo(ghi)perylene (–)	36	0	0.56	33	0	0.41	35	0	0.35	10	0	0.09
Coronene (–)	36	0	0.47	33	0	0.35	35	0	0.29	9	0	0.08
Benzo(e)pyrene (–)	37	0	0.18	34	0	0.13	37	0	0.14	11	0	0.03
Perylene (–)	27	4	0.10	22	4	0.04	23	4	0.06	9	0	0.03

[a]See Santodonato et al., 1981.
[b]N = number of samples analyzed.
[c]NBDL = number below detection limit.
[d]M_G = geometric means based on resolvable samples above quantitation limits, with BDL set at one-half of detection limit.
[e]Ringwood samples are 3-day composites.

Table 4.5. Geometric Means of PAHs at Four Sites During the Winter 1982 ATEOS Campaign (Greenberg et al., 1985)

Compound (Rel. Carc.)[a]	Newark			Elizabeth			Camden			Ringwood		
	N[b]	NBDL[c]	M_G[d] (ng/m³)	N	NBDL	M_G (ng/m³)	N	NBDL	M_G (ng/m³)	N	NBDL	M_G[e] (ng/m³)
Carcinogens												
Benzo(a)pyrene (+ + +)	30	0	1.63	21	0	1.01	29	0	0.87	10	0	0.32
Benzo(b)fluoranthene (+ +)	35	0	1.35	34	0	1.71	35	0	1.07	11	0	0.46
Benzo(j)fluoranthene (+ +)	34	1	1.06	27	0	0.92	36	0	0.58	12	0	0.24
Dibenzo(ae)pyrene (+ +)	16	0	1.21	15	0	2.67	19	0	1.18	5	0	0.47
Benz(a)anthracene (+)	32	0	1.36	25	0	1.38	32	0	1.06	10	0	0.42
Dibenz(ac)anthracene (+)	16	1	0.05	15	0	0.17	21	1	0.13	10	0	0.10
Indeno(1,2,3-cd)pyrene (+)	29	0	2.90	31	0	2.46	33	0	1.66	9	0	0.79
Chrysene (+)	19	0	4.94	34	0	5.33	36	0	2.66	9	0	1.32
Non-carcinogens												
Benzo(k)fluoranthene	16	0	0.97	15	0	0.61	20	0	0.53	10	0	0.28
Benzo(ghi)perylene	25	0	2.74	24	0	2.25	29	0	1.88	11	0	0.59
Coronene	18	0	1.62	18	0	1.62	37	1	0.92	13	0	0.34
Benzo(e)pyrene	34	1	2.38	27	1	11.15	36	2	2.55	12	0	0.35
Perylene	32	19	0.01	6	22	0.01	30	24	0.01	11	10	0.09

[a]See Santodonato et al., 1981.
[b]N = number of samples analyzed.
[c]NBDL = number below detection limit.
[d]M_G = geometric means based on resolvable samples above quantitation limits, with BDL set at one-half of detection limit.
[e]Ringwood samples are 3-day composites.

Table 4.6.   Geometric Means of PAH at four sites during the Summer 1982 ATEOS Campaign (Greenberg et al., 1985)

Compound (Rel Carc)[a]	Newark			Elizabeth			Camden			Ringwood[e]		
	N[b]	NBDL[c]	M_G[d] (ng/m³)	N	NBDL	M_G (ng/m³)	N	NBDL	M_G (ng/m³)	N	NBDL	M_G (ng/m³)
Carcinogens												
Benzo(a)pyrene (+ + +)	36	0	0.21	36	0	0.14	35	0	0.11	12	1	0.04
Benzo(b)fluoranthene (+ +)	38	0	0.34	38	0	0.24	35	5	0.17	10	0	0.07
Benzo(j)fluoranthene (+ +)	34	0	0.21	37	2	0.10	33	5	0.08	11	5	0.01
Dibenzo(a,e)pyrene (+ +)	20	5	0.06	21	0	0.21	19	3	0.07	8	3	0.19
Cyclopenta(c,d)pyrene (+ +)?	34	6	0.05	28	6	0.03	33	3	0.04	9	1	0.01
Benzo(a)anthracene (+)	24	0	0.15	33	1	0.11	27	0	0.07	13	1	0.02
Dibenzo(a,j)anthracene (+)	35	1	0.28	36	2	0.23	34	0	0.14	10	4	0.08
Dibenzo(a,c)anthracene (+)	24	9	0.06	23	13	0.05	20	8	0.02	5	0	0.01
Indeno(1,2,3-c,d)pyrene (+)	30	0	0.37	29	0	0.25	25	0	0.20	10	0	0.10
Chrysene (+)	27	0	0.52	21	0	0.31	32	0	0.22	10	0	0.12
Non-carcinogens												
Benzo(k)fluoranthene	27	0	0.15	29	0	0.11	34	0	0.09	7	0	0.04
Benzo(g,h,i)perylene	36	1	0.62	34	0	0.35	35	2	0.24	8	4	0.02
Coronene	34	0	0.37	34	1	0.23	31	0	0.14	9	0	0.07
Benzo(e)pyrene	33	3	0.16	34	9	0.08	31	15	0.03	12	5	0.03
Perylene	35	24	0.01	5	34	0.01	38	31	0.01	11	9	0.01
Pyrene	17	0	0.35	20	0	0.12	17	0	0.15	7	0	0.08
Benzo(g,h,i)fluoranthene	33	1	0.20	31	4	0.12	31	0	0.12	11	3	0.07
Dibenzo(a,l)pyrene (±)	3	0	0.14	7	1	0.05	3	0	0.35	1	0	0.01
Benzo(a)aceanthrylene(?)	34	18	0.04	33	16	0.03	28	14	0.03	8	4	0.02
Benzo(b)chrysene(?)	16	2	0.19	27	11	0.12	29	2	0.07	8	3	0.01
Benzo(a)phenanthrene(?)	22	0	0.19	23	0	0.13	14	0	0.07	1	0	0.01

[a] See Santodonato et al., 1981.
[b] N = number of samples analyzed.
[c] NBDL = number below detection limit.
[d] M_G = geometric means based on resolvable samples above quantitation limits, with BDL set at one-half of detection limit.
[e] Ringwood samples are 3-day composites.

Table 4.7. Geometric Means of PAHs at Four Sites during the Winter 1983 ATEOS Campaign (Greenberg et al., 1985)

Compound (Rel. Carc.)[a]	Newark			Elizabeth			Camden			Ringwood		
	N^b	$NBDL^c$	M_G^d (ng/m^3)	N	NBDL	M_G (ng/m^3)	N	NBDL	M_G (ng/m^3)	N	NBDL	M_G (ng/m^3)
Carcinogens												
Benzo(a)pyrene (+ + +)	38	0	1.06	37	0	0.69	37	0	0.94	14	0	0.17
Benzo(b)fluoranthene (+ +)	35	0	1.09	31	0	0.78	36	0	1.03	14	0	0.29
Benzo(j)fluoranthene (+ +)	37	0	1.04	36	0	0.70	37	0	0.86	13	2	0.17
Dibenzo(ae)pyrene (+ +)	8	0	0.83	13	0	0.55	14	0	0.51	5	0	0.14
Cyclopenta(cd)pyrene (+ + +)	37	1	0.66	37	1	0.54	37	2	0.43	14	1	0.07
Benzo(a)anthracene (+)	22	0	0.88	25	0	0.56	28	8	0.68	13	0	0.12
Dibenzo(aj)anthracene (+)	31	1	0.37	29	4	0.38	21	8	0.22	10	3	0.08
Dibenzo(ac)anthracene (+)	5	0	0.13	6	0	0.06	3	0	—	5	1	0.03
Indeno(1,2,3-cd)pyrene (+)	38	0	0.98	36	0	0.94	38	0	0.94	14	0	0.21
Chrysene (+)	9	0	2.42	9	0	1.01	3	0	0.62	7	0	0.29
Non-carcinogens												
Benzo(k)fluoranthene	32	0	0.63	21	1	0.40	27	0	0.55	11	2	0.08
Benzo(ghi)perylene	38	0	1.44	37	0	1.28	38	0	1.13	14	0	0.26
Coronene	37	0	0.52	23	0	0.59	25	0	0.56	7	0	0.19
Benzo(e)pyrene	38	0	1.83	31	2	1.09	33	1	1.35	13	0	0.32
Perylene	16	13	0.09	22	4	0.08	24	2	0.15	10	6	0.02
Pyrene	27	0	2.77	32	0	1.79	25	0	1.90	8	0	0.43
Benzo(ghi)fluoranthene	38	0	1.31	37	1	0.99	38	0	1.29	14	0	0.20
Benzo(a)aceanthrylene	15	0	0.42	15	0	0.42	20	0	0.38	3	0	0.12
Dibenzo(bk)fluoranthene	26	1	0.20	35	0	0.19	33	0	0.20	11	3	0.05

[a]See Santodonato et al., 1981.
[b]N = number of samples analyzed.
[c]NBDL = number below detection limit.
[d]M_G = geometric means based on resolvable samples above quantitation limits, with BDL set at one-half of detection limit.
[e]Ringwood samples are 3-day composites.

techniques. It is immediately obvious that the three urban locations, Newark, Elizabeth, and Camden, had 3 to 5 times the PAH levels of the rural Ringwood site during both seasons. Generally, Newark had the highest levels of PAH among the urban sites, although Elizabeth rivaled it for this distinction during winter 1982 (Table 4.5). Elizabeth usually had higher PAH levels than Camden. Winter PAH levels were usually 4 to 6 times higher than summer levels.

BaP Study Results

At this point it is worthwhile to present some of the results of the previously-mentioned 27-site study for comparison with the ATEOS study. Table 4.8 lists the sites classified according to zone type (CS = coastal; RI = rural interior; NEI = northeast industrial; SWI = southwest industrial) and provides annual averages for 1982 as well as maximum values for BaP, TSP and CX(son) (cyclohexane solubles; these data are semiquantitative and not completely comparable to the ATEOS CX values since they were obtained using TSP, not IPM, had no sample clarification, and were measured on a Mettler microbalance as opposed to a Cahn electrobalance). A map of New Jersey displaying these sites is shown in Figure 4.1. Here, one sees higher levels for the NEI and SWI sites relative to the CS and RI sites. It was gratifying to find that the lowest BaP levels were found at the Ringwood site, thus reaffirming justification for its use as the background site during ATEOS. Of the three classes of pollutants in Table 4.8, BaP showed the greatest site-to-site variability and TSP showed the least. The New Jersey site with the highest BaP average was a location in Jersey City. It was impacted by a major highway (Pulaski Skyway); an underground hazardous waste site fire, which has burned continuously for a number of years; and a coal-burning energy station, as well as the general activities of this densely populated urban site. Our windrose analysis showed no particular directionality of the pollution. The second highest BaP average, surprisingly enough, belonged to the Phillipsburg location. Here, pollution roses indicated that high BaP levels accompanied westerly winds. Although Easton, Pennsylvania and perhaps Allentown and Bethlehem were considered as likely sources, the origin may well lie with a large smelting operation less than a mile west of the sampling site. If one removes Phillipsburg from the RI class, then one finds that the NEI and SWI sites group together and have about twice the BaP levels of the CS and RI sites, which similarly group together. This finding, incidentally, may indicate that routine ambient monitoring of BaP need only be done at two types of locations.

Table 4.9 lists the monthly averages for all 27 sites for BaP and TSP. It is clear that the monthly variation in TSP is not as large as that for BaP. The highest values occur during the warm season. In contrast, the BaP levels

Table 4.8.   Mean and Maximum BaP, CX, and TSP at 27 New Jersey Sites during 1982 (Harkov and Greenberg, 1985)

Site	Zone[a]	BaP (ng/m³)	Maximum	CX (µg/m³)	Maximum	TSP (µg/m³)	Maximum
Asbury Park	CS	0.32	2.24	7.37	32.0	47.5	95.0
Atlantic City	CS	0.22	1.29	5.27	17.8	39.9	87.0
Bayonne	NEI	0.44	3.20	8.56	46.1	62.2	177.0
Bridgeton	CS	0.28	1.63	4.93	20.0	38.9	87.0
Burlington	SWI	0.40	1.51	5.64	22.5	37.9	77.0
Camden	SWI	0.47	2.44	6.49	20.2	58.3	105.0
Carteret	NEI	0.33	1.43	7.70	22.8	60.7	141.0
Cheesequake	CS	0.26	1.50	4.64	18.4	39.5	106.0
Fair Lawn	NEI	0.64	3.47	6.63	28.8	43.9	102.0
Frenchtown	RI	0.37	2.68	4.90	17.0	35.1	81.0
Hackensack	NEI	0.58	2.65	6.18	22.8	46.5	117.0
Hackettstown	RI	0.40	2.40	4.88	29.9	35.7	38.0
Hoboken	NEI	0.73	5.36	9.43	32.1	58.3	128.0
Jackson	RI	0.27	1.23	4.07	12.7	31.0	77.0
Jersey City	NEI	0.91	6.28	12.61	28.3	77.0	167.0
Kean College	NEI	0.76	4.62	8.13	28.1	48.7	124.0
Metuchen	NEI	0.62	3.85	7.14	23.7	46.0	101.0
Newark	NEI	0.71	4.09	10.92	36.3	75.7	183.0
Perth Amboy	NEI	0.50	2.09	8.45	24.6	56.4	130.0
Phillipsburg	RI	0.81	7.93	5.93	19.4	49.3	93.0
Pilesgrove	CS	0.21	2.24	4.25	15.4	32.0	92.0
Red Bank	CS	0.45	2.77	5.50	23.7	43.8	141.0
Ringwood	RI	0.19	1.06	3.86	19.0	28.6	103.0
Tom's River	CS	0.27	2.13	5.35	19.0	39.9	76.0
Trenton	SWI	0.74	3.35	7.20	23.1	45.1	98.0
Waretown	CS	0.27	1.64	3.81	8.9	33.8	70.0
Woodbury	CS	0.54	3.13	5.40	12.7	41.9	86.0

[a]Zones: CS = coastal, NEI = northeast industrial, SWI = southwest industrial, RI = rural interior.

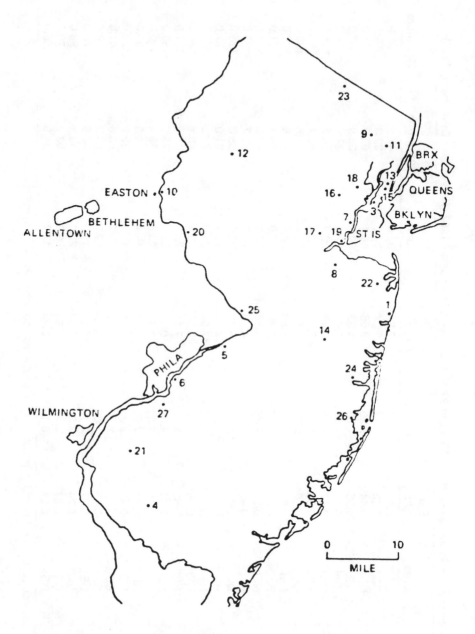

Figure 4.1.   Outline map of New Jersey showing location of BaP monitoring sites. The names and classifications of these sites are found in Table 4.5–4.10 (Harkov and Greenberg, 1985).

Table 4.9. Comparison of Monthly Means for BaP, CX, and TSP at 27 sites in New Jersey during 1982[a] (Harkov and Greenberg, 1985)

BaP ng/m³			CX (µg/m³)			TSP (µg/m³)		
a	1.22	Dec.	a	10.43	Apr.	a	62.77	Jun.
b	0.79	Jan.	ba	9.75	Feb.	b	52.98	Sep.
cb	0.67	Feb.	cb	8.86	Mar.	cb	51.28	May
c	0.57	Nov.	c	8.27	Dec.	cb	50.10	Jul.
c	0.54	Mar.	d	7.27	Jan.	cb	50.10	Oct.
d	0.37	Oct.	d	7.17	Oct.	dcb	49.48	Mar.
ed	0.28	Apr.	ed	6.35	Nov.	d	45.69	Feb.
fed	0.24	May	fe	5.36	Sep.	d	44.30	Apr.
gfe	0.17	Jun.	gf	4.47	May	d	44.30	Aug.
gf	0.13	Sep.	g	3.97	Jun.	e	39.62	Jan.
gf	0.10	Jul.	g	3.76	Aug.	e	39.56	Dec.
g	0.09	Aug.	h	2.41	Jul.	e	38.83	Nov.

[a]Duncan's Multiple Range Test—means in column following the same letter are not significantly different at the 0.05 confidence level (N = 110–130).

vary in a striking manner with season. The highest levels occurred in December, with the lowest values occurring during August. The monthly average maximum-to-minimum ratio was about 13. This is much higher than the corresponding ATEOS ratio of 4 to 6. However, the ATEOS project did not pre-identify the maximum and minimum periods, and thus there is no inconsistency between the two studies. It is worthwhile noting here that the winter/summer BaP ratio of 13 is within the range of 5 to 30 predicted on the basis of fuel use and emission rates of BaP in our earlier discussion. Generally, this suggests that higher input of BaP into the atmosphere during the winter, rather than significant decomposition during the summer, is responsible for this ratio.

PAH Concentrations During Pollution Episodes

The great differences between levels of BaP at various locations serves to emphasize the impact of local generation of this pollutant. Not surprisingly, temperature inversions have a tendency to increase local pollutant levels. Tables 4.10 and 4.11 list levels of selected PAHs during pollution episode and nonepisode periods during the Summers of 1981 and 1982, respectively. In Newark and Elizabeth, the PAH levels during pollution periods of Summer 1981 were almost double those of nonpollution periods. In contrast, there was not much change at the Camden site. This agreement emphasizes the similarity in atmospheric conditions between the Newark and Elizabeth

Table 4.10. Geometric Mean Concentrations of Six PAHs at the Three Urban Sites in Nonepisode Periods (NEP) and Episode Periods (EP)[a] during Summer 1981 (Greenberg et al., 1985)

| | Newark | | | | Elizabeth | | | | Camden | | | |
| | NEP | | EP | | NEP | | EP | | NEP | | EP | |
	N[b]	M_G (ng/m³)	N	M_G	N	M_G (ng/m³)	N	M_G (ng/m³)	N	M_G (ng/m³)	N	M_G (ng/m³)
BaP	24	0.21	9	0.33	20	0.12	8	0.22	21	0.23	8	0.22
BeP	25	0.17	12	0.20	25	0.11	9	0.25	25	0.14	12	0.16
BjF	25	0.14	12	0.23	25	0.09	9	0.11	25	0.12	12	0.15
BghiP	26	0.48	10	0.81	23	0.39	10	0.52	23	0.32	12	0.43
IcdP	20	0.55	9	0.89	17	0.30	10	0.57	16	0.44	11	0.46
Cor	26[c]	0.20	10	0.43	24	0.18	9	0.30	24	0.17	11	0.19

[a]Episode period days in Summer 1981: 18–21 July, 2–5 August, 10–13 August.
[b]N = number of samples analyzed.
[c]No data point for 21–22 July.

locations, only 8 km apart, as opposed to conditions in Camden, which is located 120 km to the southwest. Another indication is the high level of correlation between corresponding PAHs measured at the Newark and Elizabeth sites which are consistently stronger than other such correlations (Greenberg et al., 1985a).

The differences between episode and nonepisode periods during Summer 1982 were not significant. On July 19, 1981, levels at the Newark site were

Table 4.11. Episodic (EP)[a] and Non-Episodic (NEP) Levels of Seven Selected PAHs at Three New Jersey Sites during Winter 1982 (Greenberg et al., 1985)

| | Newark | | | | Elizabeth | | | | Camden | | | |
| | NEP | | EP | | NEP | | EP | | NEP | | EP | |
	N[b]	M_G (ng/m³)	N	M_G	N	M_G (ng/m³)	N	M_G (ng/m³)	N	M_G (ng/m³)	N	M_G (ng/m³)
BaP	25	1.49	5	2.51	18	0.87	3	2.41	23	0.81	6	1.11
Chry	18	4.97	1	4.36	29	4.28	6	14.08	29	2.43	7	3.90
BjF	28	1.02	6	1.27	31	0.90	6	0.98	29	0.49	7	1.16
BbF	29	1.45	6	1.07	27	1.55	7	2.49	28	0.99	7	1.46
BghiP	19	2.93	6	2.22	22	2.00	2	8.09	22	1.75	7	2.36
Cor	17	1.63	1	1.42	24	1.13	6	5.44	30	0.89	7	1.05
BaA	26	1.29	6	1.71	22	1.22	3	2.32	26	1.01	6	1.47

[a]Episode period days in Winter 1982: 19, 28, 29 January, 5, 11, 15 February.
[b]N = number of samples analyzed.

so high as to almost equal the remaining campaign days combined (the effect was to double the PAH concentration in the campaign composite – an illustration of the dangers of exclusive reliance upon the composite sample approach). No such high levels were observed at the Ringwood and Camden sites. Unfortunately, a good analysis could not be made of the Elizabeth sample, so it is impossible to say with any rigor how local the effect was. During the Winter 1983 campaign an extreme pollution episode occurred (February 13–16) in which IPM in Newark reached 201.5 $\mu g/m^3$ on February 14–15 and EOM was as high as 70.7 $\mu g/m^3$ (Lioy et al., 1985). Based upon extrapolation of COH data it would appear that TSP levels in excess of 400 $\mu g/m^3$ occurred during this period. The PAH levels in Newark and Elizabeth were 2–3 times normal levels (the increase in IPM and EOM was five- to sixfold), while the increase in levels at Camden and Ringwood were more moderate. The PAH concentrations did not increase as much as those of other pollutants measured during this episode (Lioy et al., 1985).

PAH Profiles

It is not unreasonable to assume that different combustion sources will provide different combinations and relative amounts (profiles) of PAHs, reflecting differences in fuel and combustion conditions. One extreme case is the observation of picene in the emissions from brown coal combustion; this appears to reflect the structure of compounds in the fuel (Grimmer et al., 1983). Another example is the very high levels of cyclopenta(cd)pyrene observed in automobile emissions (Grimmer et al., 1980; Grimmer, 1983c). This might allow the observer to apportion sources of PAH pollutants based upon selected indicator compounds. While a review of PAH profile data has appeared (Daisey et al., 1986), it is clear that source assignment remains elusive. Limited success has been achieved using cyclopenta(cd)-pyrene (Grimmer et al., 1980). However, the PAH mixtures from different sources seem to share much in common, making the apportionment of sources a very subtle task. Careful statistical analysis of ambient data has yielded some promising results for a lightly industrialized urban area in New Zealand where the main PAH sources are automobiles and domestic fires (Cretney et al., 1985). During periods of heavy pollution, fires were shown to be the major PAH source, and this extreme helped facilitate apportionment during days of more normal weather. Another potential complication is that many of the PAHs may be reactive under ambient conditions. Thus, aged aerosols may lose the "memory" of the sources. For example, acephenanthrylene and other cyclopenteno-PAHs are observed in fresh combustion emissions but are essentially gone from particulate matter found in the open environment (National Academy of Sciences, 1983). Cyclopenta(cd)pyrene, a representative of this class, is also very reactive due to the presence of an olefinic linkage which is readily attacked to form stabilized intermediates. Therefore, it may have a relatively short lifetime under ambient conditions. Discussions of the reactivity of PAH are to be found in the literature (National Academy of Sciences, 1983; Greenberg and Darack, 1986).

Comparison of profiles can be attained through examination of the PAH data in Tables 4.6 through 4.9. There are different numbers of PAHs in these tables because additional PAHs were added during the course of the ATEOS project. In a very few instances, a PAH was eliminated due to poor resolution during a campaign.

A useful method for comparison of PAH profiles involves indexing all PAHs to one member of the series. Ideally, this compound should be non-volatile (i.e., pentacyclic or larger) and unreactive. Benzo(e)pyrene and benzo(j)fluoranthene would be ideally suited but they co-elute under the HPLC conditions employed during the ATEOS study and the errors intrinsic to analysis of co-elutors limit their utility as index compounds. Indeno(1,2,3-cd)pyrene is another nonvolatile, unreactive PAH, but the dataset is not continuous enough to employ it as the PAH index. We employed BaP, while realizing that it has frequently been used in the past as an index of PAHs, and that it is one of the more reactive of those compounds found in the environment. Before discussing some of the profile analyses, it is worth reminding the reader that the uncertainties in individual PAH concentrations are about 25% (Greenberg et al., 1985a) and that although geometric rather than arithmetic means are employed, very high levels on only a few days may severely distort average values and the resultant indices. Also, there were slight changes in analytical protocols and calibrations between campaigns, although the final two campaigns were analyzed one after the other using the same calibration. Special caution should be exercised in the interpretation of Ringwood summer ratios since the numbers are so low.

The summer B(ghi)P/BaP ratios (i.e., ratios of means) appear generally to be higher than the winter ratios. For example, the Summer 1981 ratios for Newark and Elizabeth are 2.4 and 2.9, respectively; the Summer 1982 ratios are 3.0 and 2.5; the Winter 1982 ratios are 1.7 and 2.2, respectively; and in Winter 1983 they are 1.4 and 1.9. Similar trends are seen for coronene, although the Summer 1981 values for both compounds at the Camden site appear anomalously low. These observations are consistent with the accepted utility of these PAHs as chemically stable indicators of automotive emissions, since they evidence strong correlations with lead (Gordon and Bryan, 1973; Greenberg et al., 1981) as well as the previously mentioned importance of vehicular emissions during the summer and the relatively weak contribution of this source during winter (Harkov and Greenberg, 1985). The BkF/BaP ratio is remarkably consistent at 0.6 at the three urban sites during both summers, apparently reflecting the motor vehicle source ratio. The winter ratios were consistently higher. Loss of volatile PAHs is seen in the comparison between the three quarters of data for the tetracyclic compound benzo(a)anthracene; conclusions for chrysene are a bit more ambiguous. Although there are only two quarters of data for cyclopenta(cd)pyrene, the results are fairly striking. During Summer 1982 the C(cd)P/BaP ratio for the four sites ranged between 0.21 and 0.36, while the ratios for the Winter 1983 study varied between 0.4 and 0.8. Thus, it appears that although the PAHs differ significantly in reactivity, this is not generally reflected in large differences between winter and summer profiles, except for exceedingly reactive compounds such as cyclopenta(cd)pyrene. The significant ambient reactivity of this compound obviously limits its utility as a tracer of automotive emissions.

Pollution episode periods associated with high IPM and ozone levels were found on a number of occasions during the two-year ATEOS project. PAH levels, listed in Tables 4.10 and 4.11, could conceivably reflect the highly reactive environment in, for example, photochemical smog. No strong support for this hypothesis was found. For example, comparison of the relatively reactive BaP to the unreactive I(1,2,3-cd)P yielded episode/nonepisode (EP/NEP) ratios for IcdP/BaP of 1.0 (Newark), 1.0 (Elizabeth), and 1.1 (Camden) during Summer 1981 (see Table 4.10).

PAH Correlations with Other Pollutants

Correlations between pollutants can be done both from the point of view of qualitative intrasite comparison and intersite comparison. Intrasite comparison, using Spearman rank correlation, between PAH is quite high ($R_{sp} >$ 0.8), reflecting the general similarity of PAH emissions from various sources near the site during a particular season, and mixing due to meteorology, as well as the fact that the same sample and analytical procedures are being employed. The strongest intersite correlations are seen for the Newark and Elizabeth locations, which are only 8 km apart. For example, Spearman rank correlation coefficients of 0.59 and 0.61, respectively, were found for BaP and B(ghi)P for these two sites during Summer 1982. During Winter 1982 very strong correlations between Newark and Elizabeth were found for BaP (0.76), B(ghi)P (0.63), and coronene (0.75) and corresponding correlation coefficients of 0.81, 0.69, and 0.78 were found during Winter 1983. These correlations undoubtedly reflect the similarity of sources and proximity of the two sites, since lesser correlations are found with the Camden site. (Since Ringwood samples were three-day composites, they could not be directly compared with urban samples.)

Intrasite correlations with other classes of pollutants offer the potential of source apportionment. It was noted earlier that B(ghi)P and coronene show strong correlations with lead, thus highlighting their potential as indicators of automotive contribution. Unfortunately, most of the datasets do not show many significant correlations of this type. More such correlations are evident in the winter when compared to the summer. We feel that this is an artifact of the much lower PAH levels during the summer which sometimes approach the analytical noise level.

During Summer 1981 intrasite Spearman rank correlation coefficients (R_{sp}) involving BaP were found to be greater than 0.60 (level of significance, $p < 0.01$) only for cyclohexane-soluble matter (CX), Pb, Zn, and Fe at the Newark site. Winter 1982 R_{sp}'s involving BaP were greater than 0.60 for CX $(R_{sp} = 0.84)$, Pb, Zn, and Ni at the Elizabeth site only. During Summer 1982 BaP correlations greater than 0.60 were found for CX, Pb, and Mn at the Camden site only. During Winter 1983 many significant correlations were found, possibly representing both higher winter concentrations and improvements in technique. For BaP the following intrasite correlations were found: Newark [R_{sp}: CX (0.83), Pb (0.81), Ni (0.63)]; Elizabeth [R_{sp}: CX (0.83), Pb (0.91), Mn (0.77), Zn (0.70), Fe (0.75), Ni (0.84)]; and Camden [R_{sp}: CX (0.87), Pb (0.82), Ni (0.65)]. In light of what had been said previously about the relatively small contribution of motor vehicle emissions to winter PAH levels, it is hard to rationalize strong wintertime correlations with lead unless what is really being reduced in these correlations are general pollution levels and the variation is a function of atmospheric conditions. Significant if only weak correlations were found between BaP and Pb at Newark and Elizabeth during Summer 1981 and at all three urban sites during Summer 1982. Although our previous discussion would lead us to suspect very strong correlations since vehicular traffic is the dominant summer contributor, these weak correlations may be an artifact related to the difficulties in quantitating low PAH levels.

Although one might have anticipated extremely strong correlations between PAHs and CX, there is no a priori reason for this to be true. We have found that when one measures the dissolved mass in five fractions of the cyclohexane extract, the largest mass is in the least polar fraction (termed here fraction 1), the PAHs are in fraction 2, and the next greatest amount of mass is found in the most polar fraction of CX (A. Greenberg, unpublished results).

The reasons for the infrequent correlations between PAHs and other pollutants measured during ATEOS have to do with the nature of the sources, and differences in the physical and chemical behavior of the pollutants, as well as artifacts of experimental measurement. Thus, if there is a local intense source of zinc, correlation with PAHs is not expected, since the latter are coming from a large number and variety of area sources. The disappearance pathways of pollutants will differ. While metals such as Fe are nonvolatile, some volatility is expected for CX and the tetracyclic PAHs while the pentacyclic PAHs could show loss due to chemical reactivity, although our other discussions in this chapter indicate that this is not a major factor. The analysis of PAHs and metals takes two different routes: oxidation and acidic digestion versus organic solvent extraction. Combined with the higher (ca. 25%) uncertainty in PAH analyses compared to about 10% for the other pollutants, experimental artifact creeps into the picture.

Relationship Between PAH Levels and Mutagenicity

Although the mutagenicity studies performed during the ATEOS study are described in detail elsewhere in this book, we will briefly discuss findings relevant to our PAH results. Although five tester strains of *Salmonella typhimurium* were investigated for the ATEOS program, the TA98 strain proved most sensitive to air pollutants and will be discussed in this section. Ames assays may be run without or with enzyme activation. Enzymes are present in rat liver extract (S9) obtained following induction through administration of Aroclor. The PAH class are not direct mutagens, and their mutagenicities are manifested upon enzyme-induced (activated) assay.

Mutagenicity was found in all urban and rural composite extracts tested. During Summer 1981 the cyclohexane extracts were found to greatly increase their mutagenic activity upon enzyme activation, consistent with although not limited to the view that the PAHs play the major mutagenic role in this extract. The more polar dichloromethane (DCM) and acetone (ACE) extracts did not show increased activity with the liver extract. Furthermore, the activated (+ S9) mutagenicities of the four cyclohexane extract composites were in the same order as the PAH concentrations. Although such a correlation does not prove cause and effect, its combination with the results of the unactivated (-S9) assay appeared to support the importance of the PAHs in the direct-acting mutagenic activity of airborne particulate matter. For the Summer 1981 Newark sample, the cyclohexane extract was responsible for about 20% of the total unactivated mutagenicity of the three extracts, while the corresponding figure for the activated mutagenicity was almost 50%. However, the Winter 1982 samples did not provide such seemingly straightforward support for the importance of PAHs in biological activity. Thus, within the accuracy of the assay, the activated and unactivated mutagenicities of the cyclohexane composites were rather close, with the cyclohexane extract responsible for about 23% of the unactivated Ames mutagenicity for the Winter 1982 Newark composite and 35% for the activated assay. The ratio of Winter 1982/Summer 1981 mutagenicity (revertants/m^3) for the combined three Newark extracts was 2.7 for the unactivated assay and 2.7 for the activated assay. Subsequent summer and winter Ames assays produced results reminiscent of the Winter 1982 study. Winter 1983 mutagenicity levels were similar to Winter 1982 levels.

Recently published studies indicate the importance of derivatives of PAHs, such as nitro-PAHs, and especially the importance of the more polar extract fractions to the mutagenic response (Siak et al., 1985). This is consistent with the direct mutagenicities observed in DCM and ACE extracts from the ATEOS study (Atherholt et al., 1985). Our own unpublished studies, in collaboration with Dr. T. Atherholt of the Coriell Institute for Medical Research, indicate that of five fractions separated via thin-layer chromatography (TLC) from the cyclohexane extract, the PAH fraction shows negligible direct mutagenicity and its activated mutagenicity is approximately equal to that of the third fraction, which is slightly more polar and which contains nitro-PAHs. Using the three-solvent ATEOS extraction protocol, we found that most of the mutagenicity (activated or unactivated) is contained in the most polar fractions of five separated by TLC from the DCM extract. (Indeed, the ATEOS program had shown the DCM extract to be the most mutagenic, on the basis of revertants μg of extracted organic matter). This highly polar fraction does not contain PAHs or simple nitro-PAHs, which appear to contribute negligible mutagenicity to the DCM extract. We will return to this topic later. ATEOS and our own subsequent studies indicate mutagenic activity in the most polar acetone fractions, although these have significant levels of inorganics, including about 10% nitrate. The less polar of the acetone fractions appear to be somewhat mutagenic.

PAH DERIVATIVES AND AMBIENT REACTIVITY OF PAH

It is quite clear now that there are many other classes of organic compounds in airborne particulate matter having mutagenic and carcinogenic activity in addition to the PAHs. Some of these compounds are oxidation products, such as quinones (Pierce and Katz, 1976) and ketones (Ramdahl, 1983). An interesting PAH dicarboxylic acid anhydride having unactivated mutagenicity has been found in diesel particulate matter (Rappaport et al., 1980). Nitro derivatives of PAHs are present at very low levels in the ambient air relative to PAHs, but they are of concern as direct mutagens, some of which (the dinitropyrenes) are among the strongest known carcinogens (Rosenkranz, 1982, 1984; Gibson, 1982; White, 1985). Another reason for concern is the relatively large amount of nitro-PAH present in diesel particulates (Handa et al., 1984).

An interesting approach toward discerning what are the most biologically harmful compounds in particulate matter involves the use of biologically driven chemical analysis (Nishioka et al., 1985; Siak et al., 1985). The findings include the observation that a large fraction of mutagenic activity is due to more polar nitrated compounds, among which are hydroxynitro-PAH (HNP) (Schuetzle et al., 1982; Schuetzle, 1983; Paputa-Peck et al., 1983; Nishioka et al., 1985). Our own studies have focused on an interesting nonpolar HNP, 1-nitropyren-2-ol, which is synthesized photochemically from 1-nitropyrene (Yasuhara and Fuwa, 1983) and which, atypically for the class, is an indirect mutagen similar in activity to BaP (Lofroth et al., 1984). We have found this substance in ambient air and postulate that it may be a product of reaction of 1-nitropyrene in air (Greenberg et al., 1985b; Greenberg and Wang, 1986). Our group is also determining concentrations of airborne nitro-PAHs using the HPLC postanalytical column reducer technique of the National Bureau of Standards (MacCrehan and May, 1984). We have found this technique useful in the analysis of PAH quinones (Greenberg et al., 1985b).

Where do nitro and quinone derivatives in ambient airborne particulate matter come from? Although there is some evidence for artifacts arising from reactivity of PAHs caught on glass fiber filters (Pitts, 1979; Lee et al., 1980), recent work appears to minimize this effect (Grosjean et al., 1983). The formation of 2-nitrofluoranthene and 2-nitropyrene appears to occur in air since they have never been seen in emissions or in artifactual studies (Pitts et al., 1985). Although our own work cited here indicates that the similarity in summer and winter PAH profiles of compounds of significantly different reactivity (Greenberg and Darack, 1986) argues for little ambient reactivity, there is no inconsistency. The levels of nitro-PAHs are very low, and even if they represent a minor chemical pathway their high mutagenicity makes their presence important from a biological point of view. Similarly, quinones appear to occur at much lower levels than the corresponding PAHs (Pierce and Katz, 1976).

FUTURE DIRECTIONS

The extensions of the PAH component of the ATEOS study point in four directions. First, there will be a continuation of the current studies aimed at finding which compounds or classes of compounds are responsible for the major part of the mutagenic activity of air particulate matter. Certainly a part of these studies will be investigation into the mechanisms of PAH reaction under ambient conditions. As this chapter is being composed, current interest is focused on hydroxynitro derivatives of PAHs. In these studies, it is the biological response which drives the chemical analysis, in contrast to the situation where an investigator chooses a chemical class of preconceived importance, e.g., PAHs, and then analyzes them. A second extension of the ATEOS program will involve measurements of selected classes of nonvolatile and semivolatile compounds including PAHs, nitro-PAHs, PAH-quinones and ketones, nitrohydroxy-PAHs, heteroanalogs, chlorinated PAHs, and dioxins from the combustion of various types of incinerators. Incineration of waste fuels as well as sludge and municipal waste may become much more important in future years. A third major research direction will be the investigation of indoor pollutant levels. A number of research groups have recognized the importance of indoor air pollution from the point of view of numbers of hours normally spent indoors compared to outdoors and the poorer circulation of air in buildings sealed up to conserve energy. The fourth direction for our research studies will involve assessing human exposure under normal living conditions. We expect to assess the amount of PAHs a person is exposed to through diet and inhalation and assess what is actually absorbed and metabolized through measurement of metabolites in body fluids.

ACKNOWLEDGMENTS

I owe a debt of gratitude directly and indirectly to many people in connection with this work. I am grateful to my colleagues Professors Joseph Bozzelli and Barbara Kebbekus for bringing me into the Air Pollution Research Laboratory as an equal partner, to Dr. Arnold Allentuch, Associate Vice President for Research and Graduate Studies at NJIT for early support, to the Office of Science and Research of the New Jersey Department of Environmental Protection for continued support, to Drs. Joan Daisey, Ronald Harkov, Paul Lioy and Judy Louis, and Ms. Leslie McGeorge for continued helpful guidance and discussions, to Drs. Thomas Atherholt and Gerard McGarrity for Ames assays and guidence in interpreting results, and to Dr. Stephen Wise of the National Bureau of Standards for numerous discussions and free PAH "samples." Most of the work in this study was carried out with the able assistance of Ms. Faye Darack, Ms. Dina Natsiashvili, Ms. Nina Kovalyov and the following students: Clinton Brockway, Paul Brown, Diane Dudacik, Dean Hawthorne, Alexander Kovalyov, Roman Pazdro, Janis Racz, Orlando Rodriguez, and Yalan Wang.

REFERENCES

Ames, B. N., McCann, J., and Yamasaki, E. (1975), *Mutation Res.*, 31, 347–363.

Atherholt, T. B., McGarrity, G. J., Louis, J. B., McGeorge, L. J., Lioy, P. J., Daisey, J. M., Greenberg, A., Darack, F. (1985), In *Short-Term Bioassays in the Analysis of Complex Environmental Mixtures*, Vol. 4, Waters, M. D., Sandhu, S. S., Lewis, J., Claxton, L., Strauss, G., and Nesnow, S. (Eds.), Plenum Pub., 1985, pp. 211–231.

Atkinson, R., Aschmann, S.M., and Pitts, J. N., Jr. (1984), *Environ. Sci. Technol.*, 18, 110–113.

Bjorseth, A. (Ed.) (1983), *Handbook of Polycyclic Aromatic Hydrocarbons*, Marcel Dekker, New York.

Blumer, M., and Youngblood, W. W. (1975), *Science, 188*, 53–55.

Blumer, M., Blumer, W., and Reich, T. (1978), *Environ. Sci. Technol., 11*, 1082–1084.

Clement Associates, Inc. (1983), Review and Evaluation and Evidence for Cancer Associated with Air Pollution, U.S. EPA Report EPA-450/5-83-006.

Cretny, J. R., Lee, H. K., Wright, G. J., Swallow, W. H., and Taylor, M. C. (1985), *Envir. Sci. Technol.*, 19, 397–404.

Daisey, J. M., Cheney, J. L., and Lioy, P. J., (1986), *J. Air Pollut. Control Assoc.*, 36, 17–33.

Faoro, R. B., and Manning, J. A. (1981), *J. Air Pollut. Control Assoc.*, 31, 62–64.

Galayn, J. F., Hornig, J. F., and Soderberg, R. H. (1984), *J. Air Pollut. Control Assoc.*, 34, 57–59.

Gibson, T. L. (1982), *Atmos. Envir.*, 16, 2037–2040.

Gordon, R. J., and Bryan, R. J. (1973), *Enrivon. Sci. Technol.*, 7, 1050–1053.

Greenberg, A., Bozzelli, J. W., Cannova, F., Forstner, E., Giorgio, P., Stout, D., and Yokoyama, R. (1981), *Environ. Sci. Technol.*, 15, 566–570.

Greenberg, A., Darack, F., Harkov, R., Lioy, P., and Daisey, J., (1985a) *Atmos. Environ.*, 19, 1325–1339.

Greenberg, A., Darack, F., Hawthorne, D., Natsiashvili, D., Wang, Y., Harkov, R., and Louis, J. (1985b), Presentation at Tenth International Symposium on Polynuclear Aromatic Hydrocarbons, Columbus, Ohio, October 21–23, 1985.

Greenberg, A., and Wang, Y. (1986), Submitted to *Atmos. Environ.*

Greenberg, A., and Darack, F. (1986). In *Molecular Structure and Energetics*, Vol. 4, (Edited by Liebman, J. F., and Greenberg, A.), Chapter 1, VCH Publishers, Deerfield Beach, FL.

Greenberg, M. R. (1979), Cancer Mortality in the New Jersey Region, 1950–1969: High and Low Risk Factors, Part 1, New Jersey Department of Environmental Protection Report 79/01.

Greenberg, M. R. (1986), *The Sciences*, 26, No. 1, 40–46.

Grimmer, G. (1983a), *Environmental Carcinogens: Polycyclic Aromatic Hydrocarbons*, CRC Press, Boca Raton, FL.

Grimmer, G. (1983b), *Analysis of Polycyclic Aromatic Hydrocarbons in Environmental Samples*, IARC Vol. 3, Pub. 29.

Grimmer, G. (1983c) In *Handbook of Polycyclic Aromatic Hydrocarbons* (Edited by Bjorseth, A.), pp. 149–181, Marcel Dekker, New York.

Grimmer, G., Naujack, K. W., and Schneiden, D. (1980), In *Polynuclear Aromatic Hydrocarbons* (Edited by Bjorseth, A., and Dennis, A. J.), pp. 107–125, Battelle Press, Columbus, OH.

Grimmer, G., Jacob, J., Naujack, K.-W., and Dettbarn, G. (1983), *Anal. Chem.*, 55, 892–900.

Grosjean, D., Fung, K., and Harrison, J. (1983), *Envir. Sci. Technol.*, 17, 673–679.

Haemisegger, E., Jones, A., Steigerwald, B., and Thomson, V. (1985), The Air Toxics Problem in the United States: An Analysis of Cancer Risks for Selected Pollutants, U.S. EPA Report EPA-450/1-85-001.

Handa, T., Yamauchi, T., Sawai, K., Yamamura, T., Koseki, Y., and Ishii, T. (1984), *Envir. Sci. Technol.*, 18, 895–902.

Hangebrauck, R. P., von Lehmden, D. T., and Meeker, T. E. (1967), Sources of Polynuclear Hydrocarbons in the Atmosphere, U.S. Department HEW. Pub. No. 999-AP-33.

Harkov, R., Greenberg, A., Darack, F., Daisey, J. M., and Lioy, P. (1984), *Environ. Sci. Technol.*, 18, 287–291.

Harkov, R., and Greenberg, A. (1985), *J. Air Pollut. Control Assoc.*, 35, 238–243.

Harvey, R. (1981), *Accounts Chem. Res.*, 14, 218–226.

Harvey, R. (1982), *Am. Sci.*, 70, 386–393.

Jerina, D. M., Yagi, H., Lehr, R. E., Thakker, D. R., Schaeffer-Ridder, M., Karle, J. M., Levin, W., Wood, A. W., Chang, R. L., and Conney, A. H. (1981), In *Polycyclic Hydrocarbons and Cancer*, Vol. 1 (Edited by Gelboin, H. V., and Ts'o, P.O.P.), pp. 173–188, Academic Press, New York.

Lee, M. L., Novotny, M. V., and Bartle, K. D. (1981), *Analytical Chemistry of Polycyclic Aromatic Compounds*, Academic Press, New York.

Lee, F. S. C., Pierson, W. R., and Ezike, J. (1980), *In Polynuclear Aromatic Hydrocarbons: Chemistry and Biological Effects* (Edited by Bjorseth, A., and Dennis, A. J.), pp. 543–563, Battelle Press, Columbus.

Lioy, P. J., Daisey, J. M., Atherholt, T., Bozzelli, J., Darack, F., Fisher, R., Greenberg, A., Harkov, R., Kebbekus, B., Kneip, T. J., Louis, J., McGarrity, G., McGeorge, L., and Reiss, N. M. (1983), *J. Air Poll. Control Assoc.*, 33, 649–657.

Lioy, P. J., Daisey, J. M., Greenberg, A., and Harkov, R. (1985), *Atmos. Environ.*, 19, 429–436.

Lipfert, F. W. (1985), *Environ. Sci. Technol.*, 19, 764–770.

Lofroth, G., Nilsson, L., Agurell, E., and Yasuhara, A. (1984), *Z. Naturforsch.*, 39c, 193–195.

Lunde, G., and Bjorseth, A. (1977), *Nature*, 268, 518–519.

MacCrehan, W. A., and May, W. E. (1984), Presentation at Ninth International Symposium on Polynuclear Aromatic Hydrocarbons, Columbus, Ohio, October, 1984.

Miguel, A. H., and Friedlander, S. K. (1978), *Atmos. Envir.*, 12, 2407–2413.

National Academy of Sciences (1972), *Particulate Polycyclic Organic Matter*, Washington, DC.

National Academy of Sciences (1983), *Polycyclic Aromatic Hydrocarbons: Evaluation of Sources and Effects*, Washington, DC.

New Jersey Department of Health (1981), Report: *The Descriptive Epidemiology of Cancer in New Jersey: 1949-1976.*

Nishioka, M. G., Howard, C. C., and Lewtas, J. (1985), Presentation at Tenth International Symposium on Polynuclear Aromatic Hydrocarbons, Columbus, Ohio, October 21-23, 1985.

Paputa-Peck, M. C., Marano, R. S., Schuetzle, D., Riley, T. L., Hampton, C. V., Prater, T. J., Skewes, L. M., Jensen, T. E., Ruehle, P. H., Bosch, L. C., and Duncan, W. P. (1983), *Anal. Chem.*, 55, 1946-1954.

Pierce, R. C., and Katz, M. (1976), *Environ. Sci. Technol.*, 10, 45-51.

Pitts, J. N., Jr. (1979), *Phil. Trans. Royal Soc. London Ser. A*, 290, 551-576.

Ramdahl, T. (1983), *Environ. Sci. Technol.*, 17, 666-670.

Rappaport, S. M., Wang, Y. Y., Wei, E. T., Sawyer, R., Watkins, B. E., and Rappoport, H. (1980), *Environ. Sci. Technol.*, 14, 1505-1509.

Rosenkranz, H. S. (1982), *Mutat. Res.*, 101, 1-10.

Rosenkranz, H. S. (1984), *Mutat. Res.*, 140, 1-6.

Santodonato, J. P., Howard, D., and Basu, T. (1981), *Environ. Path. Toxicol.*, 3, 1-364.

Schuetzle, D., Riley, T. L., Prater, T. J., Harvey, T. M., and Hunt, D. F. (1982), *Anal. Chem.*, 54, 265-271.

Schuetzle, D. (1983), *Environ. Health Perspectives*, 47, 65-80.

Siak, J., Chan, T. L., Gibson, T. L., and Wolff, G. T. (1985), *Atmos. Environ.*, 19, 369-376.

Swanson, D., Morris, C., Hedgcoke, R., Jungers, R., Thompson, R., and Bumgarner, J. E. (1981), *Trends Fluor.*, 1, 2.

Swanson, D. H., and Walling, J. F. (1981), *Chrom. News*, 9, 25.

White, C. M. (1985), *Nitrated Polycyclic Aromatic Hydrocarbons*, Huethig, Heidelberg.

Wise, S. A., and Sander, L.C. (1985), *HRC&CC*, 8, 248-255.

Yamasaki, H., Kuwata, K., and Miyamoto, H. (1982), *Envir. Sci. Technol.*, 16, 189-194.

Yasuhara, A., and Fuwa, K. (1983), *Chem. Lett.*, 347-348.

You, F., and Bidleman, T. F. (1984), *Envir. Sci. Technol.*, 18, 330-333.

CHAPTER 5

Mutagenicity of Inhalable Particulate Matter at Four Sites in New Jersey

Judith B. Louis, Thomas B. Atherholt, Joan M. Daisey, Leslie J. McGeorge, Gerard J. McGarrity

CHAPTER CONTENTS

Mutagenicity of Inhalable Particulate Matter at Four Sites in New Jersey

INTRODUCTION

New Jersey is a highly urban and industrial state. A nationwide survey of cancer mortality rates published in 1973 (Mason, 1973) revealed that New Jersey had the highest rate of cancer mortality in the United States for white males, and the second highest for white females. Lung cancer mortality rankings for the state were third and fourth for white males and white females, respectively. Many past epidemiological studies have indicated that there is a higher rate of lung cancer mortality in urban areas than in rural areas (Carnow, 1978). This difference, coupled with the fact that concentrations of airborne particulate matter are generally higher in urban areas (Adamson and Bruce, 1979), has focused increased attention on the carcinogenic and mutagenic activity of the organic material associated with airborne particles.

Although air pollution has long been suspected of elevating the risk of cancer in urban dwellers, this has been difficult to demonstrate epidemiologically. There are many confounding factors in such studies, including a lack of good exposure data and accurate health records. In addition, the variables selected as surrogates for pollution, e.g., total suspended particulates (TSP—less than or equal to 35 μm diameter), and benzene-soluble organics (BSO), are not adequate surrogates for genotoxic activity. Both TSP and BSO are parameters that measure the total mass of mixtures of thousands of compounds, some of which are known to be carcinogenic or mutagenic, and others that are not. The chemical composition of the TSP and BSO mixtures can vary considerably among cities (Daisey et al., 1983; Butler et al., 1985) depending upon the local sources of particulate matter.

As a consequence, total mass is not always directly related to biological activity (Butler et al., 1986).

Animal bioassays can, in principle, provide a more direct measure of the carcinogenic potential of air pollution. Investigators have found that the extractable organic material (EOM) from airborne particles is carcinogenic in animal bioassays (U.S. EPA, 1984). However, lifetime animal bioassays are expensive, take years to complete, and require a large amount of sample.

Beginning in the mid-seventies, investigators began using short-term *in vitro* assays such as the Ames *Salmonella* mutagenicity bioassay to demonstrate the mutagenic properties of the EOM. The Ames assay is relatively simple, inexpensive, rapid, and requires less material than an animal bioassay. The use of the Ames assay as a screen for carcinogens is based on the generally accepted principle that cancer can be initiated by an alteration in DNA, and that agents that damage DNA in the bacterial strains used in the Ames assay can also damage mammalian DNA (Ames et al., 1975). Of the known animal and human carcinogens, 83% have been detected as mutagens in the Ames test (Maron and Ames, 1983). Thus, there is reason to believe that a chemical or mixture of chemicals that causes mutations in these bacteria may pose a health risk to humans. It should be recognized that bacterial metabolism often differs significantly from mammalian metabolism and, consequently, a potent mutagen in the Ames test may not necessarily be a potent carcinogen in mammals.

The Ames bacterial mutation assay can provide a more direct measure of the genotoxic activity of urban aerosols than a simple measurement of the mass of particles or the mass of extractable organics. Investigators from around the world have reported that the EOM from airborne particles is mutagenic, and that the EOM from urban sites is more mutagenic than that from less developed areas (Tokiwa et al., 1976; Pitts et al., 1977; Alfheim and Moeller, 1979). In addition, no detectable mutagenic activity was found in samples collected in pristine locations (Pitts et al., 1977; Alfheim and Moeller, 1979). These data suggest that the relative mutagenicity of the organic material associated with airborne particles may be a relevant indicator of the human health hazard associated with airborne particulate matter.

In assessing potential health impacts associated with airborne particulate matter, the size of the particles collected is a crucial factor. Most previous studies on the mutagenicity of airborne particles have examined TSP. However, it has been shown that smaller diameter particles are of prime interest, since these particles have the longest atmospheric residence time (Esman and Corn, 1971), are most readily deposited in the lung, and most slowly cleared from the lung (Yeh et al., 1976). Talcott and Harger (1980) have shown that smaller particles (less than or equal to 2.0 μm) contribute more (56 to 89%) of the total EOM from a cubic meter of air than do larger particles (2 to 11 μm) and contribute a greater percentage of the total mutagenic activity per cubic meter of air. Thus, the proportion of total mutagenic activity of airborne EOM increases as the diameter of the particles decreases. For these reasons, the mutagenic activity of inhalable particulate matter (IPM—less than or equal to 15 μm) was studied.

Some of the carcinogenic and mutagenic activity in the EOM has been attributed to the presence of polycyclic aromatic hydrocarbons (PAHs), a group of compounds that include many known animal carcinogens (Moeller and Alfheim, 1980). In the past, the concentration of one PAH, benzo(a)pyrene (BaP), has also been used as a surrogate for the carcinogenic potential of airborne particulate matter. However, the demonstration that mutagens of widely varying polarity exist in the EOM (Daisey et al., 1980; Atherholt et al., 1985), indicates that the nonpolar PAHs account for only a portion of the genotoxic material present in the EOM. Pitts (1983) has demonstrated that polar transformation products of PAHs (i.e., nitro-PAHs and oxygenated PAHs) which have been shown to be mutagens, are present in the atmosphere. Thus, BaP cannot be used as an accurate surrogate for all genotoxic activity in the EOM.

The objective of this work was to examine the mutagenicity of the EOM associated with inhalable particles at the ATEOS urban and rural sites over a two-year period. In addition, the study evaluated seasonal variations in mutagenic activity, and attempted to relate mutagenic activity to some aspects of chemical composition. These data may be used for future epidemiological studies on the effects of air pollution on human health. In addition, the mutagenicity data on ambient air in New Jersey will be essential in evaluating the results of future site-specific studies on local air pollution sources in the state, and in examining long-term trends in ambient air quality.

METHODOLOGY

Sample Collection and Preparation

Twenty-four-hour samples were collected and extracted for each of four 39-day sampling campaigns as indicated in Chapter 1. Blank filter samples were also prepared and extracted for each campaign. Details of these procedures have been described elsewhere (Daisey et al., 1979; Daisey et al., 1984).

Composite sample extracts for each of the four campaigns and each of the three organic fractions were prepared for each site and fraction by combining equivalent air volume aliquots for each day (three days for Ringwood). Composite blank filter extracts were prepared using the same number of blank filters as for the sample composites. During the Summer 1982 campaign, daily samples were also composited according to a photochemical smog or "episode" period (EP) and "nonepisode" period (NEP) for mutagenicity analysis. During the Winter 1983 campaign, daily samples (not composited) from the Newark site taken during a February 11 to 18 stagnation episode were also analyzed for mutagenic activity.

Extracts were concentrated in a rotary evaporator at 30–40°C and solvent-exchanged to acetone at 85°C under nitrogen ebullation in a Kuderna-Danish concentration tube equipped with a 3-ring Snyder column. Gravimetric analysis (sensitivity limit = 0.1 μg) was performed on each extract in its original solvent (CX, DCM, or ACE), and following solvent-exchange to acetone (Daisey et al., 1979). Extracts were further concentrated to 0.5 mL or less and dimethylsulfoxide (DMSO) was added to bring each extract to a predetermined extractable organic material (EOM) concentration prior to mutagenicity analyses. The EOM concentrations in the respective solvent fractions of the Newark, Elizabeth, and Camden samples were identical. When EOM quantity was sufficient, the concentration of the rural Ringwood extract fractions equaled that of the urban site extracts. When EOM quantity in the Ringwood fractions was insufficient, a lower concentration was chosen such that a minimum of four (and usually five) dose levels could be tested. The blank samples contained the same concentration of filter-solvent blanks per mL as the highest sample concentrations tested.

Mutagenicity Analysis

The standard Ames *Salmonella* reverse mutation plate incorporation assay (Ames et al., 1975; de Serres and Shelby, 1979; Maron and Ames, 1983) was initially conducted using bacterial strains TA98, TA100, TA1535, TA1537, and TA1538. Following the first campaign, strain TA1538 was eliminated because it provided no additional information beyond that provided by TA98. For the final two campaigns, Summer 1982 and Winter 1983, the new tester strain TA97 was added (Levin, 1982) and strain TA1535 omitted. The latter strain was dropped because none of the sample extracts were mutagenic to this strain. Due to small sample quantities, the rural sample extracts from the Summer 1982 campaign were tested only with strains TA98 and TA100. Episode and nonepisode extracts from the Summer 1982 and Winter 1983 campaigns were tested only with TA98.

Testing was conducted with and without metabolic activation in the form of three different lots of Aroclor 1254-induced liver homogenate (S9) from male Nichols-Wistar rats. The amount of liver homogenate used per plate (per 0.5 mL S9 mix) for each lot of S9 was either 25 μL or 50 μL, depending on S9 dose-response test results (the ability of various S9 dose levels to activate 2-aminoanthracene and benzo(a)pyrene). Mutagen controls were included with each assay, as were spontaneous reversion rate controls (no sample or carrier solvent), carrier solvent controls, filter-solvent blanks, and bacterial strain viability counts (see Atherholt et al., 1985).

Urban and rural sample extracts were tested at five or six dose levels in the nontoxic portion of the dose-response curve. Due to small sample quantities, all of the filter blank extracts from the Winter 1982 and Summer 1982 campaigns were tested at only four dose levels. The dose levels of the filter blank extracts were chosen using a dilution scheme similar to that employed for the urban site extracts. All sample doses were assayed in duplicate. All plates were incubated for 48 hr at 37°C. Bacterial colonies were counted on an automated colony counter. To minimize intertest variation, all assays with a given strain for each solvent fraction (Summer 1982) or all fractions (Summer 1981 and Winter 1982 and 1983) were performed on the same day. Twenty-four-hour episode sample extracts from the Winter 1983 campaign were tested at a different time than the composited sample extracts.

Data Analysis

Assay results were considered positive if: (1) the sample produced at least a twofold increase in the number of revertant colonies compared to the carrier solvent controls, and (2) there was a dose-response for at least three consecutive doses. A sample was considered marginal if only one of these two criteria was met.

The activity of each extract was expressed as the number of revertants per microgram of EOM using regression analysis on the linear portion of the dose-response curve, including correlation coefficient determinations (r^2) and 95% confidence intervals. The mass of EOM was not adjusted for blank mass, as the correction was insignificant for the CX fraction and ACE composites. For the DCM composites, omission of a blank adjustment resulted in a 5 to 9% underestimation of the slope. The number of revertants per cubic meter was determined as the product of the number of revertants per microgram of EOM and the number of micrograms of EOM per cubic meter of air.

RESULTS AND DISCUSSION

Major Observations

The total mutagenic activity (revertants/m³) of composite samples from the four sites is detailed in Tables A5.1, A5.2, and A5.3 of the appendix of this chapter for bacterial tester strains TA98, TA100 and TA1537. The data reveal that the total mutagenic activity varies among the three urban sites, from rural to urban sites, with the season, with the particular fraction, and with the bacterial strain.

Intersite Variations

Figure 5.1a,b is a plot of the sum of the mean mutagenic activity for strain TA98 of the three EOM fractions measured at the four ATEOS sites during the two summer and two winter campaigns. These data illustrate the intersite differences that were seen. The highest activity was measured at Newark and the lowest at Ringwood. These intersite variations indicate that the urban/rural differences that are so often discussed are the extremes of a continuum of variations that can be seen at sites with varying degrees of urbanization and industrialization. Similar interurban variations have been reported elsewhere in studies on New York City, Philadelphia, Elizabeth, NJ, Mexico City, and Beijing, (Butler et al., 1985; Butler et al., 1986). Urban/rural differences in mutagenic activity are greater than interurban differences, with urban dwellers being exposed to 2.4 to 5.4 times higher levels of mutagens than rural residents. This difference is partially a result of the fact that the levels of IPM and EOM were higher at the urban sites (1.5 to 2 times for IPM; 1.5 to 3.5 times for EOM), but other factors, such as differences in chemical composition, are also important (see Chapter 2). Sources of EOM, as well as emission rates, vary between rural and urban sites.

Seasonal Variations

A second major observation is the seasonal variation in the atmospheric concentration of mutagenic activity. The winter samples had 2.8 to 4.5 times more direct (-S9) mutagenic activity, and 1.4 to 1.9 times more indirect (+S9) mutagenic activity than the summer samples. This difference was observed at all four sites (Figure 5.1a,b), and probably reflects the differences in fuel use during the two seasons. During the summer, transportation is the major contributor to the EOM, while during the winter, both transportation and space heating are contributors (Morandi, 1985).

A second seasonal difference is the effect of metabolic activation. During the summer the addition of S9 increased the mutagenic activity in the CX fraction, while during the winter S9 had little or no effect. The reason for this difference is not clear. The CX fractions for both seasons contain PAHs that require metabolic activation in order to be detected as mutagens by the Ames assay, and, in fact, the PAH concentrations in the CX EOM increased during the winter. One explanation may be that there are additional direct mutagens emitted during the winter due to the contribution of space heating to the EOM. Or there may be substances present in the winter samples that bind to the S9 and inhibit its activity. Alternatively, the oxidizing atmosphere present during the summer may result in nonpolar direct-acting mutagens being converted to more polar molecules which would be present

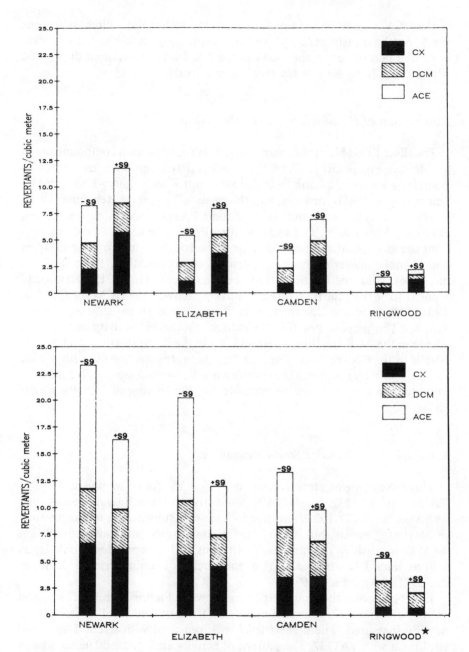

Figure 5.1. Mutagenicity of airborne particles at four sites in New Jersey. a. Average of Summer 1981 and 1982 Samples – Strain TA98 ± S9. b. Average of Winter 1982 and 1983 Samples – Strain TA98 ± S9. ★(CX data for Winter 1982 only.)

in the DCM and ACE fractions, while in the winter these direct mutagens would not be transformed and would consequently remain in the CX fraction. The percentage of the EOM in the CX fraction increased during the winter from 16 to 40% at the three urban sites.

Comparison of the Mutagenicity of the Fractions

The three EOM fractions examined in this study contain compounds with a wide range of polarity. The CX or nonpolar fraction contains such compounds as PAHs, aliphatic hydrocarbons, nitro- and dinitro-PAHs, PAH-ketones, some PAH-quinones, and thiophenes. The moderately polar DCM fraction contains compounds such as some PAH-quinones, nitroquinones, chlorinated aromatics, and hydroxynitro-PAH. The acetone fraction contains the most polar compounds, such as carboxylic acids, organic sulfates, and phenolic matter (Greenberg, personal communication, 1986; Butler et al., 1986). All three fractions contained mutagens. The ACE fraction had from 31 to 56% of the total direct mutagenic activity, the DCM fraction had 19 to 39%, and the CX fraction contained from 16 to 32% (see Figure 5.1a,b). The percentages for the indirect mutagenic activity are 17.9 to 45.5% in the ACE fraction, 17.9 to 45.2% in the DCM fraction, and 14.3 to 64.3% in the CX fraction. The fact that mutagens are present with a wide range of polarity illustrates the complex problems associated with determining which compounds are responsible for the mutagenic activity in the EOM.

Comparison of Bacterial Strain Responses

Three *Salmonella* strains were used for all four campaigns — TA98, TA100, and TA1537. Strain TA98 is sensitive to frameshift mutagens such as PAHs. Strain TA100 is sensitive to base-pair substitution mutagens such as alkylating agents, but it also detects some frameshift mutagens. Strain TA1537 is sensitive to frameshift mutagens such as epoxides of PAHs, as well as some DNA-intercalating agents such as 9-aminoacridine (Ames et al., 1973; Levin et al., 1982).

If one compares the strain responses shown in Figures 5.1a,b, 5.2a,b, and 5.3a,b, the most obvious difference is in the overall level of mutagenic activity measured. The highest level was measured with strain TA98, and the lowest with TA1537. The pattern of activity among the different strains is similar in many respects, but some differences were observed. The similarities include the following: the urban sites have higher levels of mutagenic activity than the rural sites, the winter samples had more mutagenic activity than the summer samples, and the addition of S9 was required for maxi-

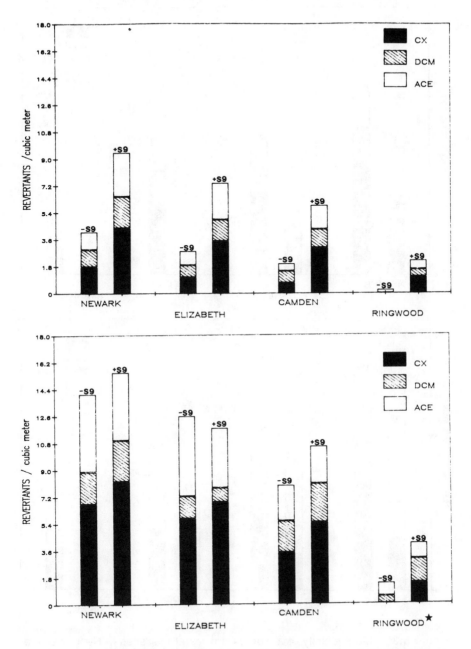

Figure 5.2. Mutagenicity of airborne particles at four sites in New Jersey. a. Average of Summer 1981 and 1982 Samples – Strain TA100 ± S9. b. Average of Winter 1982 and 1983 Samples – Strain TA100 ± S9. ★ (CX data for Winter 1982 only.)

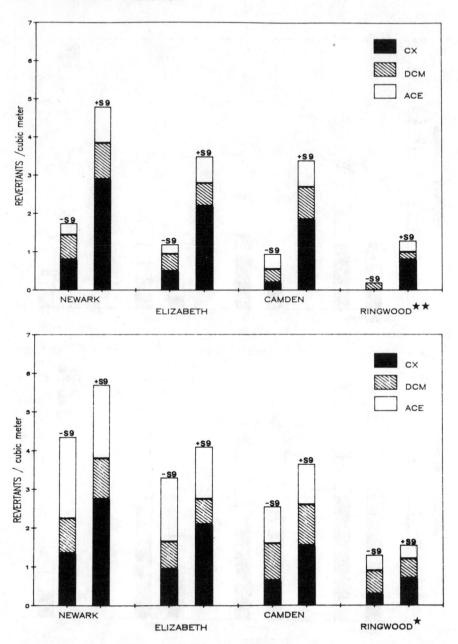

Figure 5.3.   Mutagenicity of airborne particles at four sites in New Jersey. a. Average of Summer 1981 and 1982 Samples – Strain TA1537 ± S9. ★★(CX, DCM, and ACE data for Summer 1981 only.) b. Average of Winter 1982 and 1983 Samples – Strain TA1537 ± S9. ★(CX data for the Winter 1982 only.)

mum activity in the summer campaigns. The differences include the fact that, during the summer, S9 had more of an effect on the responses of strains TA100 and TA1537 than on TA98. Also, during the winter, metabolic activation resulted in a greater increase in the activity measured by strain TA1537 at all sites and TA100 for most sites. These observed strain responses are presumed to be the result of the different spectrum of sensitivities that the three strains have toward various classes of mutagens in the particulate extracts.

Air Pollution Episodes

Summertime Episodes

Formation of secondary organic aerosol, via photochemical oxidation of gaseous precursors and gas-to-particle conversion, has long been of concern in the Los Angeles area. During the Summer 1981 ATEOS campaign, there is evidence of secondary organic aerosol formation at all four sites during air pollution episodes characterized by high concentrations of particulate matter, sulfate, and ozone. Secondary organic aerosol was estimated to have increased ambient levels of polar (ACE) particulate organic matter by 15 to 36% (Daisey et al., 1984). Because the mutagenic activity of this additional secondary organic aerosol was of interest, the activity of ACE fractions collected during an extended episode of photochemical smog was compared to that of composites of nonepisode days. This extended episode period in Summer 1982 was selected on the basis of three criteria which distinguished such periods during the earlier Summer 1981 study: (1) elevated concentrations of IPM, FPM, sulfate, ozone, and EOM, (2) higher proportions of polar (ACE) organics in the total EOM (ACE greater than 60% of EOM), and (3) stagnation conditions.

Figure 5.4 represents the variations in the concentrations of EOM at all four sites during the Summer 1982 study. In contrast to Summer 1981, where a pattern of well defined episodes occurred simultaneously at all four sites, a number of distinct episode periods and days were observed at the Newark and Elizabeth sites (Lioy et al., 1983a). At the Camden site, much of the 6-week sampling period was characterized by scattered episode days. However, the period from July 13 to 19 met all three criteria for an episode at all of the urban sites. The ranges of EOM concentrations for the extended episode were 16.0 to 30.4 $\mu g/m^3$ at Newark, 15.0 to 24.9 $\mu g/m^3$ at Elizabeth, and 10.5 to 16.5 $\mu g/m^3$ at Camden. The polar ACE fraction was more than 60% of the total EOM for the 7 days studied at Newark and Elizabeth and more than 75% of the total EOM at Camden. This compares to average values for the nonepisode of 52% for 22 days at Newark, 55% for 23 days at Elizabeth, and 63% for 17 days at Camden. The concentrations and

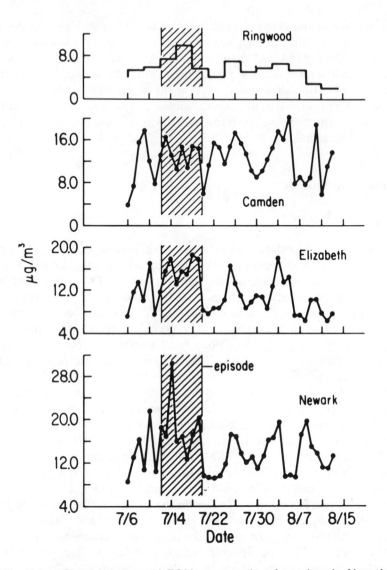

Figure 5.4. Concentrations of EOM measured at four sites in New Jersey during Summer 1982 (μg/cubic meter).

percentages of ACE during this period were similar to those observed during the Summer 1981 episode periods. Consequently, the ACE extracts from this period were composited for each urban site as an episode sample for mutagenicity analyses.

Nonepisode composite samples were also prepared for comparison. The

Table 5.1.   Geometric Mean Concentrations and Standard Deviation of
Various Pollutants for the Episode and Nonepisode Days,
Summer 1982 (in μg/m³)

Variable	Newark		Elizabeth		Camden	
	EP[a]	NEP[a]	EP	NEP	EP	NEP
No. of Days	7	22	7	23	7	17
IPM	87.7(1.3)	55.1(1.3)	75.0(1.2)	41.2(1.3)	67.1(1.2)	42.0(1.3)
FPM	65.5(1.2)	40.1(1.4)	N.A.	N.A.	55.1(1.2)	35.3(1.4)
SO_4^{-2}	20.4(1.4)	11.3(1.6)	19.1(1.4)	10.2(1.5)	21.9(1.3)	11.6(1.5)
O_3(max.)	N.A.	N.A.	111(1.2)[b]	67(1.5)[b]	86(1.2)	58(1.3)
CX	4.0(1.2)	3.8(1.3)	3.4(1.2)	2.7(1.3)	2.5(1.2)	1.8(1.5)
DCM	2.3(1.2)	1.5(1.4)	2.3(1.1)	1.2(1.4)	2.3(1.1)	1.4(1.8)
ACE	11.7(1.4)	5.8(1.3)	10.2(1.1)	4.7(1.3)	8.6(1.2)	5.5(1.4)

[a]EP = episode days; NEP = non-episode days.
[b]ppb, measured in Bayonne, NJ (closest site with O_3 data).

first criterion used to define the nonepisode days was the percentage of
ACE in the total EOM. Nonepisode days were defined as those on which
ACE was less than 60% of total EOM (less than 75% at Camden). The
second criterion for a nonepisode day was an EOM concentration of less
than 16.0 μg/m³ at the Newark and Camden sites and less than 12.0 μg/m³ at
the Elizabeth site. For a few days, the nonepisode EOM exceeded the limits
discussed. In these cases, the first criterion was used to categorize the sample.

The geometric mean concentrations of the three organic fractions, of
sulfate, IPM, and FPM for the episode and nonepisode days thus selected
are presented in Table 5.1. It should be noted that the geometric mean
concentrations of sulfate were almost identical at all sites for both periods.
Concentrations of sulfate on individual days also showed high intersite
correlation (Lioy et al., 1983b).

The mutagenic activity in the ACE fraction was primarily direct, since the
addition of S9 did not increase the level of mutagenic activity. Figure 5.5a
compares the direct-acting mutagenic activity of the ACE fraction per cubic
meter of air with TA98 for the episode and nonepisode periods at the three
urban sites. No statistically significant differences were observed between
the episode and nonepisode samples at any of the sites. Figure 5.5b examines the specific activity (revertants/μg of EOM) of the ACE composites for
the episode and nonepisode periods. Where the slopes differed by 30% or
more, the episode slope was compared to the nonepisode slope to see if the
differences were significant at the 95% confidence level. The specific activity was greater for the nonepisode than the episode period in five out of the

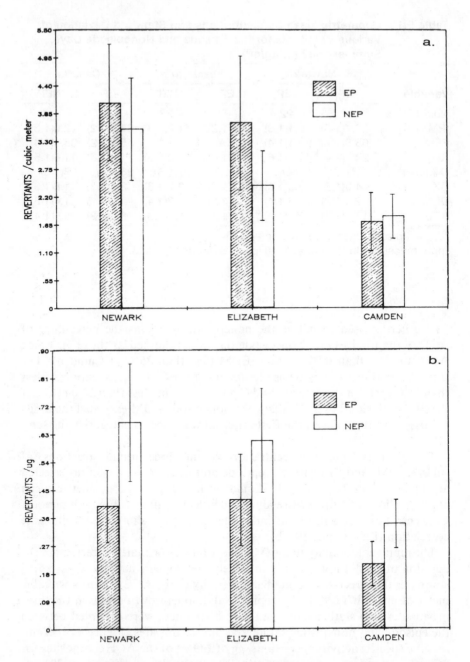

Figure 5.5. Mutagenic activity of the acetone fraction measured during the Summer 1982 with Strain TA98–S9. a. Revertants/m^3 of air. b. Revertants/µg of acetone EOM. 95% Confidence Interval Indicated.

six cases. This difference in direct-acting (-S9) specific activity was significantly different ($p < 0.05$) for all three sites.

The ACE fraction contains oxidized hydrocarbons (Daisey et al., 1982; Daisey et al., 1984). Class tests have shown that this fraction contains carbonyl compounds, carboxylic acids, and alkylating agents (Butler et al., 1985). Schuetzle et al. (1975) have shown that concentrations of compounds containing carbonyl, carboxylic acid, hydroxyl, and nitro functional groups increase during episodes of photochemical smog. However, the fact that the specific mutagenic activity (-S9) decreased during the episode indicates that at least part of the additional mass is composed of compounds that are not mutagenic. Thus, the net effect of increased concentrations of ACE and decreased direct specific activity during the episode was that the mutagenic activity per cubic meter did not change.

Winter Episode

During the winter campaign in 1983, a major air pollution episode occurred in northern New Jersey (see Chapter 6). From February 11 to 18 the values for IPM, FPM, and EOM increased dramatically at Newark and Elizabeth (Figure 5.6). The episode was centered at Newark, but also had an impact on Elizabeth. A more detailed description of this episode is available elsewhere (Lioy et al., 1985).

One-and two-day sample extracts from Newark were subjected to the Ames mutagenicity analysis. The February 11th and 12th samples and the February 17th and 18th samples were composited due to low levels of EOM in the individual samples. These samples were assayed with strain TA98 with and without metabolic activation (Figure 5.7a,b,c). The addition of S9 did not generally increase the activity of the samples, indicating that the mutagens present were predominantly of the direct-acting type.

In general, the mutagenic activity increased as the particulate mass increased, but there were some exceptions. The total mutagenic activity for all three fractions peaked on February 13th. However, the highest concentrations of IPM and FPM were measured on February 14th, indicating that some of the observed increase in mass was due to the addition of weakly mutagenic or nonmutagenic material. The total EOM measurements on February 13 and 14 were indistinguishable. This again points out the fact that IPM, FPM, and total EOM are not necessarily the best surrogates for genotoxic activity.

The day on which the maximum concentration of EOM was measured can be compared to the day on which the maximum mutagenicity was measured. For the CX fraction the concentration peaked on February 14th, while the mutagenic activity was highest on February 13th. For the DCM and ACE fractions, both the highest concentrations and the highest level of

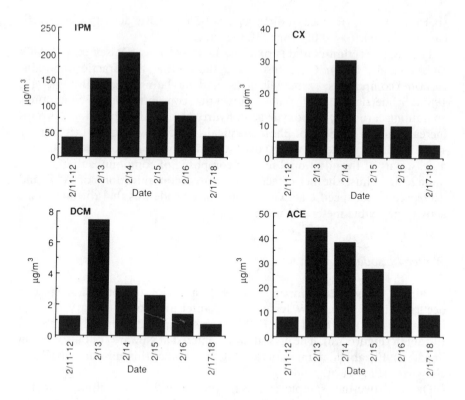

Figure 5.6.   Parameters measured at Newark during a winter episode in 1983.

the total EOM (27.7% and 42.3%, respectively), indicating that the increase in the IPM on February 14th was at least partly due to the addition of some nonpolar and nonmutagenic organics.

Composition of the EOM

Extractable organic matter is a complex mixture of many classes of compounds and individual compounds within the classes. Many of the components in EOM remain unidentified. Presently, it is not possible to completely account for the mutagenic activity of EOM in terms of its chemical composition. In some instances, it has been possible to account for a portion of the mutagenic activity of a sample in terms of certain compounds, e.g., nitro-PAH, (Peterson and Siak, 1981). Since chemical class information was available for the PAHs in the CX fractions, comparisons between the concentrations of PAHs and the mutagenic activity of the fraction were

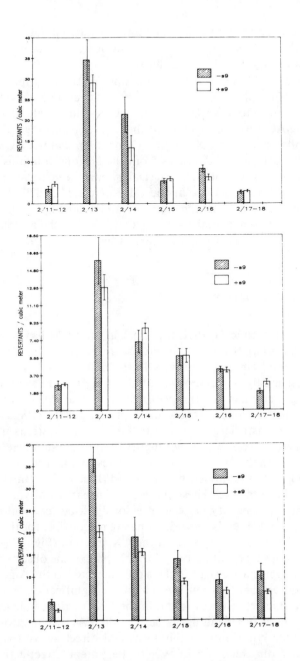

Figure 5.7.   Mutagenicity of airborne particles measured at Newark during an episode in Winter 1983. a. CX Fraction – Strain TA98 ± S9. b. DCM Fraction – Strain TA98 ± S9. c. ACE Fraction – Strain TA98 ± S9. 95% Confidence Interval Indicated.

the concentrations of PAHs and the mutagenic activity of the fraction were investigated. In addition, interurban and seasonal variations in specific mutagenic activity were also examined.

In this study, the mass of the EOM was fractionated into three groups containing chemicals of different polarity. Between 17 and 34% of the IPM was extractable into CX, DCM, and ACE. During all of the sampling periods, the ACE fraction contained the highest percentage of the IPM (11 to 21%) followed by the CX fraction (3 to 12%), and the DCM fraction (2 to 4%). At least part of the mass from the acetone fractions consisted of inorganic material such as NH_4NO_3 (Daisey et al., 1982; Daisey et al., 1984) and trace metals such as Cu, Zn, and Cd (Kneip et al., 1979). Some work on the acetone fraction from the Summer 1981 campaign suggests that the percentage of inorganic ions (NH_4^+, NO_3^-, SO_4^{2-}) in the acetone fraction at the Newark site ranged from 9 to 26% (Daisey et al., 1984).

PAHs in the CX Fraction

One class of chemicals, PAHs, present in the EOM has been extensively studied. The ATEOS results for PAHs are presented in Chapter 4. The PAHs are found almost exclusively in the nonpolar CX fraction. For the first three campaigns, composites of the CX fraction were analyzed for both mutagenicity and for the presence of several PAHs. The results for four carcinogenic PAHs (Santodonato et al., 1981) are shown in Figure 5.8a,b. There was a large increase in PAH concentrations in the winter, when the levels were 5 to 18 times higher than in the summer. This increase was seen for both the urban and the rural sites. It was also observed that for PAHs as a group, the three urban sites had three to five times higher PAH levels than the rural site. These patterns of urban/rural variations correspond to the mutagenicity patterns previously discussed, and indicate that the changes in PAH levels are at least partly responsible for the urban/rural differences in mutagenicity seen in the CX fraction (Figure 5-1a,b). However, PAH concentrations account for only part of the observed mutagenicity. The mutagenic activity of PAH is only detected in the Ames assay when metabolizing enzymes (+ S9) are added. A significant amount of direct (–S9) mutagenic activity was found in the CX fraction, indicating that this fraction contains other mutagens besides the PAHs. One group of chemicals that could contribute to this measured direct activity is the nitrated PAHs, many of which are known to be potent direct-acting mutagens (Rosenkranz et al., 1983; Vance and Levin, 1984), are emitted in diesel exhaust, and are found in the ambient atmosphere (Pitts, 1983). Current work being done on samples collected at Newark has shown that nitrated PAHs are indeed present in the CX fraction (Harkov et al., 1986).

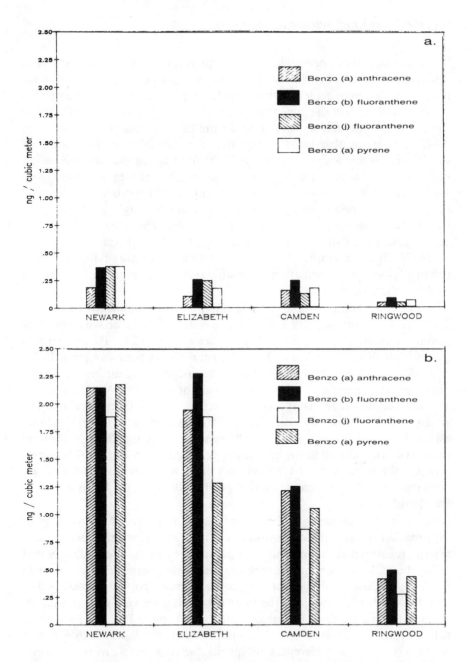

Figure 5.8. Levels of four carcinogenic PAHs measured at four sites in New Jersey. a. Average for Summer 1981 and 1982 samples. b. Winter 1982 samples.

Specific Mutagenic Activity of the EOM

Mutagenic activity per cubic meter of air is the parameter that has been discussed in detail, but additional information can be obtained by examining the specific mutagenic activity (revertants/μg of EOM). (See Tables A5-4, A5-5, and A5-6 in the appendix of this chapter.) Figure 5.9a,b illustrates the mean specific activity measured during the four campaigns for strain TA98. The major observation is that the four sites differ in the amount of specific mutagenic activity. Thus, the EOM from urban sites contains either higher concentrations of mutagens per unit mass or more potent mutagens than does the EOM from rural sites. "Aging" of the aerosol via oxidation reactions which occur during transport to rural sites might also contribute to the lower specific activity of the rural samples. This urban/rural difference in specific activity was also seen for strains TA100 (Figure 5.10a,b) and TA1537 (Figure 5-11a,b). The specific activities measured for the three urban sites are fairly similar and probably reflect a similarity of sources of EOM in these three cities.

Seasonal differences in the specific activity are also apparent with strain TA98. The winter samples had higher levels of direct activity than the summer samples (Figure 5.9a,b). This increase occurred for the three urban sites for all three fractions, and for the rural site in the more polar DCM and ACE fractions. Strain TA100 also showed seasonal differences in the direct-acting specific activity (Figure 5.10a,b) of the EOM. Again the winter samples had higher levels of mutagenic activity for all three fractions. For strain TA1537, the results were slightly different (Figure 5.11a,b). The highest levels of activity were found in the summer samples. These levels were measured with the addition of metabolizing enzymes ($+$ S9). The direct activity did increase in the winter, but to a lesser extent. The increase appeared to be due to increases in the specific activity of the DCM and ACE fractions.

Data on the mutagenic activity per unit of mass provide two pieces of information about the composition of the EOM. First, the low specific activity measured at the rural site compared to the urban sites indicates that either the EOM at the rural site contains more nonmutagenic material, and/or that the EOM at the urban sites contains more potent mutagens. The specific activities measured at the three urban sites are very similar, indicating that there are common sources contributing to the EOM at these three urban sites. In contrast, in a study of more divergent urban sites by Butler et al. (1985), intersite differences in specific activity were greater. Second, higher specific activities occurred in the winter, indicating that the composition of the EOM varies with the season.

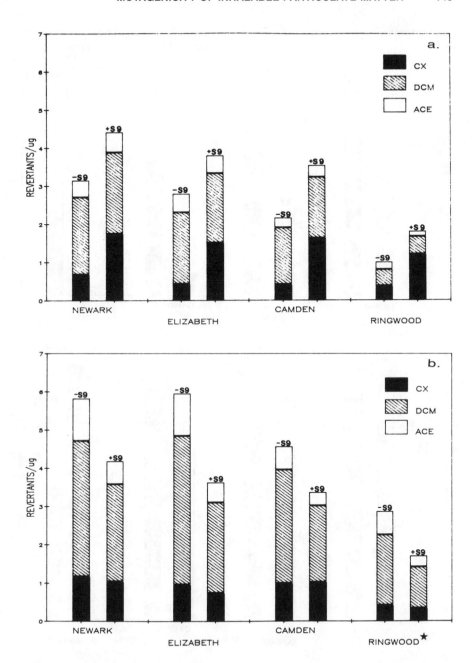

Figure 5.9.   Specific mutagenic activity measured at four sites in New Jersey.
a. Average of Summer 1981 and 1982 samples – Strain TA98 ± S9.
b. Average of Winter 1982 and 1983 samples – Strain TA98 ± S9.
★ (CX data for Winter 1982 only.)

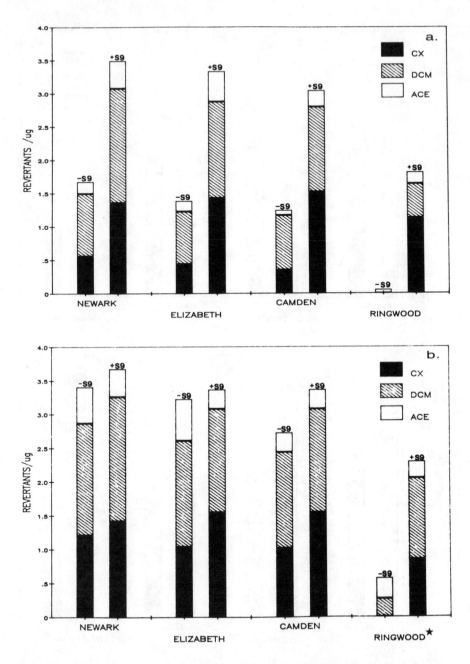

Figure 5.10. Specific mutagenic activity measured at four sites in New Jersey. a. Average of Summer 1981 and 1982 Samples – Strain TA100 ± S9. b. Average of Winter 1982 and 1983 Samples – Strain TA100 ± S9. ★(CX data for Winter 1981 only.)

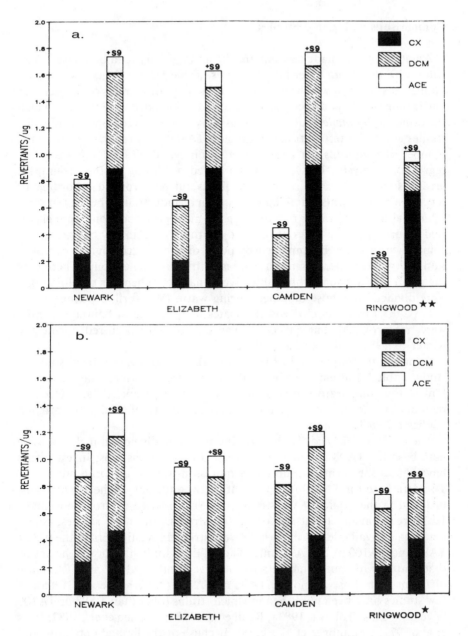

Figure 5.11.   Specific mutagenic activity measured at four sites in New Jersey. a. Average of summer 1981 and 1982 samples – Strain TA1537 ± S9. ★ ★ (CX, DCM, and ACE data for Summer 1981 data only. b. Average of Winter 1982 and 1983 samples – Strain TA1537 ± S9. ★ CX data for Winter 1982 only.)

Comparisons with Other Studies

An attempt was made to compare the mutagenicity data obtained in this study with that from other investigations. Table 5.2 is a list compiled from published studies in which the mutagenic activity of extracts of ambient air particulate matter had been measured. Studies included were those in which the Ames *Salmonella* mutagenicity assay was employed. Specifically, the studies employed tester strains TA98 and TA100, and reported data as the number of revertants per cubic meter of air based on least squares linear regression analysis. The listing is compiled according to the geographic area(s) sampled in each study. The list is further grouped according to whether the location(s) sampled were urban or industrial, suburban or non-industrial urban, rural or remote. For the most part, locations were classified according to the views of the study authors. Within any one grouping, some locations may be impacted by point or generalized sources of pollution to a greater extent than other areas within that same group. Therefore, the groupings are somewhat subjective in nature. Whenever possible, data were divided into those obtained during warm (W, April–September) and cold (C, October–March) seasons. Dates of sampling in Santiago, Chile, were not provided, but collection was said to have occurred during the winter of 1981 (Tokiwa et al., 1983a).

Sampling techniques and extraction methodologies varied from study to study. Table 5.2 attempts to highlight the differences which may be important in the comparative interpretation of the mutagenicity data. Detailed methodology could not be included and the reader is referred to the original studies for such information.

The listing is fairly comprehensive but undoubtedly not all-inclusive. The data base for TA98 is much larger than for TA100, as most investigators have found the former strain to be more sensitive to airborne mutagens. The data base for TA100 is in turn larger than for any of the other strains included in the original (Ames et al., 1975) or revised (Maron and Ames, 1983) recommended battery of tester strains. In most studies, small amounts of available test material have restricted investigators to the use of TA98 and TA100 or to TA98 only. The ATEOS study has shown, however, that patterns of mutagenic activity observed with TA1537 and TA97 are different than those found for TA98 or TA100 (Atherholt et al., 1985). A few studies have been published in which strains other than TA98 or TA100 have been used (Tokiwa, 1983a; Reali et al., 1984; Madsen et al., 1982; Pitts et al., 1977; Commoner et al., 1978). Because of the limited data base and other constraints, these studies have not been included in Table 5.2.

The range of values from the published studies (Table 5.3) indicate that direct mutagenic activity worldwide can vary by more than three orders of magnitude. Although methodological differences undoubtedly contribute to some of the variation in mutagenic activity from one study to another,

Table 5.2. Mutagenic Activity of Extracts of Ambient Air Particulate Matter Collected Worldwide as Determined in the Ames *Salmonella* Plate Incorporation Assay

Location	Year[A] Season	No. Daily Samples	Filter[B] Particle Size	Extraction[C] Method	Notes[D]	Revertants per cubic meter (range) TA98 −S9	TA98 +S9	TA100 −S9	TA100 +S9	Reference
1. USA (North America)										
a. Urban (industrial)										
New York, NY (Manhattan)	77/78–W	26*	G/≤3.5	Sox, C/D/Ac; res. Ac	1,2	4.5[a]	—	6.8[a]	—	Daisey et al., 1980
New York, NY (Manhattan)	77/79–C	26*	G/≤3.5	Sox, C/D/Ac; res. Ac	1,2	9.6[b]	—	12.1[b]	—	Ibid
New York, NY (Manhattan)	79/80–C	13*	G/≤3.5	Sox, C/D/Ac; res. Ac	1	9.9	15.2	—	—	Butler et al., 1985
Elizabeth, NJ	82–C	35	G/≤2.5	Sox, C/D/Ac; res. Ac	1	10.1	22.0	—	—	Ibid
Phila., PA	82–W	20	G/≤15	Sox, C/D/Ac; res. Ac	1	3.0	8.5			Ibid
Dearborn, MI	80–W	8	G/TSP	Sox, B-Et (8/2)		288.0				Gibson, 1985
	83–C	3				14.0	—	—	—	Ibid
River Rouge, MI	82–W	5	G/TSP	Sox, B-Et (8/2)		12.0	—	—	—	Ibid
Detroit, MI	81–W	15	G/TSP	Sox, B-Et (8/2)		20.0	—	—	—	Ibid
Detroit, MI	81–W	31	G/TSP	Sox,D; TLC Sep	3	8.0 ± 6 (1.9–26.7)	—	—	—	Wolff et al., 1985
Los Angeles, CA	9/17/80	1	T/TSP	Son,T-M-D(1/1/1)		63 (30–120)[c]	71 (50–180)[c]	—	—	Pitts et al., 1982
Los Angeles, CA (2 sites)	3/9/83	1	T/<10	Sox, D/An (combined)		(40–140)[c]	(40–140)[c]	—	—	Sweetman et al., 1984
b. Suburban (nonindustrial urban)										
Morgantown, WV	80–W	6	G/TSP	Sha, D		—	23[d]	—	—	Whong et al., 1981
Morgantown, WV	80–C	8	G/TSP	Sha, D		—	12	—	—	Ibid
Lexington, KY	80–W	6	G/TSP	Son, B/Ac (combined)		1.7	1.2	1.4	1.9	Viau et al., 1982
Lexington, KY	80–W	12	G/TSP	Son, B/Ac (combined)		3.3	3.0	2.9	2.8	Lockard et al., 1981

Table 5.2., Continued

Location	Year[A] (Season)	No. Daily Samples	Filter[B] Particle Size	Extraction[C] Method	Notes[D]	TA98 −S9	TA98 +S9	TA100 −S9	TA100 +S9	Reference
Lexington, KY	80–C	26	G/TSP	Son, B/Ac (combined)		4.4	5.0	3.2	3.6	Ibid
Warren, MI	82–C	7				5.2	—	—	—	Gibson, 1985
Warren, MI	84–W	5				5.1	—	—	—	Ibid
Riverside, CA	9/17/80	1				35 (10–70)[c]	38 (15–100)[c]			Pitts et al., 1982
c. Rural										
Delaware(coast)	82–W	7		Sox, D		1.3	—	—	—	Gibson, 1985
PA(Allegheny Mt)	79–W	13	T/≤5.5			0.6	0.3	—	—	Pierson, et al., 1983
d. Remote										
Bermuda	82–W	9				0.8	—	—	—	Gibson, 1985
	83–C	6				1.1	—	—	—	Ibid
2. Central/South America										
a. Urban										
Mexico City	82–C	14	G/TSP	Sox, C/D/Ac; res. Ac	1,2	22.1	60.3	—	—	Butler et al., 1985a
Santiago, Chile (2 sites)	81–C	5?	G/TSP	Son, D	4	157 (39–287)	—	34 (19–57)	—	Tokiwa et al., 1983a
		5?	G/TSP	Son, M	—		690 (271–1177)			
3. Europe										
a. Urban										
Oslo, Nor. (2 sites)	78–C	30	G/TSP	Sox, C; res. C	2	4 (1.5–12)	5 (1.5–10.5)	3 (0.3–10.5)	2 (0.3–5)	Moeller & Alfheim, 1980
	78–W	7	G/TSP	Sox, C; res. C		1 (1–2)	1 (0.5–20)	—	—	Ibid

Revertants per cubic meter (range)

Table 5.2., Continued

Location	Year[A] Season	No. Daily Samples	Filter[B] Particle Size	Extraction[C] Method	Notes[D]	TA98 −S9	TA98 +S9	TA100 −S9	TA100 +S9	Reference
Oslo - street	79-C	e	G/≤3	Sox, Ac	[n14] day	36 (12–55)	91 (33–180)			Moeller et al, 1982
					[n8] night	9 (8–10)	17 (10–28)			Ibid
- roof/park (2 sites)	79-C	e	G/≤3	Sox, Ac	[n10] day	16 (3–41)	15 (3–34)			Ibid
					[n6] night	12 (9–17)	10 (9–12)			Ibid
Stockholm, Swe. 78/79-C		e	G/TSP	Sox, Ac		[n7]21 (2.1–39)	[n7]16 (0.8–28)	[n5]30 (2.3–47)	[n3]26 (21–35)	Lofroth et al., 1983
79-W		15	G/TSP	Sox, Ac		10.9 (2.2–18)	–	–	–	Lofroth, 1981
78/80-C		18	G/TSP	Sox, Ac		40.2 (25–55)	–	–	–	Ibid
b. Suburban (nonindustrial urban) Bayreuth, F.R.G.	83-C	4	G/TSP	Son, D		(0.1–0.6)	(0.5–1.4)	(0.3–0.6)	(1.1–2.1)	Garner et al., 1986
Stockholm surb.	79-W	15	G/TSP	Sox, Ac		5.7 (0.9–12)				Lofroth, 1981
	78/80-C	18	G/TSP	Sox, Ac		23.7 (13–30)				Ibid
c. Rural Wageningen, Netherlands	82/83-C	77	G/≤7	Sox, M		5 (0–14)	7 (0–23)	–	–	van Houdt et al., 1984
Wageningen, Netherlands	79/80-W	38	G/TSP	Sox, M	2	2.5 (0–11)				Alink et al., 1983
Wageningen, Netherlands	79/80-C	40	G/TSP	Sox, M	2	9.6 (2.3–22)				Ibid

Table 5.2.,   Continued

Location	Year[A] Season	No. Daily Samples	Filter[B] Particle Size	Extraction[C] Method	Notes[D]	TA98 −S9	TA98 +S9	TA100 −S9	TA100 +S9	Reference
Wageningen, Netherlands	79/80–Y	78	G/TSP	Sox, M	2	6.1 (0–22)	—	—	—	Ibid
Terschelling, Netherlands	79–W	15	G/TSP	Sox, M	2	1.4 (0–12.5)	—			Ibid
Terschelling, Netherlands	79–C	8	G/TSP	Sox, M	2	15.0				Ibid
	80–W	39	G/TSP	Sox, D		(0.8–31)	1.2		—	Reali et al., 1984
4. Asia										
a. Urban										
Beijing, China	81–C&W	4	G/TSP	Sox,C/D/Ac; res. Ac	1,2	9.2	>60.0	—	—	Butler et al., 1985a
Ohmuta, Japan (6 sites)	74–C	1	G/TSP	Sox, M			182 (22–445)			Tokiwa et al., 1977
Ohmuta, Japan (1 site)	78–C	13?	G/TSP	Sox, M		—	32.7 (8.4–52.6)	10.4	33.0 (5.0–92.7)	Tokiwa et al., 1980
Ohmuta, Jpan (11 sites)	78/79–W	28	G/TSP	Sox, M		9.0 (0.1–41.2)	9.8 (1.0–30.1)	(0.1–37.6)	7.3 (0.1–29.0)	Tokiwa et al., 1983a
Ohmuta, Japan	74, 78/79–C	e	G/TSP	Sox, M		[n20]30.5 (0.1–94.9)	[n39]68.4 (5.7–445)	[n20]12.2 (0.1–45.8)	[n39]23.1 (0.1–157)	Ibid
Kawasaki, Japan (several sites)	?–C	8–14	G/TSP	Sox, B		7.3	19.4	—	—	Ohsawa et al., 1983
b. Suburban (nonindustrial urban)										
Sagamiko, Japan (several sites)	?–C	8–14	G/TSP	Sox, B		3.7	8.3	—	—	Ibid
Fukuoka, Japan (6 sites)	74–C	1	G/TSP	Sox, M		—	29 (7–78)	—	—	Tokiwa et al., 1977
Fukuoka, Japan (11 sites)	77–C?	1	G/TSP	Sox, M		—	16.0 (7.4–36.4)	—	32.9 (14.1–52.5)	Tokiwa et al., 1980

Column group header: Revertants per cubic meter (range)

Table 5.2., Continued

Location	Year[A] Season	No. Daily Samples	Filter[B]	Particle Size	Extraction[C] Method	Notes[D]	Revertants per cubic meter (range) TA98 −S9	TA98 +S9	TA100 −S9	TA100 +S9	Reference
Fukuoka, Japan (13 sites)	74, 77/79−W	e	G/TSP		Sox, M		[n27]5.1 (0.1−18.9)	[n30]11.9 (3.1−37.1)	[n27]2.3 (0.1−12.4)	[n27]11.6 (0.1−41.2)	Tokiwa et al., 1983b
Fukuoka, Japan	74/75, 77/80−C	e	G/TSP		Sox, M		[n27]11.2 (0.4−35.5) 5.4	[n30]20.5 (1.2−52.4)	[n27]7.1 (0.1−45.9)	[n27]11.3 (0.8−52.5)	
Chiba, Japan	79−W	12	G/TSP		Sox, B	5	(3.7−6.8) 6.8	−	−	−	Fukino et al., 1982
Chiba, Japan	79/80−C	10	G/TSP		Sox, B	5	(3.6−16.5)	−	−	−	Ibid

[A] W = warm, April thru Sept; C = cold, October thru March (northern hemisphere); Y = year round.

[B] Filter = G, glassfiber; T, Teflon® (or Teflon covered glassfiber). Particle Size (μm); TSP, total suspended particles (≤ 30 μm).

[C] Extraction method. Sox = Soxhlet extraction; Son = sonication; Sha = shaking; Ac = acetone; An = acetonitrile; B = benzene; C = cyclohexane; D = dichloromethane (methylene chloride); DMSO = dimethylsulfoxide; Et = ethanol; M = methanol; T = toluene; (e.g., C-D-Ac[7/1/2] = solvent mixture with proportions indicated. C/D/Ac sequential extraction with individual solvents.) Solvent extracts dried and resuspended (res.) in DMSO, unless indicated; TLC Sep = thin layer chromatography separation.

[D] Notes = 1, mutagenic activity in separate fractions from sequential extraction summed;
2, values estimated from bar graphs;
3, sum of activity of TLC fractions;
4, data available for other tester strains also;
5, preincubation assay.
n, number of daily samples for corresponding mutagenicity data

- - - - - -
a contains some data from March.
b contains some data from September.
c range of values from 3-hr samples within a single day (est. from graph).
d "heavy road and stadium construction during this period."
e see mutagenicity data.
* weekly samples collected for 7 days.

Table 5.3.   Range of Mean Values Reported in Table 5.2

| | \multicolumn{8}{c}{Revertants per Cubic Meter of Air} |
| | TA98 | | | | TA100 | | | |
	(n)	–S9	(n)	+ S9	(n)	–S9	(n)	+ S9
Urban or industrial								
W[a]	(11)	1–288	(5)	1–71	(2)	7–10	(1)	7
C[b]	(12)	4–157	(11)	5–690	(5)	3–34	(4)	2–33
Suburban, or nonindustrial urban								
W	(8)	2–35	(5)	1–38	(3)	1–3	(3)	2–12
C	(7)	1–24	(7)	1–29	(3)	1–7	(4)	2–33
Rural/remote								
W	(5)	1–3	(2)	1–1	ND[c]		ND	
C	(4)	1–15	(1)	7	ND		ND	

[a]W = Warm.
[b]C = Cold.
[c]ND = No data available

the major differences between locations have been shown by investigators to be due to differences in types and quantities of pollution sources (e.g., wood and coal burning, automobiles, industrial point sources, etc.), time of sampling, which reflects temporal patterns of source inputs (time of day, as well as time of year), and meteorological conditions prevailing at the time of sampling. In general, samples taken during the cold space-heating months are more mutagenic per unit volume of air than those taken during warm months, although exceptions to this have been published (Gibson, 1985; Whong et al., 1981). Likewise, samples from urban or industrial areas are more mutagenic than those from suburban or nonindustrial urban areas, which are in turn more mutagenic than those from rural/remote areas (Gibson, 1985; Pitts et al., 1982; Loforth, 1981; Tokiwa et al., 1977; Tokiwa et al., 1980; Tokiwa et al., 1983b). The mutagenic activity at the ATEOS urban sites was within the range of values reported for nonindustrial urban areas in general, while that at the rural Ringwood site fell within the range for nonurban sites. Levels at urban New Jersey sites, even during a wintertime air pollution episode, were lower than those measured in cities where coal is used as a fuel (e.g., Beijing), or where there are no emission controls on motor vehicles (e.g., Mexico City).

Specific mutagenicity also varies considerably from one study to another (data not shown). Specific mutagenic activity for TA98 (+ and -S9) ranged from 0.01 to 3.6 revertants/μg of unfractionated EOM (Pitts et al., 1982; Moeller et al., 1980; Siak et al., 1985; Talcott and Harger 1981). For TA100, a range of 0.01 to 1.2 revertants/μg has been reported (Reali et al., 1984; Lockard et al., 1981). In the ATEOS study, where the samples were fractionated the sum of the specific activity ranged from 0.9 to 6.5 revertants/μg for TA98 ± S9, and 0 to 5.1 revertants/μg for TA100 ± S9.

Specific mutagenic activity is influenced by the amount of nonmutagenic material, in addition to the amount of mutagenic material per unit volume of air, whereas the amount of mutagenic activity per unit volume of air is related solely to the amount of mutagens present (ignoring possible synergistic or antagonistic effects between mutagenic species and between mutagenic and nonmutagenic species). Therefore, the latter unit of measurement is considered by most investigators, including ourselves, to be more relevant in terms of potential impact on human health.

SUMMARY

During the ATEOS project, the Ames *Salmonella* assay was used to assess the mutagenicity of airborne particles over a two-year period. Three major uses of biological screening tests such as the Ames assay were demonstrated during this period. First, use of the Ames test as a "toxicological air quality" parameter (deRaat et al., 1985). As demonstrated in this study, a biological test is a more meaningful measure of human exposure to mutagens and carcinogens than the previously used surrogates such as TSP, BSO, or BaP. The use of the Ames assay in conjunction with other types of mammalian biological tests with different endpoints in conjunction with epidemiological studies should begin to answer questions about the relationship between ambient air quality and its potential impact on human health.

Second, a biological screening test, such as the Ames test, can be used as a probe to guide chemical analyses. The fact that mutagens with varying polarity were present in EOM illustrates the complexity of the analytical problems involved in determining the chemicals present in ambient air. The Ames test can be used in combination with subfractionation of the EOM to guide future chemical analyses toward the subfractions with the most mutagenic activity. Such work is currently being done on ambient airborne particulates collected at the Newark site (Harkov et al., 1986). This type of study will allow the priority for chemical identification to be directed toward the most biologically important chemicals.

Finally, the data gathered from this project will be useful in evaluating any future changes in ambient air quality in New Jersey, as well as in evaluating the impact of local point sources on the nearby environment.

REFERENCES

Adamson, L. F., and Bruce, R. M. (1979). *Suspended Particulate Matter*, a Report to Congress, U.S. EPA, p. 3.

Alfheim, I. and Moeller, M. (1979). *Sci. Total Environ. 13*:275–278.

Alink, G. M., Smit, H. A., Van Houdt, J. J., Kolkman, J. R., and Boeij, J. S. M. (1983). *Mutat. Res. 116*:21–34.

Ames, B. N., Lee, F. D. and Durston, W. F. (1973). Proc. Nat. Acad. Sci. *70*:782–786.

Ames, B. N., McCann, J., and Yamasaki, E. (1975). *Mutat. Res. 113*: 347–364.

Atherholt, T. B., McGarrity, G. J., Louis, J. B., McGeorge, L. J., Lioy, P. J., Daisey, J. M., Greenberg, A., and Darack, F. (1985). In *Short-Term Bioassays in the Analysis of Complex Environmental Mixtures*, Volume IV., Eds. Waters, M. D., Sandhu, S. S., Lewtas, J., Claxton, L., Strauss, G., and Nesnow, S., Plenum Publishing Corp., New York, 211–231.

Butler, J. P., Kneip, T. J., Mukai, F., and Daisey, J. M. (1985). In *Short-Term Bioassays in the Analysis of Complex Environmental Mixtures*, Volume IV, Eds. Walters, M. D., Sandhu, S. S., Lewtas, J., Claxton, L., Strauss, G., and Nesnow, S., Plenum Publishing Corp., New York, 233–246.

Butler, J. P., Kneip, T. J., and Daisey, J. M. (1986), *Atmos. Environ.*, in press.

Carnow B. W. (1978). *Environ. Health Perspect. 22*:17–21.

Commoner, B., Madyastha, P., Bronsdon, A., Vithayathil, A. J. (1978). *Toxicol. J. Environ. Health 4*:59–77.

Daisey, J. M., Leyko, M. A., Kleinman, M. T., and Hoffman, E. (1979). *Ann. N.Y. Acad. Sci. 322*:125–142.

Daisey, J. M., Kneip, T. J., Hawryluk, I., and Mukai, F. (1980). *Environ. Sci. and Technol. 14*:1487–1490.

Daisey, J. M., Hershman, R. J., and Kneip, T. J., (1982). *Atmos. Environ. 16*:2162–2168.

Daisey, J. M., Kneip, T. J., Wang, M.-X., Rew, L. X., and Lu, W.-X. (1983). *Aerosol Sci. Tech. 2*:407–415.

Daisey, J. M., Morandi, M., Wolf, G., and Lioy, P. J. (1984). *Atmos. Environ. 18*:1411–1419.

Esman, N. and Corn, M. (1971). *Atmos. Environ. 5*:571–578.

Fukino, H., Mimura, S., Inoue, K., and Yamane, Y. (1982). *Mutat. Res. 102*:237–247.

Garner, R. C., Stanton, C. A., Martin, C. N., Chow, F. L., Thomas, W., Hubner, D., and Herrmann, R. (1986). *Environ. Mutagen. 8*:109–117.

Gibson, T. L. (1985). *Sources of Nitroaromatic Mutagens in Atmospheric Polycyclic Organic Matter*. Proceedings of the 78th Annual APCA Meetings, Detroit, MI, Paper No. 85-36.2.

Greenberg, A. (1986). Personnel Communication, Department of Chemical Engineering and Chemistry, New Jersey Institute of Technology, Newark, NJ.

Harkov, R. (1986). Louis, J., Greenberg, A., Darack, F., and Atherholt, T. *A Study of the Mutagenicity of Extractable Organic Matter (EOM) Subfractions and Associated Substituted Polycyclic Aromatic Hydrocarbons in Newark, NJ: Preliminary Findings.* Proceedings of the 79th Annual APCA Meeting, Minneapolis, MN, Paper No. 86-57.8.

Kneip, T. J., Lippmann, M., Mukai, F., and Daisey, J. M. (1979). *Trace Organic Compounds in the New York City Atmosphere Part I— Preliminary Studies,* prepared for Electric Power Institute, EA 1121, Project 1058-1, 92pp.

Levin, D. E., Yamasaki, E., and Ames, B. N. (1982). *Mutat. Res. 94*: 315–330.

Lioy, P., Daisey, J. M., Atherholt, T., Bozzelli, J., Darack, F., Fischer, R., Greenberg, A., Harkov, R., Kebbekus, B., Kneip, T. J., Louis, J., McGarrity, G., McGeorge, L., and Reiss, N.M. (1983). *J. Air Pollut. Control Assoc. 33*:649–657.

Lioy, P. J., Daisey, J. M., Reiss, N. M., and Harkov, R. (1983b). *Atmos. Environ. 17*:2321–2330.

Lioy, P. J., Daisey, J. M., Greenberg, A., and Harkov, R. (1985). *Atmos. Environ. 19*:429–436.

Lockard, J. M., Viau, C. J., Lee-Stephens, C., Caldwell, J. C., Wojciechowski, J. P., Enoch, H. G., and Sabharwal, P. S. (1981). *Environ. Mutagen. 3*:671–681.

Lofroth, G. (1981). In *Short-Term Bioassays in the Analysis of Complex Environmental Mixtures,* Volume II, Eds. Waters, M. D., Sandhu, S. S., Huisingh, J. L., Claxton, L., and Nesnow, S. Plenum Press Corp., New York, pp. 319–336.

Lofroth, G., Nilsson, L., and Alfheim, I. (1983). In *Short-Term Bioassays in the Analysis of Complex Environmental Mixtures,* Volume III, Eds. Waters, M. D., Sandhu, S. S., Lewtas, J., Claxton, L., Chernoff, N., and Nesnow, S., Plenum Press Corp., New York, pp. 515–525.

Madsen, E. S., Nielsen, P. A., and Pedersen, J. C. (1982). *Sci. Total Environ. 24*:13–25.

Maron, D. M. and Ames, B. N. (1982). In *Second Handbook of Mutagenicity Test Procedures* Eds. Kilbey, B. J., Legator, M., Nichols, W., and Ramel, C., Elsevier Inc., New York, pp. 93–140.

Maron, D. M. and Ames, B. N. (1983). *Mutat. Res. 113*:173–215.

Mason, T. J. and McKay, F. W. (1973). U.S. Dept. of Health, Education and Welfare, Public Health Service, Nat. Inst. Health, Nat. Cancer Inst. Bethesda, MD, DHEW Pub No. (NIH 74-615).

McCann, J., Choi, E., Yamasaki, E., and Ames, B. N. (1975). *Proc. Nat. Acad. Sci. 72*:5135–5139.

Moeller, M. and Alfheim, I. (1980). *Atmos. Environ. 14*:83–88.

Moeller, M., Alfheim, I., Larssen, S., and Mikalsen, A. (1982). *Environ. Sci. Technol. 16*:221–225.

Morandi, M. (1985). Doctoral Thesis entitled "Development of Source Apportionment Models for Inhalable Particulate Matter and its Extractable Organic Fractions in Urban Areas of New Jersey." New York University, 286pp.

Ohsawa, M., Ochi, T., and Hayashi, H. (1983). *Mutat. Res. 116*:83–90.

Pederson, T. C. and Siak, J-S. (1981). *J. App. Toxicol. 1*:54–60.

Pierson, W. R., Gorse, Jr., R. A., Szkarilat, A. C., Brachaczek, W. W., Japar, S. M., Lee, F. S. C., Zweidinger, R. B., and Claxton, L. D. (1983). *Environ. Sci. Technol. 17*:31–44.

Pitts, Jr., J. M., Grosjean, D., Mischke, T. M., Simmon, V. F., and Poole, D. (1977). *Toxicol. Lett. 1*:65–70.

Pitts, Jr., J. M., Harger, Wm., Lokensgard, D. M., Fitz, D. R., Scorziell, G. M., and Mejia, V. (1982). *Mutat. Res. 104*:35–41.

Pitts, Jr., J. M. (1983). *Environ. Health Perspec. 47*:115–140.

de Raat, W. K., DeMeijere, F. A., and Kooijam, S. A. L. M. (1985). *Sci. Total Environ. 44*:17–33.

Reali, D., H. Schlitt, Lohse, C., Barale, R., and Loprieno, N. (1984). Environ. Mut. *6*:813–823.

Rosenkranz, H. S. and Mermelstein, R. (1983). *Mutat. Res. 114*:217–267.

Santodonato, J., Howard, P., and Baser, D. (1981). *J. Environ. Path. Toxicol. 3*:1–364.

Schuetzle, D., Cronn, D., Crittenden, A. L., and Charlson, R. J. (1975). Environ. Sci. Technol. *9*:838–845.

de Serres, F. J. and Shelby, M. D. (1979). *Science 203*:563–565.

Siak, J., Chan, T. L., Gibson, T. L., and Wolff, G. T. (1985). *Atmos. Environ. 19*:369–376.

Sweetman, J. A., Harger, Wm., Fitz, D. R., Paur, H. R., Winer, A. M., Pitts, Jr., J. N. (1984). *Diurnal Mutagenicity of Airborne Particulate Organic Matter adjacent to a heavily traveled West Los Angeles Freeway*. Proceeding of the 77th Annual APCA Meeting, San Francisco, CA, Paper No. 84-16.5.

Talcott, R. and Harger, W. (1980). *Mutat. Res. 79*:177–180.

Talcott, R. E. and Harger, W. (1981). *Mutat. Res. 91*:433–436.

Tokiwa, H., Takeyoshi, H., Morita, K., Takahashi, K., Soruta, N., and Ohnishi, Y. (1976). *Mutat. Res. 38*:351–359.

Tokiwa, H., Morita, K., Takeyoshi, H., Takahashi, K., and Ohnishi, Y. (1977). *Mutat. Res. 48*:237–248.

Tokiwa, H., Kitamori, S., Takahashi, K., and Ohnishi, Y. (1980). *Mutat. Res. 77*:99–108.

Tokiwa, H., Kitamori, S., Horikawa, K., and Nakagawa, R. (1983a). *Environ. Mutagen. 5*:87–100.

Tokiwa, H., Kitamori, S., Nakagawa, R., Horikawa, K., and Matamala, L. (1983b). *Mutat. Res. 121*:107–116.

U.S. EPA (1984). *Review and Evaluation of the Evidence for Cancer Asso-*

ciated with Air Pollution, Office of Air Quality, Planning and Standards, EPA-450/5-83-006R.

Vance, W. A. and Levin, D. E. (1984). *Environ. Mutagen. 6*:797–811.

Van Houdt, J. J., Jongen, W. M. F., Alink, G. M., and Boleij, J. S. M. (1984). *Environ. Mutagen. 6*:861–869.

Viau, C. J., Lockard, J. M., Enoch, H. G., and Sabharwal, P. S. (1982). *Environ. Mutagen. 4*:37–43.

Whong, W.-Z., Stewart, J., McCawley, M., Major, P., Merchant, J. A., and Ong, T. (1981). *Environ. Mutagen. 3*:617–626.

Wolff, G. T., Siak, J. S., Chan, T. L., and Korsog, P. E. (1985). *Multivariate Statistical Analyses of Air Quality Data and Bacterial Mutagenicity Data From Ambient Aerosols*. Research Publication. GMR-5060. ENV-209.

Yeh, H. C., Phalen, R. F., and Raabe, O. G. (1976). *Environ. Health Perspec. 15*:147–156.

APPENDIX

Table A5.1. Mutagenicity of Airborne Particulate Matter Strain TA98 (Revertants/m³)

Site	Summer 1981		Winter 1982		Summer 1982		Winter 1983	
	−S9	+S9	−S9	+S9	−S9	+S9	−S9	+S9
Newark								
CX	1.8±0.3	6.4±0.4	5.8±0.3	7.3±0.4	2.7±0.4	5.1±0.8	7.5±0.9	4.9±1.3
DCM	3.1±0.3	2.9±0.3	5.4±1.6	4.3±0.7	1.8±0.2	2.6±0.2	4.8±0.6	3.2±0.1
ACE	3.2±0.4	3.5±0.3	10.7±0.7	8.0±1.0	4.0±0.6	3.2±0.4	12.5±1.8	5.1±0.4
Elizabeth								
CX	1.0±0.1	4.6±0.3	4.4±0.3	4.9±0.4	1.2±0.2	2.8±0.4	6.7±1.0	4.1±0.3
DCM	2.1±0.3	2.0±0.2	6.7±0.9	3.3±0.5	1.4±0.3	1.5±0.1	3.5±0.6	2.6±0.2
ACE	3.0±0.5	2.8±0.2	6.3±0.5	3.6±0.3	2.3±0.2	2.2±0.2	13.0±2.3	5.6±0.3
Camden								
CX	0.9±0.2	4.8±0.3	3.4±0.5	4.3±0.4	0.8±0.2	1.9±0.3	3.6±0.7	3.0±0.5
DCM	1.5±0.1	1.7±0.1	5.3±1.0	4.2±0.7	1.4±0.2	1.3±0.3	4.1±0.6	2.4±0.1
ACE	1.7±0.2	2.5±0.2	6.7±0.6	4.1±0.3	1.8±0.2	1.7±0.3	3.6±0.7	1.9±0.2
Ringwood								
CX	0.3±0.1	1.8±0.2	0.7±0.2	0.6±0.2	0.5±0.3	0.7±0.1	ND[a]	ND[a]
DCM	0.6±0.1	0.5±0.1	3.2±0.3	1.9±0.2	0.2±0.1	0.4±0.1	1.7±0.2	1.0±0.2
ACE	0.6±0.2	0.5±0.1	2.9±0.3	1.7±0.2	0.8±0.2	0.6±0.1	1.5±0.3	0.6±0.1

[a]ND = not done.

Table A5.2. Mutagenicity of Airborne Particulate Matter Strain TA100 (Revertants/m³)

Site	Summer 1981		Winter 1982		Summer 1982		Winter 1983	
	-S9	+S9	-S9	+S9	-S9	+S9	-S9	+S9
Newark								
CX	1.2±0.4	5.0±0.5	4.9±1.0	11.2±2.3	2.4±0.4	3.8±0.7	8.6±1.8	5.3±0.8
DCM	1.3±0.3	2.5±0.2	1.0±0.4	3.3±0.9	1.0±0.2	1.7±0.2	3.3±0.3	2.2±0.3
ACE	Neg.	3.6±0.5	3.7±0.6	5.3±0.6	2.4±0.2	2.3±0.3	7.2±1.1	3.8±0.5
Elizabeth								
CX	1.1±0.3	3.8±0.2	3.3±1.1	10.3±1.9	1.1±0.2	3.2±0.6	8.2±1.5	3.4±0.6
DCM	0.8±0.3	1.5±0.3	Neg.	1.1±0.5	0.8±0.2	1.4±0.2	3.0±0.5	0.8±0.2
ACE	Neg.	2.9±0.4	2.8±0.6	3.6±0.4	1.9±0.3	2.0±0.3	7.9±0.8	4.4±0.5
Camden								
CX	0.7±0.3	3.6±0.3	2.4±0.6	6.6±1.3	0.7±0.1	2.5±0.9	4.5±0.7	4.3±0.8
DCM	0.8±0.2	1.4±0.2	1.6±0.3[a]	3.6±0.7	0.8±0.3	1.1±0.2	2.6±0.3	1.6±0.1
ACE	Neg.	2.1±0.4	2.3±0.7	3.7±0.4	1.0±0.3	1.1±0.3	2.5±0.5	1.3±0.5
Ringwood								
CX	Neg.	1.6±0.2	Neg.	1.4±0.5	Neg.	0.7±0.1	ND[a]	ND
DCM	Neg.	0.6±0.3	Neg.	2.2±0.4	Neg.	0.4±0.1	1.0±0.2	1.0±0.2
ACE	Neg.	0.7±0.2	0.9±0.2[b]	1.7±0.3	0.5±0.2	0.5±0.2	0.9±0.2	0.4±0.1

[a]ND = not done.
[b]Marginal response.

Table A5.3. Mutagenicity of Airborne Particulate Matter Strain TA1537 (Revertants/M³)

Site	Summer 1981		Winter 1982		Summer 1982		Winter 1983	
	−S9	+S9	−S9	+S9	−S9	+S9	−S9	+S9
Newark								
CX	0.3±0.1	2.8±0.3	1.4±0.2	4.0±0.3	1.3±0.4	3.0±0.4	1.3±0.3	1.5±0.4
DCM	0.7±0.2	1.0±0.1	0.8±0.1	1.4±0.2	0.6±0.1	0.9±0.1	1.0±0.1	0.7±0.1
ACE	Neg.	1.1±0.2	2.1±0.3	2.3±0.2	0.6±0.1	0.8±0.1	2.1±0.4	1.5±0.3
Elizabeth								
CX	0.1±0.1	2.6±0.2	0.7±0.2	3.0±0.3	0.9±0.2	1.8±0.4	1.2±0.4	1.2±0.2
DCM	0.4±0.1	0.6±0.1	0.6±0.1	0.7±0.1	0.5±0.1	0.6±0.1	0.8±0.1	0.6±0.1
ACE	Neg.	0.8±0.2	0.9±0.2	1.3±0.1	0.5±0.1	0.6±0.1	2.4±0.2	1.4±0.1
Camden								
CX	0.1±0.1	2.6±0.2	0.4±0.1	2.5±0.4	0.3±0.1	1.1±0.2	0.9±0.2	0.6±0.1
DCM	0.2±0.03	0.7±0.1	1.0±0.1	1.3±0.2	0.4±0.1	1.0±0.1	0.9±0.1	0.8±0.1
ACE	0.4±0.2	0.8±0.3	1.0±0.2	1.5±0.2	0.4±0.1	0.6±0.1	0.9±0.2	0.6±0.1
Ringwood								
CX	Neg.	0.8±0.1	0.3±0.1	0.7±0.1	ND[a]	ND	ND	ND
DCM	0.2±0.1	0.2±0.1	0.8±0.1	0.6±0.1	ND	ND	0.4±0.1	0.4±0.1
ACE	Neg.	0.3±0.1	0.5±0.1	0.5±0.1	ND	ND	0.3±0.1	0.2±0.1

[a]ND = not done.

Table A5.4. Mutagenicity of Airborne Particulate Matter Strain TA98 (Revertants/μg)

Site	Summer 1981		Winter 1982		Summer 1982		Winter 1983	
	−S9	+S9	−S9	+S9	−S9	+S9	−S9	+S9
Newark								
CX	0.55±0.08	1.95±0.12	0.95±0.05	1.18±0.07	0.83±0.12	1.57±0.23	1.41±0.17	0.91±0.25
DCM	3.08±0.33	2.88±0.34	3.07±0.89	2.44±0.39	0.95±0.10	1.38±0.10	4.01±0.46	2.63±0.11
ACE	0.43±0.05	0.48±0.05	0.88±0.06	0.66±0.08	0.59±0.09	0.46±0.05	1.33±0.20	0.54±0.04
Elizabeth								
CX	0.40±0.05	1.93±0.12	0.64±0.05	0.71±0.06	0.48±0.09	1.10±0.14	1.30±0.19	0.79±0.06
DCM	2.82±0.26	2.62±0.20	4.08±0.55	1.99±0.30	0.92±0.21	1.02±0.09	3.67±0.58	2.73±0.16
ACE	0.61±0.10	0.57±0.04	0.67±0.05	0.38±0.04	0.37±0.03	0.36±0.03	1.55±0.08	0.67±0.04
Camden								
CX	0.40±0.09	2.24±0.16	0.89±0.13	1.13±0.11	0.44±0.10	1.04±0.15	1.11±0.22	0.92±0.15
DCM	2.28±0.15	2.53±0.12	2.68±0.89	2.11±0.36	0.69±0.10	0.67±0.09	3.26±0.50	1.89±0.10
ACE	0.25±0.04	0.37±0.03	0.76±0.07	0.46±0.03	0.26±0.03	0.25±0.04	0.46±0.08	0.24±0.03
Ringwood								
CX	0.28±0.13	0.71±0.22	0.42±0.10	0.34±0.10	0.48±0.13	0.71±0.11	ND[a]	ND
DCM	0.61±0.07	0.58±0.08	2.74±0.25	1.61±0.15	0.25±0.04	0.36±0.09	0.93±0.14	0.55±0.09
ACE	0.19±0.06	0.14±0.02	0.50±0.05	0.29±0.04	0.20±0.04	0.14±0.02	0.74±0.12	0.28±0.03

[a]ND = not done.

Table A5.5. Mutagenicity of Airborne Particulate Matter Strain TA100 (Revertants/µg)

Site	Summer 1981 −S9	Summer 1981 +S9	Winter 1982 −S9	Winter 1982 +S9	Summer 1982 −S9	Summer 1982 +S9	Winter 1983 −S9	Winter 1983 +S9
Newark								
CX	0.38±0.11	1.55±0.14	0.81±0.16	1.84±0.38	0.74±0.14	1.16±0.21	1.61±0.35	0.99±0.15
DCM	1.35±0.28	2.55±0.17	0.57±0.21[b]	1.88±0.50	0.53±0.08	0.89±0.09	2.74±0.27	1.80±0.22
ACE	Neg.	0.50±0.07	0.31±0.05	0.44±0.05	0.35±0.03	0.34±0.04	0.77±0.12	0.40±0.05
Elizabeth								
CX	0.45±0.12	1.59±0.10	0.47±0.16	1.48±0.28	0.42±0.07	1.26±0.23	1.60±0.28	0.66±0.11
DCM	1.05±0.26	1.96±0.30	Neg.	0.68±0.33[b]	0.53±0.12	0.94±0.12	3.14±0.54	0.86±0.22
ACE	Neg.	0.58±0.08	0.30±0.06	0.38±0.04	0.31±0.05	0.33±0.05	0.94±0.09	0.52±0.06
Camden								
CX	0.33±0.12	1.67±0.17	0.64±0.15	1.75±0.34	0.36±0.07	1.37±0.50	1.40±0.22	1.34±0.26
DCM	1.24±0.32	2.02±0.34	0.80±0.16[a]	1.79±0.35	0.39±0.15	0.53±0.10	2.04±0.26	1.27±0.10
ACE	Neg.	0.32±0.06	0.26±0.08	0.42±0.05	0.16±0.04	0.18±0.05	0.32±0.06	0.16±0.06
Ringwood								
CX	Neg.	1.49±0.23	Neg.	0.85±0.27	Neg.	0.76±0.12	ND[a]	ND
DCM	Neg.	0.64±0.32	Neg.	1.84±0.38	Neg.	0.37±0.10	0.53±0.10	0.55±0.12
ACE	Neg.	0.22±0.08	0.15±0.04[b]	0.29±0.04	0.12±0.04	0.13±0.06	0.46±0.11	0.21±0.04

[a]ND = not done.
[b]Marginal response.

Table A5.6. Mutagenicity of Airborne Particulate Matter Strain TA1537 (Revertants/μg)

Site	Summer 1981		Winter 1982		Summer 1982		Winter 1983	
	−S9	+S9	−S9	+S9	−S9	+S9	−S9	+S9
Newark								
CX	0.09±0.02	0.87±0.09	0.23±0.03	0.65±0.05	0.40±0.11	0.90±0.11	0.25±0.06	0.29±0.08
DCM	0.70±0.15	0.99±0.07	0.45±0.05	0.81±0.09	0.33±0.03	0.45±0.02	0.80±0.04	0.59±0.05
ACE	Neg.	0.14±0.03	0.17±0.02	0.19±0.01	0.09±0.01	0.11±0.02	0.22±0.04	0.16±0.03
Elizabeth								
CX	0.06±0.02	1.07±0.09	0.10±0.03	0.44±0.04	0.34±0.09	0.71±0.14	0.24±0.06	0.23±0.04
DCM	0.51±0.07	0.79±0.09	0.36±0.05	0.42±0.07	0.30±0.03	0.42±0.03	0.79±0.07	0.64±0.09
ACE	Neg.	0.16±0.04	0.10±0.02	0.14±0.01	0.09±0.02	0.10±0.01	0.29±0.03	0.17±0.02
Camden								
CX	0.06±0.03	1.22±0.09	0.12±0.02	0.66±0.10	0.18±0.07	0.59±0.10	0.26±0.07	0.20±0.03
DCM	0.32±0.04	1.02±0.12	0.49±0.07	0.65±0.11	0.22±0.02	0.47±0.06	0.74±0.05	0.66±0.04
ACE	0.06±0.02	0.12±0.04	0.11±0.02	0.17±0.03	0.06±0.01	0.09±0.02	0.11±0.03	0.07±0.02
Ringwood								
CX	Neg.	0.71±0.11	0.20±0.07	0.40±0.07	ND[a]	ND	ND	0.29±0.08
DCM	0.22±0.08	0.22±0.06	0.65±0.06	0.53±0.04	ND	ND	0.21±0.05	0.21±0.03
ACE	Neg.	0.09±0.03	0.08±0.02	0.09±0.01	ND	ND	0.13±0.01	0.08±0.01

[a]ND = not done.

CHAPTER 6

Air Pollution Episodes During the ATEOS—Their Nature and Significance

Paul J. Lioy

CHAPTER CONTENTS

Air Pollution Episodes During the ATEOS—Their Nature and Significance

INTRODUCTION

In the past, and probably for the foreseeable future, our attention is rather vividly directed toward the occurrence of air pollution problems during what have come to be defined as episodes, or sudden hazardous releases. Air pollution episodes, which are the subject of this chapter, are defined as periods in which the concentrations of one or more primary or secondary pollutants significantly exceed those generally observed and can pose a potential health risk.

The nature of individual episode events can vary significantly, depending upon the sources, the chemicals released, the cause of the release(s), and/or the local and regional meteorological conditions. Air pollution episodes have been qualitatively or quantitatively described since 2000 B.C. (Heidron, 1978). The most famous of these occurred in London, England; Donora, Pennsylvania; Meuse Valley, Belgium; and New York City, New York. The most tragic episode was the London Smog of 1952, which is shown graphically in Figure 6.1 (Stern, 1962). As can be seen, there was a substantial increase in the daily death rate over a relatively short period of time, and this effect was associated with increases in sulfur dioxide and British Smoke. The measurement of British Smoke is considered to be a surrogate for respirable particulate matter and most specifically of the carbonaceous components of the seasonal mass. Residential coal burning was the primary source of these types of emissions during that era.

Throughout the 1970s and 1980s episodes of the type observed in London have been virtually nonexistent in the United States. What is usually the case today are situations in which one or more criteria pollutants exceed a

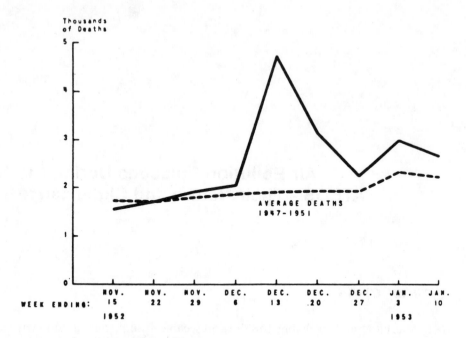

Figure 6.1.   London Acid Smog Episode in which over 3,000 excess deaths occurred in one day. (Permission from Her Majesty's Stationery Office, Norwich, England.)

national standard or a pollutant indicator, such as coefficient of haze (COH), or a criteria pollutant exceeds a value that corresponds to locally or regionally established alert stage conditions.

Most recent episodes in the New York-New Jersey Metropolitan area have been associated with the occurrence of ozone and other products of photochemical smog. Although the frequency of smog events is highest in the Los Angeles area, most presently occur in and downwind of major urban areas in the eastern half of the U.S. (EPA, 1978).

Fall and wintertime episodes can still occur in urban centers. They can also develop in isolated communities where woodburning is the predominant fuel for space heating (Cooper, 1980). In most cases the accumulated pollutants are primarily related to emissions from combustion processes, e.g., motor vehicles and space heating. The local increments in pollution will be enhanced by material transported in by nearby and mesoscale urban emissions.

The following discussion examines the types of episodes that occurred during the ATEOS project. Each will be characterized by excursions in concentrations of pollutants or indicator species above a standard or alert level. The general features of the winter and summer episodes that occurred can be used as a guide by individuals who may wish to design future characterization studies, to regulate specific pollutants, or to design acute health effects field studies.

GENERAL CHARACTERISTICS OF EPISODES

Although controlled by different chemical processes, episode periods are characterized by high concentrations of single or multiple pollutants which can persist from one to ten days. Situations will ensue where either a broad peak or spikes in concentrations will develop within a given day or over a series of days.

As has been demonstrated in a number of investigations (Wolff et al., 1977; Lioy and Samson, 1979) summertime episodes will take place when the meteorological conditions of high temperature, sunlight, and low or high relative humidity are conducive to the formation of photochemical smog. The work of Wolff and Lioy (1980) demonstrated that certain meteorological conditions within the high emission density area can lead to the transport of photochemical smog-related pollutants over thousands of kilometers. Photochemical reactions produce an oxidizing atmosphere which can produce ozone, other oxidants (e.g., peroxyacetylnitrate), and secondary particulate sulfate and organics. Precursor compounds include nitrogen oxides, olefin and paraffin hydrocarbons, and sulfur dioxide. Details on the basic chemical reaction schemes can be found in an excellent text by Seinfeld (1986). From Table 1.2 in Chapter 1 it is apparent that these compounds are emitted in the counties that contain each ATEOS site. Regional emission inventories of EPA also show a substantial burden in the metropolitan area and throughout the eastern United States (U.S. EPA, 1978).

The wintertime episodes, which have been traditionally called reducing episodes, occur at low temperatures, high relative humidity, and with local atmospheric stagnation. In many cases, nocturnal temperature inversions produce conditions conducive for producing a wintertime episode. Such events trap locally produced rooftop space heating, industrial and motor vehicle emissions. This will result in the accumulation of high primary particulate matter concentrations as well as gaseous pollutants. Finally, emissions from sources characteristic of a particular subsection of an urban, suburban or rural area can result in the accumulation of specific compounds from point or fugitive emission sources (e.g., storage tanks, gasoline stations). Obviously, these sources will contribute to the volatile hydrocarbon air pollutants during the summer, but the effect may not be observed as higher concentrations. The source emissions may be consumed and transformed to secondary materials, since most volatile hydrocarbons are precursors for photochemical reactions.

ATEOS EPISODES

The summer and wintertime episodes (IPM > 70 $\mu g/m^3$ or > 16 $\mu g/m^3$ EOM or > 20 $\mu g/m^3$ SO_4^{-2} at least one site) which occurred during the course of the study are shown in Table 6.1 along with some information on the nature and magnitude of each event. It is obvious that summertime episodes dominated in terms of duration, and as could be expected by oxidant materials. The peak concentrations (24-hr basis) of particulate matter occurred during a wintertime episode. The two major mass fractions of the $IPM - SO_4^{-2}$ and EOM — had their peak concentrations in the summer and winter, respectively. From the results of other studies, the peak in summertime SO_4^{-2} would be anticipated. The accumulation of SO_4^{-2} species results from the oxidation of SO_2 emitted by regional power plant plumes via a number of heterogeneous and homogeneous chemical reactions. These can occur during the development of photochemical smog episodes (Husar et al., 1978). Reaction products such as hydrogen peroxide, the hydroxyl radicals (OH), and other radicals are important constituents in the oxidation of ambient SO_2 to H_2SO_4. The SO_4^{-2} may be further transformed to a more neutral form (ammonium bisulfate or ammonium sulfate) after transport some distance downwind and interaction with pockets of ammonia over urban or agricultural areas. In the wintertime, the lack of ultraviolet radiation minimizes the formation of smog-derived SO_4^{-2}. The dominant reaction mechanisms will be heterogeneous, e.g., vanadium or manganese catalytic oxidation of SO_2, with a primary source of the SO_2 being local heating sources rather than the regional-scale power plant emissions (Husar et al., 1978).

The accumulation of winter and summer SO_4^{-2} and the seasonal dichotomy in potential population exposure is shown explicitly in Figure 6.2, using data obtained from the SURE (Sulfate Regional Experiment). The results indicate a rather broad regional distribution of SO_4^{-2} in summer episodes, with daily concentrations in excess of $30 \mu g/m^3$. In the winter, the regional extent of SO_4^{-2} in an episode contracts, although the New York-New Jersey metropolitan area remains a focus, but with much lower peak concentrations. (Mueller and Hidy, 1983).

Lioy and Lippmann (1986), in their review of available data bases on sulfur species, have indicated that one or more of the species H_2SO_4 and $(NH_4)_2SO_4$ can be present in the atmosphere during an episode. The distribution of species can range from acidic (H_2SO_4) to basic (($NH_4)_2SO_4$) depending upon the availability of gaseous ammonia to neutralize the particles. In the northeast, the acidic species are found either downwind of major SO_2 sources or in rural areas. Work by Morandi et al. (1983) and Lioy et al. (1980) suggests that the rural SO_4^{-2} may be more acidic during the initial phases of an episode.

Chapter 2 dealt extensively with the nature of the average contributions

Table 6.1. Episodes and Their Characteristics during the Summers and Winters of ATEOS

Peak Values ($\mu g/m^3$) on Each Pollutant (Keyed on each material not an IPM sample)

Year	Dates	Duration (days)	Newark IPM	Newark EOM	Newark SO_4^{-2}	Elizabeth IPM	Elizabeth EOM	Elizabeth SO_4^{-2}	Camden IPM	Camden EOM	Camden SO_4^{-2}	Meteorological Characteristics
81	7/6–7/10	5	63	12	17	65	10	17	94	15	32	Summer heatwave regional transport, W-SW winds, O_3 > 100 ppb
81	7/16–7/22	6	109	29	28	81	20	26	66	14	25	Partial collapse of SW flow of Bermuda High, light variable winds (7/19–21) O_3 > 100 ppb
81	7/31–8/5	6	81	20	30	61	10	28	79	11	32	High pressure system passing across NE, stagnation (8/2–4)
81	8/7–8/15	8	84	25	22	59	10	29	74	12	28	Weak stationary front, SW flow most of period – regional transport moderate, O_3 > 100 ppb
82	7/10–7/20	10	124	30	23	97	18	21	86	15	30	Weak flow through 7/15, stagnation peaked 7/15–7/20, O_3 > 120 multiple days
82	7/25–7/28	4	75	17	21	68	17	20	66	15	23	High pressure off New England SW & W flow
82	7/31–8/6	7	103	9	23	84	14	25	79	20	25	Weak ridge of high pressure produced
82	1/18–1/19	1	62	21	11	72	23	14	73	24	16	Local stagnation (nocturnal) at all sites
82	1/27–1/30	3	96	37	10	77	40	13	66	26	14	Weak high pressure on east coast light & variable winds
82	2/5–2/6	1	95	27	16	106	34	17	64	19	16	Inversion affecting northern New Jersey
82	2/14–2/16	2	77	32	15	75	29	15	58	20	17	Local nocturnal inversion
83	1/29–1/30	1	86	30	16	72	32	14	73	28	8	Nocturnal inversion northeastern New Jersey
83	2/1–2/2	1	92	33	13	76	31	13	50	22	10	Nocturnal inversion northeastern New Jersey
83	2/13–2/18	5	202	70	28	117	64	15	104	52	14	Persistent stagnation period after large snow fall. Moderating daytime temperatures into 40's. Regional accumulation.
83	2/21–2/23	2	86	27	16	74	32	16	102	46	20	Persistent stagnation, especially in the southern section of state. Daytime temp. max. >50°F

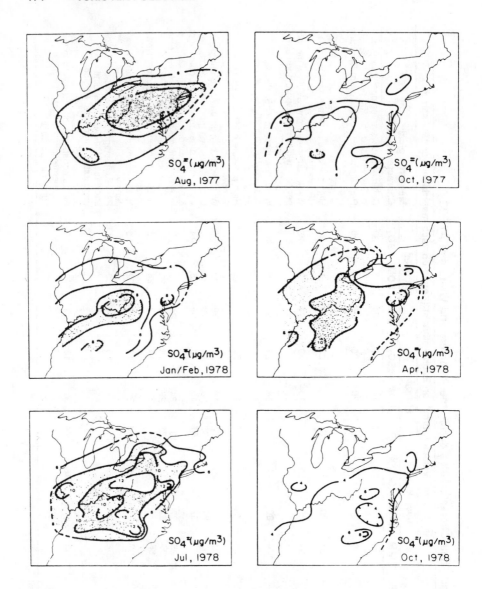

Figure 6.2.   Regional Distribution of SO_4^{-2} aerosol during the Sulfate Regional Experiment (SURE) in all seasons. (1983, Electric Power Research Institute Report–EA–1901 "The Sulfate Regional Experiment–Report of Findings"–Vol. 2 with permission.)

of organic and inorganic material to the inhalable particulate mass. In contrast to SO_4^{-2}, the extractable organic matter (EOM) maximum is found in the winter and is related to the presence of space heating and local motor vehicle sources in each city. These increased the primary emissions of both the cyclohexane-soluble fraction (CX) and the acetone-soluble fraction (ACE) of particulate matter. The EOM concentrations were also different at each site. In Chapters 2 and 5 it was explained that this was due to the emissions density and number of potential organic emissions from area sources found in areas surrounding the section studied within each city.

An example of the importance of local contributions to EOM was found by Wilson (1985) in his analysis of areas with high hydrocarbon emissions versus wind direction during summertime episodes. He focussed on summertime to minimize confounding directional factors caused by the fairly uniform distribution of space heating sources in the winter. The density of local EOM emissions was either defined by (1) an industrial pocket or center including petrochemical plants, refineries, etc., (2) multiple small sources for a given wind direction, or (3) areawide sources. Details on the source distribution have been discussed in Chapters 2 and 7. In Chapter 1, the individual site characteristics were described, and it was noted that the areas around Elizabeth and Newark had the most diverse array of sources and types.

Summary data from Wilson (1985) for the three urban sites are found in Tables 6.2a and 6.2b for days when the EOM concentrations were above 16 $\mu g/m^3$ in the summers of 1981 and 1982. The data for the summer of 1981 were more closely associated with the southerly to west-northwest wind direction, which if taken alone would have been suggestive of a limited array of sources contributing to the EOM at each location. The 1982 data were used to get a clearer picture of the variety of emission sources that could affect each site, since a number of wind directions affected the sites.

For summertime conditions, and probably for wintertime conditions (although as stated above an area could be dominated by the space heating sources), a source section classification scheme based upon surface winds was developed for the elevated EOM days ($> 16\ \mu g/m^3$). Trajectory analyses were also attempted, but (in contrast to the case for SO_4^{-2}) produced no meaningful transport relationships. For each sampling location the principal local source areas were:

Newark

1. Sector 150° – local impact from Bayonne
2. Sector 210° – local impact from Elizabeth and Linden
3. Sectors 300° and 330° – local impact from downtown
4. Sectors 360° and 30° – local impact from Harrison-Kearny

Table 6.2a.   Daily Surface Wind Sector Frequency Distributions (Percent) at Newark and Philadelphia Airports on Days When the [EOM] ≥ 16.0 µg/m³ in 1981

Monitoring Station(s)[a]	Date	SECTOR FREQUENCY												
		360°	30°	60°	90°	120°	150°	180°	210°	240°	270°	300°	330°	Calm
C	7/9 – 7/10	16.7			12.5		29.2	20.8	20.8	4.2	41.7	25.0	12.5	
N,E	19 – 20					4.2				4.2				
N	8/2 – 8/3								29.2	50.0	12.5	8.3		12.5
C	3 – 4						4.2	8.3	4.2	20.8	20.8	20.8	8.3	
N	4 – 5								4.2	50.0	29.2	16.7		
N,E	10 – 11						8.3	16.7	12.5	33.3	29.2			
N	11 – 12	12.5		4.2		4.2	20.8	4.2	8.3	8.3	16.7	16.7		4.2
N	12 – 13	8.3						4.2	20.8	45.8	8.3	4.2	8.3	
N	13 – 14		4.2	4.2	4.2	8.3			12.5	16.7	37.5	12.5		
C	13 – 14	4.2		4.2				8.3		20.8	45.8	16.7		

[a]C = Camden (Philadelphia Airport Data); N = Newark (Newark Airport Data); E = Elizabeth (Newark Airport Data).

Table 6.2b. Daily Surface Wind Sector Frequency Distributions (Percent) at Newark and Philadelphia Airports on Days When the [EOM] ≥ 16.0 μg/m³ in 1982

Monitoring Station(s)[a]	Date	360°	30°	60°	90°	120°	150°	180°	210°	240°	270°	300°	330°	Calm
N	7/8 – 7/9	12.5	16.7	4.2					4.2	16.7	29.2	16.7		
C	9 – 10	20.8	16.7		20.8	4.2					8.3	16.7	12.5	
N,E	10 – 11				4.2	20.8	25.0	41.7	8.3					
N	12 – 13	12.5		4.2				16.7	16.7	4.2	16.7			12.5
N	13 – 14	8.3	25.0		4.2	4.2	4.2		8.3	8.3	8.3	33.3	4.2	4.2
C	13 – 14					20.8	8.3	12.5	29.2	12.5		12.5		8.3
N,E	14 – 15			4.2	4.2	25.0	54.2	4.2	25.0	12.5	12.5	8.3		
N	15 – 16					8.3	29.2	12.5	45.8	33.3				
N	16 – 17					4.2	4.2	12.5	12.5	62.5				
N,E	18 – 19										20.8	4.2	4.2	
N	19 – 20		25.0					12.5	12.5	25.0	16.7	4.2	4.2	
N,E	25 – 26								8.3	66.7	20.8	12.5	20.8	8.3
N	26 – 27	4.2	20.8	4.2			4.2	12.5		4.2	20.8	20.8	25.0	
C	26 – 27	29.2	12.5	4.2		8.3	4.2	4.2		33.3	4.2		8.3	
N	8/1 – 8/2	4.2		8.3					4.2	8.3	25.0	20.8		
N	2 – 3	16.7	33.3	4.2	4.2	12.5					12.5		12.5	8.3
N,E	3 – 4		12.5				33.3	12.5	4.2			8.3	29.2	4.2
C	3 – 4	37.5						4.2	45.8	41.7	12.5			
C	4 – 5							8.3	8.3	16.7	4.2			
C	5 – 6	4.2	20.8	20.8	4.2	4.2	4.2		8.3	50.0	4.2	4.2		8.3
N	7 – 8						12.5	25.0		16.7				
N	8 – 9					4.2	41.7	25.0			4.2			
C	10 – 11	20.8	16.7	12.5		8.3			4.2	12.5	4.2	16.7	16.7	

[a] C = Camden (Philadelphia Airport Data); N = Newark (Newark Airport Data); E = Elizabeth (Newark Airport Data).

Elizabeth

1. Sector 120° — local impact from Bayonne

Camden

1. Sectors 300°, 330°, 360° and 30° — local impact from Pennsylvania

The main conclusions from this analysis were that elevated summertime EOM concentrations observed at urban sites in New Jersey may primarily be the result of local industrial and commercial activities. This is consistent with the compositional analyses completed by Daisey et al. (1984). However, regional transport from Pennsylvania and the Washington to Philadelphia corridor is contributing to EOM concentrations observed during the episodes at these sites with westerly to southwesterly winds.

The elevated EOM levels observed at Newark and Elizabeth are due to various combinations of local emissions from the oil refineries and petrochemical plants of the Bayonne and Linden area, and local emissions from the urban centers of Harrison-Kearny, as well as the downtown centers of Newark and Elizabeth. Regional transport from industrial areas in Pennsylvania and other urban centers will occur but qualitative and quantitative differentiation is difficult. The local contribution to elevated EOM levels observed at Camden is due primarily to the various industrial and commercial activities in Philadelphia.

Selected Episodes Occurring in ATEOS

Summertime — July 16 through 22, 1981. The period was characterized by a partial breakdown of normal summertime southwesterly flow around the Bermuda High (Figure 6.3). Air circulation near the ground can best be described as light and variable, but primarily from the south, probably dominated by subsynoptic-scale sea breezes. An interval of stagnation conditions persisted from July 19 to 21. At 850 mb, however, there was a persistent southwesterly flow over the eastern U.S. As is usually the case, the period of high concentrations was terminated with the passage of a cold front on July 22 (Lioy et al., 1983).

As previously stated, with the added summertime conditions of high temperature and relative humidity, these meteorological events were conducive to the accumulation of secondary particles and O_3. On July 19 the O_3 levels increased to a peak of 192 ppb in the general region around Newark and Elizabeth (Figures 6.4a,b). Throughout the period there were consecutive days during which the daily 1-hr peak O_3 levels exceeded 120 ppb (NAAQS), at all sites. Typical of photochemical smog episodes in the eastern U.S., multiple hours of O_3 above 100 ppb were noted at many locations

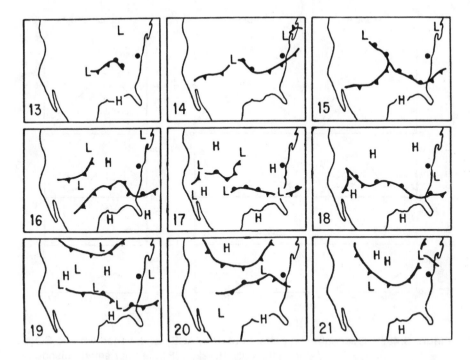

Figure 6.3. The movement of the high pressure system associated with the
July 16–22 episode in 1981.

in the state monitoring network throughout a given day (NJDEP,
1980–1983).

On July 19 an approximately twofold increase from the July 18 values
was observed for the fine particle mass, EOM, the polar organic fraction
(ACE) and SO_4^{-2} at Newark and Elizabeth (Figure 6.4). Sulfate showed a
similar, but somewhat smaller increase in Camden. The simultaneous SO_4^{-2}
increases at each site were indicative of SO_4^{-2} generation and transport
combination with the regional accumulation of ozone. The absolute concentrations of SO_4^{-2} were essentially identical at all urban sites on July 19.
The increases in polar EOM were most apparent at the Newark and Elizabeth sites, which are situated only 7 km apart. The total EOM and the ACE
concentrations were approximately 30% higher in Newark than Elizabeth.
In addition, Newark had approximately double the EOM observed in Camden. Comparisons of the concentration differences between Ringwood and
each urban site for this episode made by Daisey et al. (1984) indicate that
local sources produced moderate increases in EOM at Elizabeth and Cam-

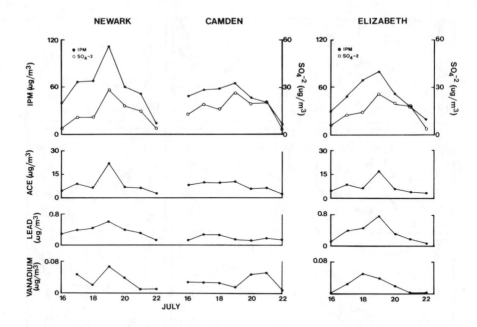

Figure 6.4a.   Concentration patterns of IPM, ACE, lead, vanadium and SO_4^{-2} observed during the July 16–22, 1981 summer smog episode in Newark, Elizabeth, and Camden. (Adapted from Lioy et al., 1983.)

den, and substantial increases at Newark. The remainder, 17–25% of the EOM, was estimated to be associated with regional sources.

Because the wind direction was previously from the south and west during the summer of 1981, the analysis used to determine these estimates appeared to differentiate the regional influence. However, the range of wind direction that occurred in 1982 precluded the completion of a similar estimate for that summer. At all three sites, the IPM and EOM were significantly correlated ($r \geq 0.7$), and EOM usually was 20 to 30% of the IPM. Therefore, the sum of EOM and SO_4^{-2} accounted for 40 to 60% of the IPM mass during the 1981 summertime episodes.

As shown in Chapter 4, the highest levels of volatile organic compounds were generally observed for benzene and toluene. During this episode, between site relationships for these species were not apparent, although the mean benzene concentrations were similar at all locations. High toluene levels were most pronounced at Newark, and the Newark peak level of 137 ppb (approximately 10 times the summer of 1981 mean) was observed during the stagnation associated with this episode.

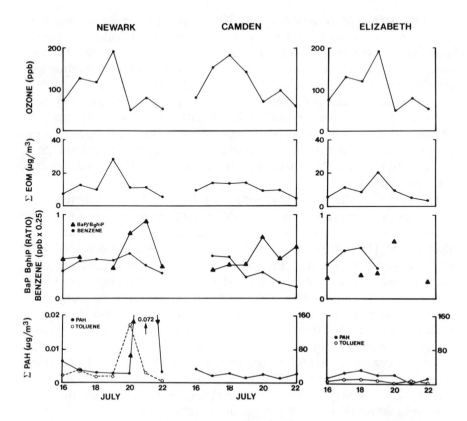

Figure 6.4b.   Concentration patterns of ozone, EOM, benzene, PAHs, and BaP and BghiP observed during the July 16–22, 1981 summer smog episode in Newark, Elizabeth, and Camden. (Adapted from Lioy et al, 1983.)

The sum of the concentrations of PAH compounds measured was relatively low throughout the summer. However, these reached a maximum concentration of 71.3 ng/m³ for compounds in Newark during this episode. When automobile emissions are a predominant source of PAH, the ratio of benzo(a)pyrene to benzo(ghi)perylene (BghiP) is generally between 0.2 and 0.4 (Greenberg et al., 1985). As can be seen in Figures 6.4a and 6.4b, this range was apparent at Elizabeth, while the Newark and Camden data suggested the presence of additional source types. The July 21 PAH excursion at Newark was associated with a BaP/BghiP ratio close to 1 (Greenberg et al., 1985), which would be consistent with a local source emitting PAHs in the area and not being efficiently diluted because of the stagnation conditions.

From the preceding analysis, the SO_4^{-2} concentration excursions were coincident and nearly equivalent from day to day for Elizabeth, Newark, and Camden, and only slightly lower in Ringwood. Also, the SO_4^{-2} during all episodes had high intersite correlations ($r > 0.89$). This observation was consistent with the earlier work of Wolff et al. (1979) and Lioy et al. (1980). Each showed that during the summer, sites in the New York subregion (New York–New Jersey–Connecticut) will be influenced simultaneously by increases in SO_4^{-2} when the sites are affected by transport conditions associated with the presence of a high pressure system in the northeastern U.S. It can be inferred from these data that little if any of the SO_4^{-2} was related to local emission sources.

In contrast to other major components of the inhalable particulate matter (IPM), extractable organic matter (EOM) concentrations were normally not equivalent at any of the urban sites during this episode. Thus, although Daisey et al. (1984) have shown that to some extent the EOM is associated with the regional accumulation processes occurring in a photochemical smog episode, the local sources of EOM and its precursors played a significant role in determining what apparent EOM concentrations are observed. In this example episode, on July 19 the Newark EOM value was 30% higher than observed in Elizabeth and approximately twice the concentrations found in Camden. This is due to both primary emissions of EOM and secondary organic matter (dichloromethane-soluble fraction and ACE) produced from reactions of volatile organic compounds (VOCs) in photochemical smog. However, on the day immediately before and after the 19th, Camden had equivalent or higher values than Newark.

The toluene, benzene, and PAHs measured at each site appeared to be related to local sources, since toluene and benzene peaks were observed sporadically and were not associated with the highest mass concentration days of the episode. For toluene this was most apparent in Newark, while for benzene the most significant excursions were observed at Elizabeth.

The PAH variation, however, is somewhat more complicated. When individual PAH compounds are examined for variations during the episode (Figure 6.5), it is apparent that although the absolute concentrations were different, the overall variations of the individual compounds were similar. As in the case of the EOM, this probably reflects the influence of the meteorological conditions prevailing throughout New Jersey.

Available information on the local sources that may be affecting the Newark site was given in Chapter 1. A qualitative microinventory was taken of all sources in the area surrounding the neighborhood, and it can be seen that there are numerous small sources (100 tons/yr) with the potential to affect the site. Most are located to the south-southwest, and during this episode that was the most frequent wind direction. Consequently, it is reasonable to suggest that these sources were linked to the sporadic excursions

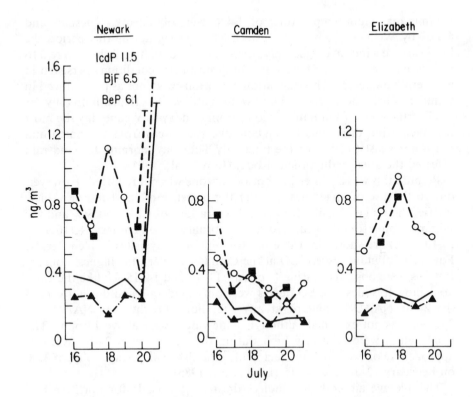

Figure 6.5.   The variation of indeno(cd)pyrene, benzo(j)fluoranthene, and benzo(a)pyrene in Newark, Elizabeth, and Camden throughout the July, 1981 episode. (Pergamon Press, Ltd., with permission, from Lioy et al., 1983.)

of PAHs and VOCs not observed at the other sites, and to a portion of the Newark EOM concentration.

Wintertime—February 13 through 18, 1983. On February 11 an intense winter storm moved up along the Atlantic Coast from the southeast. Snow began to fall during the late morning and reached blizzard conditions by the late afternoon and throughout the night. On Saturday morning (February 12), between 40 and 55 cm of new snow had fallen. By the next morning an area of high pressure moved down from Quebec and centered over the New York-New Jersey metropolitan area. This high pressure system persisted from Sunday to Wednesday. Although the temperatures were much lower than summertime conditions, a gradual warming trend was observed, and daytime maximum temperatures of 4.4°C were obtained by Tuesday, and 8.9°C by Wednesday. In northeastern New Jersey, during this period the local surface winds averaged only between 4 and 6 mph, and there were 3 to 6 hr of calm each day. Thus, stagnant atmospheric conditions persisted in northern New Jersey. The stagnation conditions were not as pronounced in Camden. There the average surface wind speed was less than 6 mph only for the February 13–14 sampling period. From Sunday to Wednesday the most prevalent wind directions throughout the state were from the north and north-northeast (>75% of the time). By Thursday morning fog and rain affected the area, ending the episode. (Lioy et al., 1985).

Because this was a wintertime episode, ozone was not reported. However, due to the use of space heating and the presence of local motor vehicle traffic, the range of daily average concentrations of CoH and SO_2 and the 1-hr maximum for CO measured from February 13 to February 18 (10 a.m. to 10 a.m.) are shown in Table 6.3 for representative sites in New Jersey. For each pollutant (except CO at the Camden Trailer), the highest concentrations were observed during February 13–14 and 14–15. Unlike the London smog episodes, the SO_2 levels were only moderate and did not exceed the 24-hr NAAQS standard at any site. For CO, the 1-hr NAAQS of 25 ppm was not exceeded, although some values were above 15 ppm. The CoH values were relatively high during the period, with 24-hr averages approaching or exceeding the regionally established alert stage value of 3.00 on February 13–14 and 14–15 (Lioy et al., 1985).

The average air pollution indices during the episode for northern and southern New Jersey are shown in Figure 6.6. Using the CoH values and the air pollution index, an estimated peak total solid particulate matter (TSP) in northern New Jersey would have been between 375 and 450 $\mu g/m^3$ (Ott and Hunt, 1976).

From the data provided from the State Monitoring network it is apparent that particulate soot pollution (as inferred by CoHs) increased substantially in the northeast part of the state after the storm. From Figure 1.1 in Chapter 1 it can be seen that the ATEOS urban sites were located in places where increases in pollution could be observed. In contrast, the Ringwood site was an excellent control site: during this episode winds were primarily from the north-northeast, and it would not be affected by urban emissions. The levels of IPM and fine particulate matter (FPM) measured at Ringwood on February 13–14 and February 14–15 were 30.4 $\mu g/m^3$ and 28.8 $\mu g/m^3$, respectively, and were close to the average wintertime concentrations observed previously in the Ringwood area (Lioy et al., 1984).

Figure 6.7 shows that the urban ATEOS sites did not have similar values for IPM and FPM during the intense portion of the episode. Again, Newark had the highest IPM concentrations, but the concentrations on February 13–14 and 14–15 increased for very specific reasons. The difference between the Newark and Elizabeth IPM concentrations on February 13–14 was 32

Table 6.3. Range of Concentration of Sulfur Dioxide (24 hr), Carbon Monoxide (1 hr) and Coefficient of Haze (24 hr) Measured at Selected Sites in New Jersey during the 13–18 February Episode[a]

	EO	NWK	JC	ES	ET	CT
CoH	0.8 – 2.6	1.1 – 3.5	1.2 – 3.3	1.1 – 2.6	0.6 – 2.6	1.2 – 2.3
CO (ppm)	1.9 – 8.4	4.2 – 17.9	3.9 – 11.9	4.7 – 24.8	2.0 – 8.4	1.4 – 10.8
SO_2 (ppm)	0.016 – 0.057	0.011 – 0.042	0.013 – 0.052	0.010 – 0.039	0.013 – 0.047	0.013 – 0.042

[a]All data based on a 10 a.m. to 10 a.m. sampling interval. Key: EO, East Orange; NWK, Newark Trailer; JC, Jersey City; ES, Elizabeth Station; ET, Elizabeth Trailer; CT, Camden Trailer.

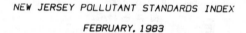

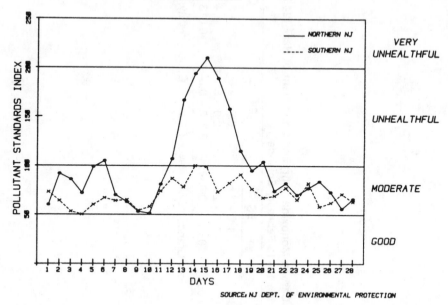

SOURCE: NJ DEPT. OF ENVIRONMENTAL PROTECTION

Figure 6.6.   The change in the particulate pollutant index in northern and southern New Jersey for the month of February in 1983. (With permission, from Lioy et al., 1985.)

μg/m^3, on the following day this difference tripled to 97 μg/m^3. On the same days, the IPM values at the Camden site were 48.4 and 144.7 μg/m^3 less than the Newark values. The local meteorology was similar for Newark and Elizabeth; however, in the Camden area, the surface wind speed averaged 9 mph on February 14–15, which was approximately twice the average observed at Newark Airport. Greater dilution and fewer upwind sources along the northeast wind direction probably accounted for the much lower Camden mass values observed on February 14–15.

The effects of the characteristics of each urban area on increases in the total EOM during the episode are most apparent from comparisons with data collected at the Ringwood Site. The three-day EOM composites collected at Ringwood covered the period from February 13 to 16 (10 a.m. to 10 a.m.). The concentrations of ACE measured for this composite sample averaged 4.85 μg/m^3, which was only 13.4, 18.0 and 22% of the three-day average concentrations calculated for the same interval in Newark, Elizabeth and Camden, respectively. In contrast to the summertime, these would

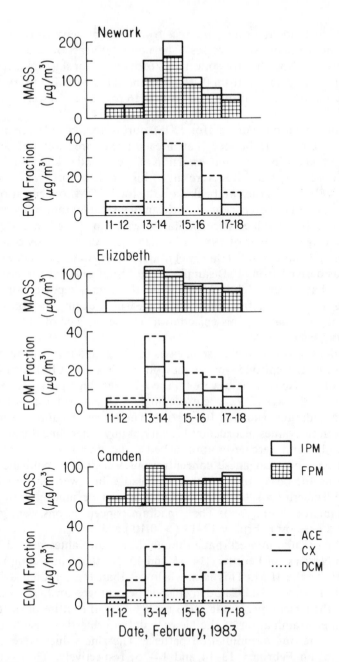

Figure 6.7.   Measured concentrations of IPM, FPM, and organic fractions at all urban ATEOS sites. (With permission, from Lioy et al., 1985).

be related to condensation of organics from local primary emission sources and not photochemical processes. The nonpolar fraction did not have a well-defined episode/nonepisode rural/urban relationship. Normally, the rural/urban ratio varied from 0.1 to 0.5, and during the February 13 to 16 sampling interval, the ratio varied from 0.16 to 0.21 in Newark and Elizabeth.

The concentration patterns for EOM during the episode are shown in Figure 6.7, and it can be seen that in each urban area well-defined peaks were recorded during the intense portion of the episode. The actual concentrations observed at all sites were much higher than observed at all other times in ATEOS. On the two peak days the total EOM concentrations at all urban sites (with the exception of one Camden sample) ranged from 43.5 to 70.9 $\mu g/m^3$. These values were similar to values observed in a study conducted during the winter of 1982 in Mexico City, Mexico (Lioy et al., 1983) and Beijing, China in 1981 (Daisey et al., 1983). However, in those cases the EOM was derived from TSP samples. The actual EOM at the New Jersey sites may have been slightly higher than the values reported since EOM available in the coarse fraction was not measured during the study. In any case, a major feature of this episode was the occurrence of unusually high concentrations of EOM.

The values recorded in almost all cases for SO_4^{-2} and trace elements on the peak days of the episode were highest in Newark and Elizabeth. Striking features of the Newark data were (1) the relatively high peak concentration for SO_4^{-2} of 28.3 $\mu g/m^3$, (2) the exceedingly high zinc values: $> 10 \ \mu g/m^3$, and (3) a cadmium value of 0.1 $\mu g/m^3$. These concentrations were much higher than the values recorded at Newark at any other time during the two winter studies and were never approached at the other sites. In contrast, the nickel, iron, and manganese concentrations were nearly equivalent at all sites during the peak episode days. The lead values were highest on both days in Elizabeth ($> 1.8 \ \mu g/m^3$), and copper was elevated in both Newark and Elizabeth (0.15 mg/m^3). The vanadium concentrations were generally high at all sites on February 13–14 ($> 0.10 \ \mu g/m^3$).

It is of particular interest that although the sulfate values were above 20.0 $\mu g/m^3$ in Newark on February 14–15 and 15–16, the values comprised less than 15% of the IPM. This is much lower than the seasonal average of 25%. The Elizabeth and Camden episode percentages for SO_4^{-2} were much closer to their mean percentages (23 to 28%) for the entire project.

A further examination of the Newark data during the episode indicates another interesting accumulation pattern. The zinc values were 14.3 and 26.4 $\mu g/m^3$ on February 13–14 and 14–15, respectively. These elemental concentrations were 9.4% and 13.2% of the total IPM measured on each day.

In Newark, the IPM and EOM on the worst days increased by factors between 4.5 and 6.5 times the mean. Similar or greater increases occurred

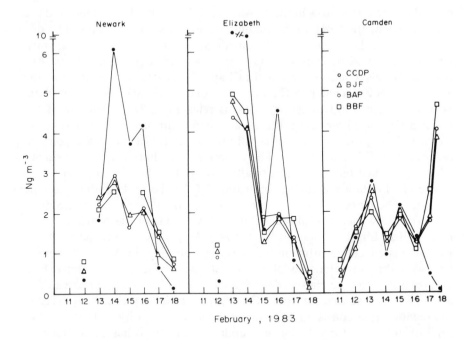

Figure 6.8.   Absolute concentrations of cyclopenta(cd)pyrene, benzo(a)py-
rene, benzo(j)fluoranthene, and benzo(b)fluoranthene for all
urban ATEOS sites in the February 11 through 18, 1983, episode.
(With permission, from Lioy et al., 1985.)

for Ni, Cd, Cu, and Zn. However, only moderate increases occurred for
SO_4^{-2}, Fe, Mn, and Pb. The other sites had less pronounced concentration
increases above the mean in most cases, but were more than five times the
mean for V, Cd, Pb, and Zn in Elizabeth, and Ni and Zn in Camden.

The variation in the levels of selected polycyclic aromatic hydrocarbon
compounds, cyclopenta(cd)pyrene (CcdP), benzo(a)pyrene (BaP), and ben-
zo(j)fluoranthene (BjF), benzo(b)fluoranthene (BbF) measured during this
episode followed similar trends at the three urban sites, although the absolute concentrations were generally highest at Elizabeth (Figure 6.8). This is
consistent with mean concentration patterns for both the 1982 and 1983
winters. Although the PAH levels were elevated during this episode, the
concentrations found were similar to PAH values observed in the winter of
1982 during the short episodes (1 day) associated with nocturnal temperature inversions. One exception was the relatively high CcdP levels found at
all three urban sites in the 1983 episode.

The spatial extent of the episode had concentration boundaries, as evidenced by the differences in the Newark and Elizabeth IPM values, and the distribution of the CoH values among the state monitoring sites. The distance between the Newark and Elizabeth sites is less than five miles; thus, normally it would be expected that during a local stagnation episode, the pollution levels would be similar. In Chapter 7, evidence is reported of the presence of a Zn smelter to the northeast of the Newark site, which from New Jersey Emission Inventory data, is released as ZnO. Because of the northeasterly wind direction, there was a strong influence of the smelter in Newark during the episode. In addition, this source influenced Elizabeth, especially on February 13–14. The concentration, however, was 3 $\mu g/m^3$, which was much higher than normally observed at the Elizabeth site.

The CoH data are a further indication of the spatial boundaries of the episode. The CoH at East Orange, which is to the west but adjacent to Newark, was a factor of about 1.5 times lower than at the Newark, Elizabeth trailer, Elizabeth station, and Jersey City sites on February 14–15. From the site location information, it is apparent that this would be consistent with the characteristics of the worst day of the episode, since East Orange is in a commercial-residential area, and the other sites are located in areas with high source densities. Therefore, the Newark-Elizabeth ATEOS site dichotomy is consistent with differences in the density of local sources (industrial and motor vehicle) surrounding each site. It has been shown in Chapter 1 that there are a number of small industrial sources and a high density of local diesel truck traffic within the Iron Bound section of Newark, and idling diesel train engines just east of the ATEOS sampling site. The presence of such sources would always affect the IPM on a given day. However, the influence of local industrial activities and truck traffic was significantly enhanced because of stagnation and light winds. The ATEOS Elizabeth site does not have the same mix of sources and is affected mainly by commercial business traffic and activities, space heating, and refineries, although it can also be affected by plumes from Newark on north winds. The CoH values for sites in Elizabeth operated by New Jersey were similar to those at the Newark sites on February 14–15. These latter sites were located in areas impacted by a high density of industrial and commercial sources, as was Newark.

During the episode, the concentrations of PAH compounds were elevated. The concentrations of cyclopenta(cd)pyrene (CcdP), however, increased disproportionately during the middle of the episode at both Newark and Elizabeth. Based on the work of Grimmer et al. (1980), this suggests an increased influence of motor vehicle sources during this episode. These investigators have reported a ratio of CcdP to benzo(a)pyrene (BaP) of about 4 for tunnel samples and a ratio of about 0.4 for ambient aerosol samples collected in an area of Dusseldorf, West Germany influenced by oil burning for space heating. During the episode, the ratios of CcdP/BaP varied between 2 and 3 at Newark and Elizabeth, respectively, compared to an average of 1.2 at other times. The concentration of CcdP increased by 5 to 10 times during the episode, while other PAH increased by only 2 to 4 times. Other motor vehicle-associated emissions, e.g., Pb and CO, also increased disproportionately, e.g., 3 to 10 times. Furthermore, number 2 fuel oil and natural gas are the major fuels used for space heating in New Jersey, and these emit relatively small amounts of particulate organic emissions per Btu. Thus, it is unlikely that the relatively small increase in PAHs compared to CX, observed at all sites during the episode, was from this source category.

HISTORICAL PERSPECTIVE

Looking back in time, when increased morbidity was noted with air pollution incidents, comparisons can be made with the severe fall and winter episodes of 1953 and 1966 in the New York metropolitan area using routinely monitored variables (Greenberg et al., 1962; Glasser et al., 1967). At that time, the investigators were aware that the environmental variables measured — SO_2 and CoH — were only surrogates for "more toxic species," but these were the only ones available to compare with health statistics. Fortunately, these are still available today for comparisons. In the 1953 and 1966 episodes, the peak levels of SO_2 reached approximately 1.0 ppm, and the daily averages were about 0.5 ppm. The data for the 1983 episode indicate that the peak SO_2 and the mean values were lower by a factor of 10 or more. During the earlier episodes, the CoH values in the northeastern New Jersey area reached 4.8, and the peak daily mean value was 3.4. From the above, it is apparent that the episode in 1983 was not nearly of the same magnitude as those observed in the preregulatory period of 1970, and the differences in intensity are probably a result of the elimination of high-sulfur oil and coal for heating and energy production (Eisenbud, 1978). However, based upon the composition data derived from the 1983 episode, the historic episodes were in all probability affected by significant contributions of particular sulfur species and organic material.

Photochemical smog episodes have been reported in Los Angeles since the 1950s. Today, the northeastern United States is one of the three areas which experience the highest 1-hr ozone concentrations. The others are the gulf coast and southern California. Peak values in New Jersey have reached in excess of 250 ppb, and were approached in the ATEOS study area during the July 16 to 21, 1981 and July 10 to 20, 1982 episodes. Recent health data have indicated that changes in pulmonary function and respiratory symptoms can occur in healthy exercising children and adults during ozone episodes (U.S. EPA, 1985). Unfortunately, no epidemiological studies were conducted to determine if there was an increase in morbidity within the immediate ATEOS areas. However, during the summer of 1982 a field air pollution epidemiological study was conducted simultaneously in a semi-rural area of New Jersey to the west of the Newark and Elizabeth sites. The results of the field epidemiological study showed that during and immediately after the extended episode from July 12 to 20, the lung function of active normal children was altered. The change in function was due to the persistence of high ozone and possibly sulfur species (Lioy et al., 1985) as well as a daily ozone dose-response relationship (Bock et al., 1985).

REFERENCES

Bock, N., Lippmann, M., Lioy, P. J., Munoz, A., and Speizer, F. E. (1985), *Transactions of APCA*, TR-4, 297–308.

Cooper, J. A. (1980), *JAPCA*, 30, 855–861.

Daisey, J. M., Morandi, M., Wolff, G. T., and Lioy, P. J. (1984), *Atmos. Environ.* 18, 1411–1419.

Daisey, J. M., Kneip, T. J., Wang, M.-X., Ren, L.-X., and Lu, W.-X. (1983), *J. Aerosol Sci. Technol.* 2, 407–415.

Eisenbud, M. (1978), *Bull. NY Acad. Med.*, 54, 991–1011.

Elston, J. (1983), New Jersey Department of Environmental Protection, Continuous Monitoring Network Data — 1980–1983, Trenton, NJ.

Glasser, M., Greenberg, L., and Field, F. (1967), *Arch. Envir. Hlth.*, 15, 684–694.

Greenberg, L., Jacobs, M. B., Drolette, B. M., Field, F., and Braverman, M. M. (1962). *Public Hlth. Rep.*, 77, 7–15.

Greenberg, A., Darack, F., Harkov, R., Lioy, P. J., and Daisey, J. M. (1985), *Atmos. Environ.*, 19, 1325–1339.

Grimmer, G., Naujack, K. W., and Schneider, D. (1980). In "Fourth International Symposium on Polynuclear Aromatic Hydrocarbons" (Edited by Bjoreth A. and Dennis, A. J.), Battelle Press, pp. 107–175.

Husar, R. B., Lodge, J. P., Moore, D. J., Eds. (1978). *Sulfur in the Atmosphere*, Pergamon Press, Oxford, England, 1–816.

Heidron, K. C. (1978), *Bull. Amer. Meteor. Society*, S9, 1589–1597.

Lioy, P. J., Falcon, Y., Morandi M., and Daisey J. M. (1983). *J. Aerosol Sci. Technol.*, 2, 166.

Lioy, P. J., Vollmuth T. A., and Lippmann, M. (1985), *JAPCA, 35,* 1068–1071.

Lioy, P. J., and Samson, P. J. (1979), *Environ. Intern.*, 2, 77–83.

Lioy, P. J., Samson, P. J., Tanner, R. L., Leaderer, B. P., Minnich, T., and Lyons, W. (1980), *Atmos. Environ.*, 14, 1391–1407.

Lioy, P. J., Daisey, J. M., Greenberg, A., and Harkov, R. (1985), *Atmos. Environ.*, 19, 429–436.

Lioy, P. J., and Lippmann, M. (1986), In *Aerosols*, Lewis Publishers, Chelsea, MI, 743–752.

Lioy, P. J., Kneip, T. J., and Daisey, J. M. (1984), *J. Geophys. Res.*, 89, 1355–1359.

Lioy, P. J., Daisey, J. M., Reiss, N. M., and Harkov, R. (1983), *Atmos. Environ.*, 17, 2321–2330.

Morandi, M. T., Kneip, T. J., Cobourn, W. G., Husar, R. B., and Lioy. P. J. (1983) *Atmos. Environ.* 17, 843–848.

Seinfeld, J. H. (1986), *Atmospheric Chemistry & Physics of Air Pollution*, Wiley Interscience, John Wiley & Sons, New York.

Stern, A. C. (1962), *Air Pollution, Vol. 1*, Academic Press, New York.

Wilson, J. (1985), Local and Regional Meterology: Its Use in Discriminating the Source Regions of Atmospheric Organic Matter Summertime Episodes, M.S. Thesis, NYU Medical Ctr.

Wolff, G. T., and Lioy, P. J. (1980), *Environ. Sci. Technol.* 14, 1257–1261.

Wolff, G. T., Lioy, P. J., Wight, G. D., Meyers, R. E., and Cederwall, R. T. (1979), *Atmos. Environ.* 11, 797–802.

U.S. EPA (1978), Air Quality Criteria Document for Ozone and Other Photochemical Oxidants, EPA-600/8-78-004.

U.S. EPA (1985) Air Quality Criteria Document for Ozone and Other Photochemical Oxidants EPA-600/8-84/20B.

CHAPTER 7

Inhalable Particulate Matter and Extractable Organic Matter Receptor Source Apportionment Models for the ATEOS Urban Sites

Maria T. Morandi, Joan M. Daisey, Paul J. Lioy

CHAPTER CONTENTS

(continued)

Inhalable Particulate Matter and Extractable Organic Matter Receptor Source Apportionment Models for the ATEOS Urban Sites

INTRODUCTION

Control strategies for airborne contaminants are based on characterization of the substances present in the atmosphere, as well as the identification and apportionment of the sources that contribute to ambient pollutant concentrations. The relationship between source emissions and the corresponding ambient contaminant concentrations is difficult to establish directly because: (1) the number of individual sources is very large, (2) pollutant sources and their relative emission rates are, at best, only partially known, (3) the chemical and physical transformations of primary emissions in the atmosphere are not completely understood, and (4) the effects of changing meteorological conditions are not totally quantifiable. As a result, models are used to identify and apportion the sources of environmental pollutants. These models are also an important research tool for the investigation of airborne contamination.

The ambient data obtained during ATEOS are some of the most extensive to date in terms of the variables, sites, number of days, and seasons sampled. Most source apportionment models have been developed for just one fraction of the ambient aerosol, at either one single location, or at multiple sites with similar sources that are usually easily identified. The complexity and characteristics of the three ATEOS urban sites provided the opportunity to apply the same modeling approach to areas where the nature of and impact from potential sources could be very different, and thus test the possibilities and limitations of the modeling methods developed. Besides providing an approach applicable to source identification and apportionment in urban atmospheres, this work: (1) contributes to the further understanding of how source apportionment techniques can be used to assess atmospheric aerosols, (2) further develops the currently available methods for source apportionment modeling research, (3) increases our understanding of the characteristics of atmospheric aerosols in a complex airshed where environmental health concerns exist, and (4) contributes to our knowledge of airborne particulate organic matter sources and their contributions, about which relatively little is known.

HISTORICAL PERSPECTIVE ON SOURCE IDENTIFICATION AND APPORTIONMENT MODELS

As previously indicated, apportionment models attempt to describe and quantify the impact of different sources on ambient concentrations of one or more airborne substances. Models provide the information necessary to assist in the resolution of nonattainment situations for regulated air pollutants. They are also an aid in the identification of sources of nonregulated airborne substances that may impact the health of the general population.

Dispersion and Receptor Modeling Methods

There are two broadly defined approaches to source identification and apportionment: dispersion models and receptor models. Dispersion models estimate airborne pollutant levels from emission composition and rates measured at the source. Receptor models estimate source contributions by analyzing relationships between airborne pollutants measured at a sampling or receptor site.

Dispersion models have a number of limitations, particularly when applied to urban atmospheres: (1) it is usually not possible to test all sources present in an airshed, (2) methods currently available for source stack testing are still limited, (3) the nature and quantity of substances emitted at the source can change because of deposition and/or chemical processes, (4) any changes in emission parameters usually require further source testing, (5) the emissions from small sources and soil resuspension are usually not inventoried, and (6) the micrometeorological variables in urban airsheds are difficult to characterize.

Receptor source apportionment models are based on the assumption that differences in the composition of emissions measured at their point of origin are reflected in the ambient aerosol composition at a receptor site. Minimum a priori knowledge of source emission rates or meteorology is necessary, although some of these models require emission composition data. Validation of receptor models is not simple, and requires at least qualitative knowledge of the types of sources present in the area (Parkinson, 1980; Cooper and Watson, 1980). While dispersion models can predict impact from individual point sources, receptor models can generally identify only source type contributions.

The fundamental assumptions of receptor modeling methodology were first proposed by Hidy and Friedlander (1970). They are: (1) source identities and their respective contributions to ambient pollutant concentrations can be inferred from the chemical composition of the aerosol at the receptor site (for this reason they are also called chemical receptor models), (2) concentrations of airborne substances measured at a receptor site are the linear sum of contributions from the different sources impacting the site (i.e., principle of mass conservation), (3) elemental compositions of source emissions are relatively constant in time and space, and (4) different source types can be identified from a limited number of characteristic elements or tracers.

There are two generally recognized classes of receptor models: (1) chemical elemental balance or mass balance (CEB/CMB), and (2) multivariate or statistical. While CEB/CMB methods apportion sources using extensive qualitative and quantitative source emission information, statistical approaches infer source contributions without a priori need of quantitative source composition data. Extensive reviews of the various source apportionment methodologies have been presented by Gordon (1980a, 1980b, 1983), Cooper and Watson (1980), Watson et al. (1981), Stevens et al. (1982), Dattner and Hopke (1983), Watson (1984), and Henry et al. (1984).

CEB/CMB methodology has contributed significantly to the receptor modeling field. Through this modeling approach, the basic tenets of receptor modeling were first established. It has been successfully applied to identify and quantify the major source contributions to various constituents of the ambient aerosol in a number of different urban atmospheres. The major drawback of this method is the need to obtain source emission composition for the sources in each airshed of interest. Most CEB/CMB applications utilized published source emission composition information rather than the results from local source testing. In studies where local emission measurements were performed, they were limited to a fraction of the time alloted for ambient air sampling.

Multivariate/Statistical Methods

The major statistical methods used in air pollution modeling are linear multiple regression, factor analysis/multiple regression (FA/MR), regression on principal components, and target transformation factor analysis (TTFA). A summary of applications of multivariate apportionment models is presented in Table 7.1.

Table 7.1. Source Apportionment of Ambient Aerosols in U.S. Cities—Multivariate Methods

City/ Period of Sampling	Ambient Aerosol Parameter	Method	No. of Elements Analyzed	References
Boston, MA 1970	TSP Variance	FA and cluster analysis	18	Hopke et al., 1976
Tucson, AZ 1973–1974	TSP Variance	FA and cluster analysis	20, NH_4^+, NO_3^-, SO_4^{-2}	Gaarenstroom et al, 1977
St. Louis, MO 1973–1975	TSP Variance	PCA	10–20	Gatz et al., 1977
New York City 1968–1975	TSP Mass	FA/MR	9, SO_4^{-2}, NO_2^-, NO_3^-	Kleinman, 1977; Kleiman et al., 1980
Charleston WV 1976	TSP Variance Fine (D ≤ 3.5μm) Coarse (D ≥ 3.5μm)	PCA	19, NH_4^+, NO_3^-, SO_4^{-2}	Lewis and Macias, 1980
New York City 1978–1979	Organic RSP Mass (D ≤ 3.5μm)	FA/MR	4, SO_4^{-2} CX, DCM, and ACE	Daisey et al, 1981
New York City 1978–1980	RSP Mass Coarse (D > 3.5μm)	FA/MR	4, SO_2^{-2}	Kneip et al, 1983
New York City 1975–78–79	TSP Carbon RSP Carbon (D ≤ 3.5μm)	FA/MR	11, Organic, Elemental-C	Shah, et al., 1985

Table 7.1., Continued

City/ Period of Sampling	Ambient Aerosol Parameter	Method	No. of Elements Analyzed	References
Boston, MA 1970	TSP Mass	TTFA	18	Alpert and Hopke, 1980
St. Louis, MO 1975–1977	Fine Mass (D ≤ 2.4μm) Coarse Mass (2.4μm ≤ D ≤ 20μm)	TTFA	15 (10)	Alpert and Hopke, 1981
St. Louis, MO Granite City 1976	Fine Mass (D ≤ 2.4μm)	TTFA	12	Liu et al., 1982
Newark, NJ 1981–1982	IPM (D ≤ 15μm)	FA/MR	$8, SO_4^{-2}, CO$	Morandi et al., 1983
Watertown, MA 1979–1981	Fine (D ≤ 2.5μm) Coarse (2.5 ≤ D ≤ 15μm)	Regression PCs	16	Thurston et al., 1983
New York City 1979–1980	Organic RSP (D ≤ 3.5μm)	FA/MR	$11, SO_4^{-2}$	Daisey et al., 1986

Factor Analysis/Multiple Regression (FA/MR)

Kleinman et al. (1977, 1980) first developed FA/MR to apportion the sources of total suspended particulate matter (TSP) in New York City. The method consists of first identifying source types and their respective unique tracers using exploratory common factor analysis. TSP is then regressed against the identified unique tracers using forward stepwise multiple regression analysis. The final model can be expressed as follows:

$$Y = \sum_{i=1}^{p} K_i X_i + R \qquad (1)$$

where Y = dependent variable concentration (TSP, etc.)
K_i = regression coefficient for the ith source tracer
X_i = atmospheric concentration of the ith source tracer
p = number of different source types
R = residual

The tracer regression coefficients are related to the tracer content of the respective source emissions and thus can be used as evidence of the validity of the model (Daisey et al., 1981). This relationship can be expressed as follows:

$$K_i = \alpha_{ij} Y_j / X_{ij} \qquad (2)$$

where Y_i = mass associated with emissions from source j
α_{ij} = coefficient of fractionation of species i in source j as measured at the receptor site
X_{ij} = atmospheric concentration of ith tracer from j^{th} source

This modeling approach has also been applied by Daisey et al. (1981, 1984), Kneip et al. (1983), and Shah et al. (1985) to apportion various fractions of the ambient particulate aerosol.

The advantages of FA/MR over other receptor modeling methods are (1) it is relatively simple to use, (2) it does not require a priori source testing in the area studied, and (3) it is developed using generally available statistical software. The main disadvantages are that, as with other statistical source apportionment methods, large data sets are required, and FA/MR is of limited applicability when one or more tracers are not unique to individual source types. Kleinmann (1977) and Willan and Watts (1978) have discussed the inherent limitations of using regression analysis for statistical inference: underspecification, overspecification, and multicolinearity. These considerations are of particular importance in FA/MR since predictor variables are usually not independent. Morandi (1985) and Morandi et al. (1986) further developed the FA/MR approach for the ATEOS study. The approach was modified to partially overcome the limitations imposed by the use of non-unique tracers in source apportionment by regression analysis. The procedure is described below.

If the major source types emitting a tracer, X_i, can be successfully resolved by factor analysis (i.e., the communality of the tracer under consideration is very close to 1), and there are other unique tracers for all the identified sources of X_i except one, the ambient concentration of X_i due to emissions from the source type without a recognizable unique tracer can be estimated based on the equation:

$$X_i = \sum_{i=1}^{p-1} K_i \,' \, M_i + R \qquad (3)$$

where $K_i\,'$ = regression coefficient for the ith source type that contributes to X_i

M_i = atmospheric concentration of the unique tracers for source types that also contribute to X_i

R = concentration of X associated with the remaining source of X_i

p = number of source types contributing to X_i

Therefore,

$$R = X_i - \sum_{i=1}^{p-1} K_i \,' \, M_i \qquad (4)$$

R can be used in the final apportionment equation (i.e., Equation 1) as the unique tracer for the unidentified source of X_i. As each apportionment model is developed, the residuals (i.e., actual minus predicted dependent variable concentration) are estimated and regressed against all other variables in the data. Significant correlations between residual values and one or more variables may indicate that not all sources have been resolved and identified, and therefore the model should be further refined. The number of identified source types is thus maximized by complementing the FA results with analyses of model residuals. This development allowed the use of FA/MR methodology in the urban ATEOS sites.

Regression on Absolute Principal Components

This procedure uses principal component analysis (PCA) not only to identify but also to apportion sources (Thurston, 1983). Exact factor score coefficients are first calculated from the rotated factor pattern matrix. The scores can be related to source mass contributions by regression analysis (Hopke, 1981; Henry et al., 1984). However, the factor scores are standardized (i.e., they have means of 0 and standard deviations of 1), and if mass is regressed against them, the coefficients obtained will represent the fraction of the total independent variable variance explained by each PCA, not individual source mass contributions (Blifford and Meeker, 1967; Gaarenstroom et al., 1977; Henry and Hidy, 1979, 1982; Lewis and Macias, 1980; and Lioy et al., 1982). Thurston (1983) reported that absolute PCA scores can be used to apportion mass. The absolute scores are estimated by first calculating the z score for absolute zero concentration for all variables included in the PCA analysis, as follows:

$$z_0 = \frac{0 - x_i}{\sqrt{x_i}} = \frac{-x_i}{\sqrt{x_i}} \tag{5}$$

where z_0 = z score corresponding to zero ambient mass concentration

The absolute PCA score is

$$f_{i0} = F z_0 \tag{6}$$

where f_{i0} = absolute zero PCA factor score matrix
      F = matrix of actual factor score coefficients

Absolute PCA scores are then estimated by subtracting f_{i0} from the actual z scores. Multiple regression of mass on the absolute PCAs produces estimates of each source contribution. Individual source profiles can be obtained by regressing each variable on the estimated source contributions.

The predictor variables, i.e., the absolute principal components, are statistically independent. However, because PCA rather than common FA is used, it is possible to interpret a factor as a source even if its presence is only due to error variance. In addition, the theory underlining the calculation of absolute principal component scores has not yet been presented.

Target Transformation Factor Analysis

This method was first developed by Hopke et al. (1980) and Alpert and Hopke (1980). Target transformation factor analysis (TTFA) is based on the idea that some preliminary assumption can be made about the nature of the sources in the airshed under study and, consequently, about the factors into which the data can be resolved. Initial factors are first obtained from a matrix of correlations between samples (Q mode analysis). Each individual factor is then rotated in order to associate its loadings with an input source profile or target vector. In practice, the initial target source profile is usually a unique test vector, b, (i.e., a vector with loading 1 on one element and 0 on the rest). A rotation vector, r, is then found by least squares fit to b. From r and b, a predictor vector, b′, is calculated. If the difference between the initial and predictor vectors falls within certain criteria, b′ is then used as a new test vector. The procedure is repeated until a satisfactory solution is found. Because the test vectors provide only relative concentrations of the component elements, they are scaled by regression against the factor loadings before apportioning mass. Final source apportionment is accomplished by least squares fit to ambient mass.

TTFA has been used by Alpert and Hopke (1980, 1981), Liu et al. (1982), and Severin et al. (1983), with various modifications. Similar to regression on principal components, TTFA produces independent predictor variables (i.e., final source profiles of the rescaled predictor vectors). Software for this procedure was not readily available at the time of the ATEOS study.

Reasons for Selecting FA/MR in the ATEOS Urban Sites

The FA/MR modeling approach was selected for use in the ATEOS study for the following reasons:

1. Although many of the major sources present in the ATEOS cities had been inventoried, there was no quantitative source emission composition for these sources.
2. There were many small, uninventoried industrial sources, particularly in Newark. Therefore, the use of methods such as dispersion modeling or CEB/CMB was seriously limited since qualitative and quantitative knowledge of the sources would have been necessary.
3. The number of samples available from the ATEOS project was extensive enough to permit use of factor analysis-based statistical methods.

Therefore, source identification and apportionment were done using the FA/MR model first described by Kleinman (1977) and further developed by Morandi (1985). As one of the methods of model validation, the results of the FA/MR approach were compared with those obtained from regression on absolute principal components.

SOURCE APPORTIONMENT OF INHALABLE PARTICULATE MATTER IN ATEOS

Statistical Methods

Data screening and distribution analyses were done with BMDP software (BMDP Statistical Software, 1981). Multivariate analyses were performed

Table 7.2.   Variables Preselected for IPM Model Development at Newark, NJ[a]

IPM	BghiP
Pb	COR
Mn	BeP
Cd	BjF
Cu	PER
V	BbF
Zn	SO_{2avg}
Fe	O_{3max}
Ni	HEADD
SO_4^{-2}	COODD
CX	WSPINV
DCM	MAXT
ACE	MINT
CO_{max}	VISMD
BaP	PECIP

[a]Variables are defined in Chapter 1.

with the Statistical Package for the Social Sciences (SPSS), version 8 (Nie et al., 1975). A CDC Cyber computer was used for all analyses.

Exploratory common factor analyses with orthogonal (varimax) rotation was used to resolve the data into factors. The variables considered suitable for model development were those which would provide robust FA solutions with at least 100 degrees of freedom, calculated according to the method described by Henry et al. (1984). Variables that met these criteria are presented in Table 7.2. Values at or below the lower limit of detection were retained, since it was empirically determined that their exclusion from the analyses did not affect the final results. Factors were extracted to a minimum eigenvalue of 0.2 prior to rotation. A maximum of 50 iterations were used to reach final communality estimates. Heywood cases were avoided by excluding values larger than 4 s.d. from each variable mean. (Approximately 12% of the cases were in this category.) Factor interpretation and tracer selection were based on the results of previous applications of FA/MR, the reported source emission composition analyses, and the Newark source microinventory results (Chapter 1). As a general rule, factors with at least one variable with a loading of 0.3 or greater were considered interpretable. If more than one element appeared suitable as a tracer, the one with the lowest relative analytical uncertainty and/or minimal communality explained by other factors was selected for the apportionment step.

Multiple regression apportionment models were developed using forward stepwise regression with listwise deletion of missing data and the SPSS default criteria of $F = 1.00$, and $T = 0.001$.

IPM Source Apportionment Models

Newark

Source Identification

Several combinations of variables were used in the factor analytical procedure. Only the final solution for each of the sampling sites will be presented, since there were no qualitative differences between the various trials. The results for the city of Newark are summarized in Table 7.3. Of the nine factors obtained, seven complied with the factor interpretation criteria. Together they accounted for 97.9% of the variance in the data.

The first factor explained 42.5% of the variance in the data. COODD and HEADD were the variables most highly correlated with this factor (0.853 and –0.830, respectively). These associations indicated that Factor 1 was probably related to the seasonal character of the data rather than a source type. Therefore it was not included in the apportionment model.

Factor 2 accounted for 30.7% of the variance in the data. The high correlation of this factor with Mn (0.825) and Fe (0.751) indicated that it was related to resuspended soil. Weaker associations (0.3–0.4) with Cd and Pb were probably due to soil contamination from sources such as motor vehicle exhaust and industries (Lagerwerff and Specht, 1970; Miller and McFee, 1983). Manganese was selected as the tracer for this source because Factor 2 accounted for 91% of its communality and only 64% of that of Fe.

Factor 3 accounted for 7.3% of the variance in the data. The high loadings for V (0.817) and Ni (0.766), and lower correlations (0.3–0.4) with Pb and HEADD were indicative of an oil-burning source type, related to distillate oil used for residential space heating during winter, and residual oil burning probably related to industrial use and/or contamination of home heating oil (Winchester et al., 1971; Lee et al., 1973; Gartrell et al., 1975; Kowalczyk et al., 1978; Watson, 1979; Homoloya et al., 1981). Vanadium was selected as the most suitable tracer because Factor 3 accounted for 85% of its common variance, while it only explained 59% of the Ni communality. In addition, V has less analytical uncertainty than Ni.

Factor 4, which accounted for 6.3% of the variance in the data, was strongly correlated with Pb (0.739) and CO_{max} (0.702%), explaining 54% and 49% of their respective communalities. It was also weakly associated with Cd, Cu, and Ni. These results suggest that Factor 4 was related to motor vehicle emissions. Lead was not an appropriate tracer for this source

Table 7.3. Newark—Factor Loadings[a]

Newark FA-2	Factor 1	Factor 2	Factor 3	Factor 4	Factor 5	Factor 6	Factor 7	Factor 8	Factor 9	Communality (Factor 1–8)
Pb	-0.067	0.338	0.348	0.739	0.140	0.384	0.068	0.200	0.047	0.99
Mn	0.054	0.825	0.070	0.170	0.105	0.078	0.143	-0.104	0.001	0.74
COODD	0.853	0.110	-0.215	-0.164	0.017	-0.165	0.232	0.011	0.053	
HEADD	-0.830	-0.095	0.311	0.095	-0.068	0.109	-0.025	-0.014	0.048	
Cd	-0.008	0.338	0.000	0.371	0.448	0.143	-0.040	0.022	0.279	0.48
Cu	0.138	0.239	0.187	0.240	0.811	0.276	0.164	-0.001	-0.055	0.93
V	-0.252	-0.029	0.817	0.189	0.008	0.075	0.094	0.100	0.071	0.79
Zn	-0.145	0.028	0.092	0.060	0.148	0.647	0.008	-0.007	0.010	0.47
Fe	0.399	0.751	0.033	0.114	0.372	-0.062	0.048	0.304	0.026	0.97
Ni	-0.273	0.240	0.766	0.262	0.284	0.165	0.005	-0.193	-0.143	0.93
SU_4^{-2}	0.360	0.194	0.107	0.084	0.120	0.021	0.481	0.004	0.007	0.43
CO_{max}	-0.137	0.082	0.174	0.702	0.167	-0.028	0.048	-0.064	-0.012	0.58
Variance (%)	42.5	30.7	7.3	6.3	5.3	3.6	2.2	1.9	0.8	
Probable Source type	Seasonal	Soil Resuspension	Oil Burning/ Space Heating	Motor Vehicles	Industrial	Zinc	$SO_4^{-2}/$ Secondary			

[a] n = 137

in Newark because, as the FA results indicate, it was also associated with other source types. Stocks (1960) and Sawicki (1963) have indicated that benzo(ghi)perylene (BghiP), benzo(a)pyrene (BaP), and coronene (COR) are enriched in motor vehicle exhaust. When these three PAHs were included separately in the FA procedure, they loaded highly on Factor 4 (0.71, 0.62, and 0.53 correlations, respectively). However, their use as tracers is questionable because they are also emitted by other combustion sources, are subject to evaporative and/or reaction losses during sampling (Commins, 1962), and have a relatively short atmospheric half-life under photochemical smog conditions (Daisey, 1980). Alternatively, CO is a long-lived gas strongly associated with motor vehicle emissions, which are its main source in urban areas. Therefore, CO_{max} could be a suitable tracer for these emissions in Newark (Morandi et al., 1983). Since there were no clearly unique tracers for motor vehicles in Newark, all the previously discussed variables were considered during development of the apportionment model.

Copper had a strong correlation (0.811) with Factor 5, which accounted for 5.3% of the variance in the data. This factor explained 71% of Cu communality. Factor 5 also had lower correlations (0.3–0.5) with Cd, Fe, and Ni. Kleinman (1977) and Kneip et al. (1983) interpreted a Cu-associated factor as being related to refuse incineration in apartment buildings in New York City. Greenberg et al. (1978) reported a 47:70:1 average ratio for Zn, Pb, and Cu concentrations in municipal incineration emissions in Washington DC. Jacko and Neuendorf (1977) have indicated that Zn emissions from scrubber-controlled municipal incinerators are only an order of magnitude lower than those resulting from uncontrolled zinc smelters. The low correlation of the fifth factor with Pb and Zn, coupled with the lack of municipal incinerators in Newark and the presence of only a few apartment building incinerators, indicated that Factor 5 was probably related to a different source type. It was interpreted as being related to the industrial, nonferrous metal processing, fabricators, platers, and illegal wire recovery operations previously described in the Newark area. Copper was the most suitable tracer for this source.

Zinc was strongly correlated with the sixth factor, which was interpreted as being mostly associated with smelters (Zn and other metals), primarily those located northeast of the sampling site. Zinc concentrations were highest with northeasterly winds, particularly under stagnation conditions. Emissions from this source type consist largely of ZnO.

Sulfate concentrations were strongly correlated with Factor 7. When ACE and/or O_{3max} were included in the analysis, they were also loaded on Factor 7, and the SO_4^{-2} communality increased to 0.64. This result indicated that the relatively low SO_4^{-2} communality is partly due to specificity (Harman, 1976) rather than error variance. Factor 7 was interpreted as being related to sulfate and secondary aerosol formation. Sulfate was selected as the tracer for this source type.

Multiple Regression Source Apportionment Models

As indicated above, all the identified sources had suitable tracers, with the exception of motor vehicles. CO_{max}, BghiP, BaP, and COR were sequentially tried in the IPM apportionment equations as motor vehicle tracers, but their respective regression coefficients were nonsignificant. Therefore, Pb was apportioned (as per Equation 3) to estimate the fraction of ambient Pb (PbA) associated with motor vehicle emissions. By successively combining the methods of tracer apportionment and analysis of residuals, a previously unresolved Fe source and its respective tracer, FeR (i.e., residual iron), were discovered. The FeR source also contributed to ambient Pb concentrations in Newark. The final models for PbA, FeR, and IPM are presented in Table 7.4.

The identity of the FeR source was investigated. The association of Factor 8 (not previously discussed since it did not comply with factor interpretation criteria) with Fe and Pb suggested that the eighth factor was related to the FeR source. In addition, FeR correlated significantly with dichloromethane-soluble organics (DCM; $p = 0.001$). FeR concentrations were higher in the summer. These relationships and careful reexamination of the microinventory observations suggested that the most likely sources of FeR were the numerous auto and truck body repair shops present in this area of Newark. Fugitive emissions from these source types are the result of stripping, preparation, and coating of surfaces. They are produced primarily by evaporation of primer and paint formulation carriers, and particle resuspension during surface preparation and spray painting. Paint pigments and fillers can include organic pigments (such as Pb and Co naphthanates), metal-based pigments (such as iron oxides), and TiO_2 (Malek, 1984). Therefore, Fe and Pb would be present in emissions from this source type. In addition, organic compounds such as ketones and alcohols present in paint formulations could be extracted in dichloromethane. A large pigment manufacturing facility was also located southwest of the sampling site, and it may have also contributed to this source type. Based on these considerations, the FeR source was interpreted as paint spraying/paint pigment.

Actual source contributions to Fe, Pb, and IPM in Newark are presented in Figure 7.1. In order of importance, source types contributing to ambient Fe concentrations were soil resuspension (51%), paint spraying/paint pigment (33%), and industries (18%). Ambient Pb concentrations were determined by motor vehicle exhaust (36%), soil resuspension (24%), fuel oil burning/space heating (18%), industrial emissions (17%), paint spraying/paint pigment (9%), and zinc (5%). The most important contributor to

Table 7.4.   Fe, Pb, and IPM Source Apportionment Models for Newark, NJ[a]

FeR^b = Fe − (23.1 Mn + 4.4 Cu)   (7.4.1)

PbA^c = Pb − (1.0 Cu + 2.0 V + 5.4 Mn + 4.5 × 10⁻² Zn + 1.3 × 10⁻¹ FeR)   (7.4.2)

IPM = (2.1 ± 0.1) SO_4^{-2} + (101 ± 25) Cu + (24.4 ± 3.3) FeR   (7.4.3)
+ (440 ± 86) Mn + (115 ± 24) V + (18.1 ± 5.4) PbA
+ 1.9 ± 2.3
n = 137
Overall F = 108 (p = 0.000)
Multiple R = 0.91

[a]Concentrations are expressed in µg/m³. Regression coefficients are presented with their standard errors.
[b]Amount of ambient Fe associated with the paint/paint pigment source.
[c]Motor vehicle-related Pb.

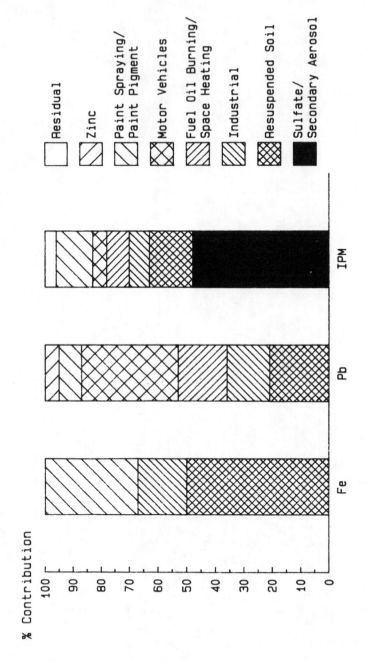

Figure 7.1.   Source contributions to Fe, Pb, and IPM in Newark, NJ.

Table 7.5. Partial Elemental Source Emissions Composition in Newark, NJ[a]

Source	Source Composition (%)								
	Pb	Mn	Cd	Cu	V	Zn	Fe	Ni	SO_4^{-2}
SO_4^{-2}/Secondary									48±4
Soil	1.2±0.6	0.23±0.08					5.2±1.2		
Industrial	1.0±0.8			1.0±0.4		$(10±7)^b$	4.3±1.6		
Fuel Oil Burning	1.8±0.6				0.9±0.4				
Motor Vehicles	5.5±0.6								
Paint Spraying/ Paint Pigment	0.5±0.4						4.1±1.2		

[a]Reported uncertainties were estimated based on the 95% confidence limit of the corresponding tracer regression coefficient.
[b]Nonsignificant.

ambient IPM concentrations was sulfate/secondary aerosol (48%), followed by soil resuspension (15%), paint spraying/paint pigment (13%), fuel oil burning/space heating (8%), industrial emissions (7%), and motor vehicle exhaust (5%). Zinc was the only tracer with a nonsignificant regression coefficient (r = 0.045, p = 0.061) in the IPM model. Analysis of Pearson product moment correlations between the residuals of the IPM model and other variables in the data indicated significant associations with IPM, FPM, all extractable organic fractions of IPM, and WSPINV. On average, the model underestimated IPM concentrations during Summer 1981 and Winter 1983, while it overestimated them during Summer 1982 and Winter 1982. It also overestimated IPM concentrations on days with predominant southeasterly winds by an average of 15%. These associations indicate that not all pertinent variables may have been included in the IPM model, and that at least some of the variables are related to meteorology.

IPM Model Validation

As previously indicated, Equation 2 can be used as an important validation tool in FA/MR models by estimating the fractional emission tracer content for each apportioned source type and comparing it with published source emission composition. The source emission tracer contents determined from the Newark models are presented in Table 7.5. A summary of previously reported source emission compositions is presented in Table 7.6.

There are no published data on the composition of the sulfate/secondary aerosol source. The regression coefficient for SO_4^{-2} is within the range of values reported by Cass and McRae (1983) for California, and Kleinman (1977) for New York City. This coefficient is greater than the ratios

Table 7.6. Concentrations of Measured Components of IPM in Various Source Type

Source Type	Pb	Mn	Cd	Cu	V	ZN	Fe	Ni	SO_4^{-2}	Measured in	Reference
					Tracers (%)						
Road dust	0.18	0.03	NR	0.16	2.5	0.05	2.5	6.0	NR	TSP	Winchester et al., 1971
Residual Oil	0.07	0.06	NR	0.2	7.0	0.02	6.0	–	NR	TSP	Gartrell et al., 1975
	0.51	0.13	NR	0.11	3.0	0.21	0.36	0.51	NR	TSP	Kowalczyk et al., 1978
	0.0064–0.17	0.038–0.067	NR	0.05–0.08	2.64–4.42	0.26–0.70	2.15–3.29	3.75–6.54	42.2–61.6	FPM	Watson, 1979[a]
	<0.001–<0.05	0.019–0.064	NR	0.24–0.127	0.65–4.13	0.0072–0.551	0.80–2.4	0.58–2.65	3.06–10.8	CPM	Watson, 1979[a]
	0.11–0.44	0.50	NR	0.01–0.04	1.72–4.55	NR	0.48–0.63	0.36–0.89	16.24–22.16	TSP	Homoloya et al., 1981[l,m]
Distillate	0.016–1.16	0.0076–0.03	NR	0.067–0.19	0.0013–0.20	0.01–0.056	0.078–0.31	0.01–0.03	1.0–24	FPM	Watson, 1979[b]
Oil Furnace	<0.01–<0.01	0.01–0.033	NR	0.055–0.14	0.001–0.01	0.005–0.027	0.03–0.43	0.01–0.02	0.5–1.5	CPM	Watson, 1979[b]
Fuel Oil	10^{-6}–10^{-4}			10^{-5}–1.5×10^{-2}			10^{-4}–10^{-2}			TSP	Lee et al., 1973[c]
Municipal	9.7±2.6	0.15±0.14	0.11±0.04	0.20±0.12	NR	12±6	0.90±0.33	0.02±0.008	NR	TSP	Greenberg et al., 1978[d,h]
Incinerators	7.7±1.1	0.041±0.014	0.019±0.002	0.17±0.003	NR	13±5	0.71±0.14	0.017±0.007	NR	TSP	Greenberg et al., 1978[d,h]
	6.9±1.0	0.027±0.008	0.15±0.002	0.17±0.003	NR	11±3	0.33±0.15	0.079±0.029	NR	TSP	Greenberg et al., 1978[d,h]
Soil Dust	0.006	0.06	NR	0.002	0.004	0.01	2.0	0.002	NR	TSP	Miller et al., 1972[e]
	0.02	0.11	NR	0.008	0.006	0.01	3.2	0.004	NR	TSP	Miller et al., 1972[f]
	0.47	0.062	NR	0.072	0.02	NR	4.72	0.067	NR	TSP	Adams, 1977
	0.25	0.053	NR	0.044	0.012	0.073	6.14	0.038	NR	TSP	Adams, 1977
	0.09	0.13	NR	0.026	0.026	0.038	6.2	NR	2.3	TSP	Watson, 1979
	0.093	0.11	NR	0.027	0.021	0.047	7.5	0.009	NR	TSP	Watson, 1979
	0.093	0.09	NR	0.087	0.017	0.047	7.8	0.006	2.4	TSP	Watson, 1979
	<0.002	0.033	NR	<0.0005	<0.0002	0.068	0.76	0.0004	5.4	FPM	Watson, 1979
Street Dust	0.0021–0.035	0.090–0.32	NR	0.014–0.024	0.015–0.033	0.023–0.086	3.75–8.85	0.0073–0.013	0.05	CPM	Watson, 1979[b]
	0.029–0.057	0.057–0.126	NR	NR	0.012–0.027	NR	3.75–5.63	NR	0.0024–0.0033	TSP	Watson, 1979[b]
	0.24–0.58	0.099–0.140	NR	0.013–0.039	0.017–0.030	0.068–0.15	5.82–6.35	0.0071–0.013	0.05–0.76	FPM	Watson, 1979[d]
	NR	0.037	NR	0.032	0.023	0.11	6.92	0.012	0.62	FPM	Watson, 1979[e]
	0.030	0.092–0.121	NR	NR	0.022–0.025	<0.005	5.43–6.2	NR	0.11	CPM	Watson, 1979[d]
		0.112		0.2	0.024		5.89	0.01	0.79	CPM	Watson, 1979[d]
Street Dust	0.1	0.035	0.0002	NR		0.032	6.2	0.025	NR	TSP	Hopke et al., 1980
	0.211	0.030	NR	0.008		0.045	2.75	0.004	NR	TSP	Weber et al., 1979[i]
	0.252	0.145	NR	0.32		0.258	12.80	0.984	NR	TSP	Weber et al., 1979[j]
	0.830	0.033	NR	0.05		0.111	3.80	0.005	NR	TSP	Weber et al., 1979[k]
Motor Vehicle (mixed traffic)	1.00						0.19			TSP	Feeney et al., 1975
	1.00			5×10^{-3}			~0.1			TSP	Dzubay et al., 1979
	1.00	1.2×10^{-3}	5×10^{-5}			0.02	0.09	~5×10^{-4}		TSP	Pierson et al., 1983
	1.00	$(3.0 \pm 1.0) \times 10^{-3}$		$(7.2 \pm 2.6) \times 10^{-3}$		0.017±0.004	0.08±0.4	0.8±0.4	0.7	TSP	Ondov et al., 1982

NR = not reported. [a]Range of 5 to 6 individual samples. [b]Range of 5 individual samples. [c]Secondary reference; range of 100 oil samples. [d]Complete sample. [e]Gross soil sample. [f]Resuspended soil sample. [g]Range of 4 samples. [h]Computed as % from original reference; reported % s.d. [i]Street sweeping (particles <0.63μm) in residential area sampled at Lodi, NJ. [j]Same as i but in industrial area. [k]Same as i but at a traffic intersection. [l]Range of samples obtained in four different boilers burning 0.32 hydrodesulfurized residual oil. [m]Mn used as anticorrosive additive in one boiler.

$(NH_4)_2SO_4/SO_4^{-2}$ or $(NH_4)HSO_4/SO_4^{-2}$. Thus, it accounts for other sulfate-related materials in the aerosol.

Reported soil and street dust Mn concentrations values range from 0.06% (soil dust; total particle composition) to 0.32% (soil dust; fine particle composition). Fe concentrations vary between 2% and 8%. The corresponding soil compositions found in this study fell within reported ranges. The estimated soil Pb content (1.2%) is higher than reported values (0.006%–0.83%). However, this is expected, given the industrial character of Newark.

Published composition information on complex industrial emission sources is not available. Data on municipal incineration emissions, which is an alternate interpretation for the source traced by Cu, indicate these emissions are relatively enriched in Pb and Cu, and poorer in Fe content with respect to the source found in Newark (Greenberg et al., 1978). This evidence, in combination with the microinventory results, supports the interpretation given to this source.

The elemental content of fuel oil burning emissions depends on the origin and type of oil, and the characteristics of the furnace used (U.S. Department of Commerce, 1983; Von Lehmden et al., 1974). Distillate oil (low ash content) is more common in residential use, while residual oil (high ash content) is prevalent in industrial operations. The Pb and V content values determined in this study are higher (1.8% and 0.9% respectively) than those reported by Watson (1979) for distillate oil. The concentration of V is within the range of values reported for residual oil, but the Pb concentration was higher than indicated in the literature. However, reports of transportation into and sale of Pb-contaminated waste oil in New Jersey (New York Times, 1983) and the residential/industrial character of the area are consistent with the interpretation given to the fuel oil source in Newark.

The low Pb fractional composition of motor vehicle contributions to IPM in Newark (5.5%) is consistent with the presence of diesel truck traffic in the area (Pierson and Brachaczek, 1983; Kowalczyk, 1979; Ondov, 1982), and the reduction in the use of leaded gasoline in recent years. The results of the model indicate that motor vehicles contribute approximately half of the ambient Pb levels in this city.

Dzubay (1980) described a paint/paint pigment manufacturing source in St. Louis. The emissions were predicted to contain approximately 20% Fe, 42% Ti, and 0.3% Mn in the coarse particulate matter (2.4 μm < D < 20 μm). Iron-containing pigments may account for 11% and 20% of automotive paint and primer formulations, respectively (Malek, 1984). These observations are consistent with the interpretation given to the FeR source in Newark.

Although the Zn tracer did not have a significant regression coefficient in the IPM model, the value obtained would indicate a content of 79% Zn in emissions from this source. Emissions from Zn smelters are mainly ZnO, which is 81% Zn. Overall, analysis of the tracer regression coefficients support the results of the Pb, Fe, and IPM models.

Further validation of the Newark IPM source apportionment modeling results was obtained by applying the regression on absolute principal components approach on the same set of data. The method was modified to include analysis of regression residuals. The results are summarized in Figure 7.2. The contributions from the SO_4^{-2}/secondary aerosol, oil burning/ space heating, paint spraying/paint pigment, and motor vehicle emission were similar for both modeling approaches. Soil contributions to IPM were 7% lower when estimated by FA/MR, while the industrial contributions were double when estimated by regression on APCs. These values do not, in fact, differ significantly if the standard errors of estimation are taken into consideration. The regression coefficient for Zn is significant in the regression on APCs model, while it was not (0.061) in the FA/MR model. However, the contributions from the Zn source calculated from the FA/MR Zn coefficient (had it been significant) would have been approximately 0.7% of IPM, quite comparable to the regression on APCs results. In general, the agreement between the two modeling approaches is good, well within the factor of two observed for previously reported comparisons among different modeling approaches (Stevens et al., 1984).

Elizabeth

IPM Source Identification

The Elizabeth data set was analyzed utilizing the factor selection and retention criteria previously applied to the Newark data set. The final FA results are presented in Table 7.7. Six factors met the FA resolution and interpretation criteria, and together accounted for 96.5% of the variance in the data.

The first factor, accounting for 51% of the common variance in the data, presented strong correlations with HEADD (0.934), V (0.785), Ni (0.782), and COODD (-0.773), and lower (0.3-0.4) correlations with Pb, Mn, and Zn. These relationships indicated that this factor was associated with an oil-burning/space-heating source type. Factor 2 accounted for 25.6% of the common variance. Iron, Mn, and Pb were highly loaded on this factor (0.908, 0.744, and 0.555, respectively), while V and Ni had lower loadings (0.356 and 0.395, respectively). The associations indicated that Factor 2 was related to soil resuspension. Factor 3, representing 8% of the common variance in the data, had high loadings for Cd (.670), Cu (0.665), and Pb (0.455), and lower correlations with Zn (0.319) and Mn (0.306). This factor was most probably associated with industrial type emissions. Factor 4 accounted for 6.3% of the communality in the data. Sulfate and COODD

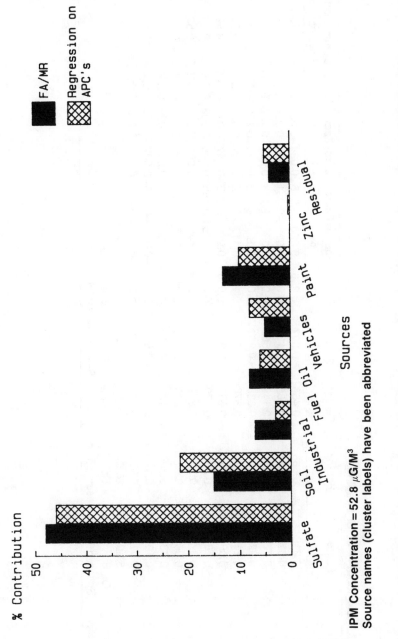

IPM Concentration = 52.8 μG/M^3
Source names (cluster labels) have been abbreviated

Figure 7.2.   Newark—IPM source contributions: comparison of FA/MR and regression on APCs model estimates.

Table 7.7. Elizabeth—Factor Loadings[a]

Elizabeth FA-2	Factor 1	Factor 2	Factor 3	Factor 4	Factor 5	Factor 6	Factor 7	Factor 8	Factor 9	Factor 10	Communality (Factor 1–6)
Pb	0.319	0.555	0.455	0.007	0.290	0.020	0.346	0.034	-0.007	0.010	0.70
Mn	0.323	0.744	0.306	0.163	0.080	0.075	-0.031	0.035	0.218	-0.045	0.78
COODD	-0.773	0.081	-0.119	0.508	-0.028	-0.096	0.133	0.016	0.126	0.051	
HEADD	0.924	-0.100	0.085	-0.151	0.092	0.121	0.023	-0.154	0.123	-0.129	
Cd	0.116	0.174	0.670	-0.037	0.177	0.112	-0.012	0.191	0.023	0.016	0.52
Cu	0.090	0.240	0.665	0.073	0.060	0.012	0.033	-0.147	-0.014	-0.005	0.52
V	0.785	0.356	0.179	0.042	0.043	-0.105	0.155	0.278	0.003	0.035	0.79
Zn	0.370	0.257	0.319	-0.098	0.223	0.449	0.003	-0.006	0.005	0.010	0.57
Fe	-0.062	0.910	0.243	0.123	-0.011	0.073	0.020	0.007	-0.115	0.050	0.91
Ni	0.782	0.395	0.133	-0.046	0.110	0.167	0.036	0.049	-0.029	0.250	0.83
SO_4^{-2}	-0.196	0.171	0.054	0.633	0.321	-0.030	-0.018	-0.002	-0.016	-0.008	0.58
CO_{max}	0.011	0.022	0.149	0.168	0.629	0.060	0.017	0.008	0.002	0.006	0.45
Variance(%)	51.0	25.6	8.0	6.3	3.1	2.5	1.3	1.0	0.9	0.4	
Probable Source type	Oil Burning/ Space Heating	Soil Resuspension	Industrial	SO_4^{-2}/ Secondary	Motor Vehicles	Zinc					

[a]n = 116

were the two more highly loaded variables (0.633 and 0.508, respectively). Therefore, Factor 4 was interpreted as being associated with sulfate/ secondary aerosol. Factor 5 correlated strongly with CO_{max} (0.629) and had lower correlations with SO_4^{-2} (0.321) and Pb (0.290). This factor was suspected of being associated with motor vehicle emissions. To further resolve Factor 5, BghiP, COR, and BaP concentrations were added to the FA procedure. BghiP correlated with several factors in the data, while inclusion of COR and BaP reduced the number of cases available for analysis to less than 100. Although this source was not as clearly identifiable in Elizabeth as in Newark, its presence in that city was supported by the microinventory results. Factor 6 showed a relatively high loading (0.449) for Zn, and was interpreted as related to Zn source type emissions. Zinc concentrations at the Elizabeth sampling site were higher, on average, with prevailing northeasterly winds, which is the direction of source emissions from Newark.

The identifiable IPM sources in Elizabeth were oil burning/space heating, soil/street dust resuspension, SO_4^{-2}/secondary aerosol, industrial emissions and Zn. Although the motor vehicular source was not clearly resolved, its existence was corroborated by the qualitative microinventory survey. The selected source tracers were V, Fe (Mn was also associated with other factors), SO_4^{-2}, Cu, and Zn. The fraction of Pb associated with motor vehicle emissions, PbA, was estimated following the methodology first developed for the Newark IPM model.

IPM Source Apportionment

Source apportionment models for IPM in Elizabeth were developed following the FA/MR methodology used in Newark. Residual analysis of preliminary Pb and IPM FA/MR models suggested the presence of a Mn source other than soil. The fraction of Mn associated with the unresolved source, MnR, was estimated and used in the Pb and IPM source apportionment models. The coefficient of MnR was significant in the IPM model but not in the Pb regression equation. Inclusion of MnR in the IPM source apportionment model resulted in a significant negative intercept ($p = 0.017$), which indicated that IPM was overpredicted by 10%. The overall F value was also lower than for the regression model, which did not include MnR (146 vs 188). Based on these statistical considerations, and since the MnR source could not be identified, it was not possible to categorically decide which apportionment model was best for IPM in Elizabeth, so both are presented together with the Mn and Pb apportionment equations in Table 7.8. Actual source contribution estimates are summarized in Figure 7.3.

Approximately one third of the ambient Pb concentration in Elizabeth was related to soil resuspension, 18% was associated with the oil burning sources, and 8% each with the industrial and Zn sources. Only one-third of

Table 7.8.   Mn, Pb, and IPM Apportionment Models for Elizabeth, NJ[a]

MnR = Mn − (0.0089 Fe + 0.044 V + 0.0032 Zn)   (7.8.1)

PbA = Pb − (0.23 Fe + 1.8 V + 0.17 Zn + 0.98 Cu)   (7.8.2)

IPM = (2.0±0.11) SO_4^{-2} + (127±17) V + (17.6±2.1) Fe + (1046±214) MnR[a]   (7.8.3)
+ (9.02±2.0) Zn + (23.7±5.4) PbA − 4.6±1.9
n = 145
Overall F = 146 (p = 0.000)
Multiple R = 0.93

IPM = (2.1±0.11) SO_4^{-2} + (18.5±2.1) Fe + (138±17) V + (24.2±5.4) PbA   (7.8.4)
+ 0.024±1.76
n = 144
Overall F = 188 (p = 0.000)
Multiple R = 0.92

[a]Concentrations are expressed in $\mu g/m^3$. Regression coefficients are presented with their standard errors.

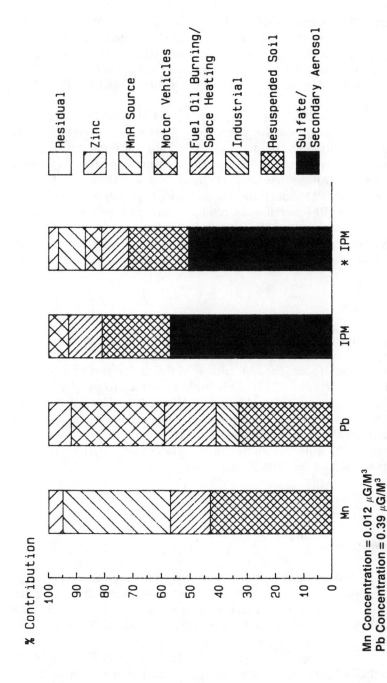

Mn Concentration = 0.012 μG/M^3
Pb Concentration = 0.39 μG/M^3
IPM Concentration = 44.7 μG/M^3; * IPM overestimated

Figure 7.3.   Source contributions to Mn, Pb, and IPM in Elizabeth, NJ.

the ambient Pb concentration in this city could be attributed to motor vehicle exhaust. However, the Elizabeth Pb apportionment equation could be underspecified, since CO_{max} was not included in the equation because CO in Elizabeth was measured at a very different sampling site. Therefore, PbA for Elizabeth is best defined as the minimum fraction of ambient Pb related to motor vehicles.

The results of the IPM apportionment model showed that secondary aerosol formation accounted for approximately 56% of the ambient IPM concentration in Elizabeth, followed by 23% from soil resuspension, 11% from oil burning/space heating, 6% from motor vehicle exhaust, 11% from the unidentified MnR source, and 4% from the Zn source. If MnR is excluded from the IPM model, the Zn coefficient is nonsignificant.

Analysis of the IPM model daily residuals showed a pattern similar to that found in the Newark model. This observation tends to support the hypothesis that there were as yet unidentified, areawide meteorological factors and/or sources affecting the model predictions.

Model Validation

The tracer content of sources identified in Elizabeth were similar to those previously determined in Newark for similar sources present at both sites, with the exception of soil. The Mn content of soil in Elizabeth was 0.05%, while that of Newark was 0.22%. This could be related to the character of the areas surrounding each sampling site. Whereas in Newark there are several large unpaved lots, in Elizabeth all areas are either covered with grass, paved, or blacktopped. In addition, soil contamination from industrial sources in Elizabeth should be lower, as indicated by the microinventory observations and the IPM model results.

Camden

Source Identification

Sources of IPM in Camden were identified following the methodology developed for Newark and Elizabeth IPM. The final FA results for Camden are presented in Table 7.9. Five factors were extracted that complied with factor resolution, retention, and interpretation criteria. Together, they accounted for 94.4% of the variance in the data.

Factor 1 showed high loadings for Ni (0.857), V (0.852), HEADD (0.493), and COODD (-0.365), suggesting an association with oil burning/space heating sources. Vanadium was selected as the tracer for this source. The second factor showed strong correlations with COODD (0.879),

Table 7.9. Camden—Factor Loadings[a]

Camden F.A.-2	Factor 1	Factor 2	Factor 3	Factor 4	Factor 5	Factor 6	Factor 7	Factor 8	Factor 9	Factor 10	Communality (Factor 1-5)
Pb	0.196	-0.084	0.246	0.429	0.669	-0.088	0.031	0.108	0.148	0.095	0.74
Mn	0.211	-0.052	0.814	0.142	0.139	0.088	-0.008	0.010	0.135	-0.014	0.75
Cd	0.138	-0.088	0.109	0.765	0.038	-0.068	-0.001	-0.007	-0.004	-0.001	0.63
Cu	0.206	0.016	0.130	0.426	0.277	0.042	0.371	0.027	-0.002	0.002	0.32
V	0.852	-0.012	0.178	0.237	0.097	-0.084	0.097	-0.033	0.083	0.051	0.82
Zn	0.230	-0.208	0.164	0.625	0.136	0.383	0.088	0.028	0.007	-0.001	0.53
Fe	0.085	0.177	0.806	0.134	0.161	-0.043	0.075	0.008	-0.133	0.020	0.73
Ni	0.857	-0.198	0.211	0.215	0.236	0.198	0.002	0.094	-0.107	-0.040	0.92
SO_4^{-2}	0.196	0.647	0.102	-0.071	-0.138	-0.006	0.045	0.161	-0.013	0.110	0.49
CO_{max}	0.084	-0.113	0.110	0.003	0.672	0.059	0.049	-0.029	-0.013	-0.030	0.49
HEADD	0.493	-0.699	0.033	0.121	0.076	0.087	0.128	0.327	-0.001	0.002	
COODD	-0.365	0.879	0.033	-0.114	-0.198	-0.026	0.007	-0.112	0.012	-0.167	
Variance(%)	48.9	20.4	10.0	8.5	6.6	2.2	1.6	1.1	0.6	0.3	
Probable Source type	Oil Burning/ Space Heating	SO_4^{-2}/ Secondary	Soil Resuspension	Industrial/ Incineration	Motor Vehicles						

[a] n = 139

HEADD (–0.699), and SO_4^{-2} (0.647), suggesting a sulfate/secondary aerosol source type; SO_4^{-2} was selected as its tracer. Factor 3 was associated with Mn (0.814) and Fe (0.806), suggesting soil resuspension. Manganese also had weak correlations with the oil burning/space heating, industrial/ incineration, and motor vehicle-related factors. The nonsoil-associated factors accounted for 9% of the Mn common variance. Fe was chosen as tracer for this source. Factor 4 was strongly correlated with Cd (0.766), Zn (0.625), and, to a lesser extent, with Pb (0.429) and Cu (0.426), again suggesting industrial and/or incineration sources. It is not possible to conclusively establish the identity of this source. The microinventory observations (Chapter 1) indicated the presence of a municipal incineration facility operating northwest of the sampling site, in Philadelphia, which could impact the sampling site, as well as industrial facilities. Copper was selected as the tracer for the incineration/industrial source, since over half of the Cd concentrations measured in Camden were at or below detection limit. Factor 5 showed high loadings for CO_{max} (0.672) and Pb (0.669), which would indicate the presence of motor vehicle exhaust. Lead also showed minor associations (0.2–0.3) with the oil burning/space heating, soil, and industrial/incineration source types. Lead was tentatively chosen as the tracer for this source.

Apportionment Models

Sources of IPM in Camden were apportioned following the methodology developed for Newark and Elizabeth IPM. The first attempt at modeling IPM in Camden using Pb as the motor vehicle tracer was not successful. Inclusion of Pb increased the p values for the regression coefficients of Cu, V, and Zn, while the use of Fe had a similar effect on the Zn regression coefficient. Since neither Pb nor Fe could be used, tracers for both the motor vehicle and soil resuspension source types were obtained by apportioning Pb and Mn, and estimating the corresponding regression residuals, PbA and MnR. CO_{max} was included in the Pb model, since FA results indicated that it was almost exclusively related to motor vehicle emissions. The Mn apportionment model included Fe so as to obtain a fully specified equation. Two IPM apportionment models were developed using MnR and Fe separately as soil resuspension tracers. The final Pb, Mn, and IPM models are presented in Table 7.10, and the corresponding source contributions are shown in Figure 7.4.

Approximately two-thirds of the ambient Mn concentration was soil resuspension related, while the rest was associated with emissions from oil burning/space heating and zinc. One half of the ambient Pb concentration was related to motor vehicle emissions, while the remaining ambient levels were almost equally distributed among the soil, oil burning/space heating,

Table 7.10.   Mn, Pb, and IPM Source Apportionment Models for Camden, NJ[a]

$MnR = Mn - (0.010 Zn + 0.046 V)$ (7.10.1)

$PbA = Pb - (0.27 Zn + 2.04 Cu + 1.03 V + 3.1 MnR)$ (7.10.2)

$IPM = (1.9 \pm 0.1) SO_4^{-2} + (24.7 \pm 2.8) Fe + (29.5 \pm 4.9) PbA + (68 \pm 24) V$ (7.10.3)
$+ 1.3 \pm 2.0^a$
$n = 142$
Overall $F = 156 (p = 0)$
Multiple $R = 0.91$

$IPM = (2.0 \pm 0.1) SO_4^{-2} + (558 \pm 94) MnR + (31.1 \pm 5.2) PbA + (127 \pm 47) Cu$ (7.10.4)
$+ (67 \pm 27) V + 3.0 \pm 2.1^a$
$n = 142$
Overall $F = 105 (p = 0)$
Multiple $R = 0.89$

[a]Constants are nonsignificant ($p > 0.10$). Concentrations are expressed in $\mu g/m^3$. Regression coefficients are presented with their respective standard errors.

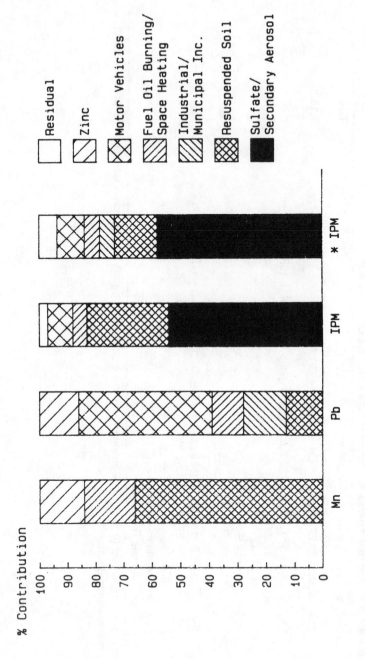

Mn Concentration = 0.015 μG/M^3
Pb Concentration = 0.30 μG/M^3
IPM Concentration = 47.1 μG/M^3; * IPM eq. 7.11.4

Figure 7.4.   Source contributions to Mn, Pb, and IPM in Camden, NJ.

industrial/municipal incineration, and zinc sources. The sulfate/secondary aerosol source accounted for approximately 58% of the IPM mass in Camden, followed by soil resuspension (15%), motor vehicles (10%), oil burning/space heating (6%), and industrial/municipal incineration (6%). The use of MnR as the soil tracer resulted in a 50% reduction in soil contributions as compared to the previous model, as well as increased significance in the industrial/municipal incineration tracer regression coefficient. The tolerance level for Fe was relatively low (0.74), which indicates the presence more than one source type for this tracer in Camden.

Model Validation

With the exception of V and PbA, the tracer content of the identified source emissions was in the range of values previously discussed for Newark. As in Elizabeth, the modeling results suggest that Mn had a multiplicity of sources. Approximately 18% of the Mn concentration was associated with the oil burning/space heating source. The estimated Mn concentration in the fuel oil burning source emissions was 0.06%, within the reported range of residual and distillate fuel oil burning emissions.

In common with Newark and Elizabeth, there were several sources of airborne Pb in Camden. The oil source emissions contained approximately 1.3% Pb, again within the Pb content range expected for fuel oil. The industrial/municipal incineration source emissions were approximately 1.6% Pb, which is comparable to the Pb content of the Newark industrial source type. The concentration of Pb in soil was approximately 0.6%, also similar to that found in Newark for the same source. Motor vehicle source contributions contained approximately 3.2% Pb, a value lower than that determined for Newark vehicular emissions. Approximately half of the ambient Pb concentration in Camden was the result of motor vehicle emissions. The lower V content of the oil burning/space heating emissions of Camden as compared to Newark could be due to a relatively small proportion of residual oil being used in Camden.

COMPARATIVE ANALYSIS OF POLLUTANT SOURCES IN THE URBAN ATEOS SITES

The final results of the IPM apportionment models for Newark, Elizabeth, and Camden are summarized in pie chart form in Figure 7.5. The SO_4^{-2}/secondary aerosol contributions to IPM were similar at all three sites. Approximately 50% of IPM was contributed by this source. Absolute SO_4^{-2}/secondary aerosol contributions to IPM were also similar, on the order of 25 $\mu g/m^3$. This is consistent with results from a number of previous

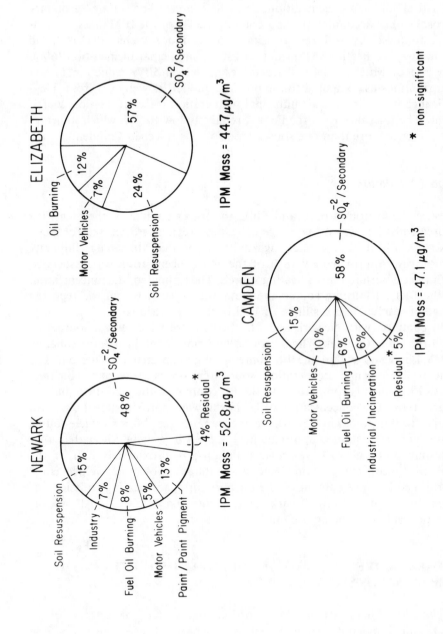

Figure 7.5. Source contributions to IPM in Newark, Elizabeth, and Camden, NJ.

studies which indicate that SO_4^{-2} concentrations in the Northeast are determined, to a large extent, by regional rather than local sources, and by overall atmospheric conditions (Lioy et al., 1980). Transport of SO_4^{-2} into the area is also important under certain conditions. The SO_4^{-2} content, as determined by multiple regression analysis in several U.S. cities, is always in the 40–60% range. It can be hypothesized that the consistency of this value is related to atmospheric reaction parameters which establish lower and upper bounds of SO_4^{-2} and other secondary pollutants' formation.

Soil resuspension contributions to IPM varied, on average, from 7.1 μg/m³ (15%) in Camden, to 8.2 μg/m³ (15%) in Newark, to 10.8 μg/m³ (24%) in Elizabeth. These concentrations are not significantly different among the cities, considering the associated uncertainties. Soil Mn content at the three sites was within the range of reported source values. Differences observed in Mn soil contribution concentrations between Camden and Newark and those of Elizabeth could be related to the fact that the former sampling sites were surrounded by unpaved areas, while in Elizabeth there were primarily asphalted roads, parking lots, and grass lawns. The Fe content of soil contributions to IPM was similar at the three sites, and within reported source composition values. The Pb content of soil was comparable in Newark and Elizabeth and lower in Camden. These results are at least in part related to local industrial emissions deposition in Newark, and influences from industrial areas located immediately to the north and west in Elizabeth.

The oil burning/space heating source contributed 4.3 μg/m³ (8%) to Newark IPM, 5.2 μg/m³ (12%) in Elizabeth, and 2.6 μg/m³ (6%) in Camden. The tracer content of this source varied from site to site, but in all cases was within reported ranges of elemental composition for residual oil. Although V concentrations are generally lower in distillate oil emissions, V should also trace this source.

In contrast to Newark, neither the industrial sources nor the zinc source were apportioned by the regression model in Elizabeth, indicating that they did not constitute important contributors to average IPM to this adjacent city. The Cu-associated factor was important in Camden. The Pb and Cu contents of the industrial/incineration source in Camden and industrial emissions in Newark were comparable, suggesting similarity of origin. Emissions from municipal incinerators and potential industrial sources in the Philadelphia area would impact the Camden sampling site. However, the exact identification of the Cu-associated source contributions in Camden was not possible.

Motor vehicle contributions to IPM were 2.7 μg/m³ (5%) in Newark, 2.9 μg/m³ (6%) in Elizabeth and 4.6 μg/m³ (10%) in Camden. The Pb content of motor vehicular emissions was also higher in Newark and Elizabeth, and lower in Camden. These results are a reflection of traffic density, the diesel/gasoline vehicle mix, and/or the relative age of the fleet present at each site.

Only between 30% to 60% of the ambient Pb concentration could be attributed to direct motor vehicle emissions. We suspect that this may be true for other U.S. cities. Therefore, Pb can no longer be assumed to be a unique tracer for motor vehicle emissions. In addition, due to the significant reductions in the use of leaded gasoline during the last five years, source composition profiles currently available in the literature may no longer be applicable for CMB modeling.

The apportionment models did not identify the presence of the paint spraying/paint pigment source either at Elizabeth or Camden, which is consistent with the results of the microinventory surveys (Chapter 1). In Newark, this source was more significant than the industrial, fuel oil burning, or motor vehicle contributions to IPM.

NEWARK – EXTRACTABLE ORGANIC MATTER SOURCE APPORTIONMENT MODELS

Background

Extractable organic matter (EOM) constituted, on average, approximately 30% of the IPM in Newark. Many of the organic compounds identified in this fraction of the ambient urban aerosol have been shown to be carcinogens and cocarcinogens in experimental animals (National Academy of Sciences, 1972). The mutagenic activity of urban EOM fractions, as determined by short-term microbial bioassays, has been reported by a number of authors (Talcott and Wei, 1977; Pitts et al., 1977; Commoner et al., 1978; Daisey et al., 1979). Fractions of urban EOM have also been shown to induce tumors and act as promoters in in vivo tests (Hueper et al., 1962; Hoffmann and Wynder, 1977). Particle-associated organic compounds are generally concentrated in the 0.1–1.0 μm diameter range, and can penetrate and deposit deep in the lung, in areas of slow clearance. Thus, given the potential health effects of airborne particulate organic matter, identification of sources that contribute to EOM is important.

Limitations of EOM Modeling

Modeling of EOM sources presents unique difficulties. Whereas sampling and analysis of elemental particle composition is fairly well understood, organic sampling and analysis is still under investigation. Sampling methods can affect the concentration and composition of EOM. Sampling artifacts have been shown to depend on the type of sampler (Van Vaek et al., 1980) and filter media used (Lee et al., 1980; Daisey et al., 1986). Other variables that can affect sampling artifact formation are sampling time (Appel et al., 1981; Konig et al., 1980; Schwartz et al., 1981) and filter loading (Schwartz et al., 1981; Gorse et al., 1982). Meteorology can also affect the nature and quantity of EOM collected on a filter. For example, temperature changes can shift vapor particle equilibria of compounds present in EOM, resulting in increased or decreased vaporization losses (DeWiest, 1978; Yamasaki et al., 1982). In general, EOM sampling artifacts are related to conditions which favor evaporative losses, and/or chemical reactions.

Extraction and analysis of EOM samples also present unique problems. During extraction and storage, in situ and in solution reactions, and evaporative losses can affect the quantity and nature of EOM. Many of the compounds present in EOM fractions are photosensitive and can degrade under sunlight or fluorescent illumination. Temperature can also affect the rates of reaction and decomposition of the extracted compounds. In addition, extraction methods can remove inorganic materials together with the organic compounds (Daisey et al., 1982; Lioy and Daisey et al., 1984).

Although many of the difficulties associated with organic particulate sampling and the relevant parameters have been identified, a comprehensive and quantitative understanding of organic artifact formation and the probable solutions are still lacking. In ATEOS, extreme care was taken to minimize evaporative and reaction losses during transport, storage, and extraction of samples. The 24-hr sampling time used in ATEOS was a compromise between minimization of artifact formation due to sampling time, and collection of EOM samples large enough to allow for posterior analyses, characterization, and source apportionment modeling. The filter media utilized, however, could also be a source of artifacts (Daisey et al., 1986). Because of the preceding considerations, the EOM modeling results have to be interpreted with caution.

Sources of EOM

Information about EOM sources and their possible contribution to airborne particulate organic matter is limited (Daisey et al., 1986). As in the case of all airborne materials, sources of EOM can be natural or anthropogenic. On a global basis, natural sources produce most of the particulate organic carbon. Anthropogenic sources predominate in urban areas (Duce, 1978). Any combustion process, either man-made, as in the case of fossil fuel burning, or natural, such as forest fires, can produce both gas- and particle-phase organic compounds, and inject them into the atmosphere. Airborne microorganisms, organic particle and gaseous emissions from vegetation, such as pollens and terpenes (Fish, 1972; Rasmussen, 1972), resuspension of soils containing organic matter (Delany and Fenchelsky, 1976), and spraying of water from oceans and lakes (Baier, 1972) are all natural sources of airborne organic compounds. Gas-to-particle conversion of anthropogenic and natural volatile emissions may lead to secondary organic particulate aerosol formation. In addition, interregional transport of organic compounds has been documented by several authors (Bjorseth et al., 1979; Daisey et al., 1981; Daisey and Lioy, 1981). Since tracers for many of these sources are not currently known or cannot be identified with available data, it is likely that not all possible sources of EOM in Newark were included in the models presented in this work.

Review of EOM Apportionment Models

Source apportionment modeling of EOM and/or its components has been conducted for only a few locations. Chemical elemental and mass balance methods have been used by Daisey et al. (1979) to estimate source contributions to BaP in New York City. Unfortunately, this approach to source apportionment of organic compounds was seriously limited by the lack of source emission data. Source measurements of organic emissions are notoriously difficult to obtain (Jones et al., 1977). In addition, due to physical and chemical transformation processes, the coefficient of fractionation of the organic species in the emissions at the source is probably very different from that measured at a receptor. These considerations largely preclude the effective use of CMB techniques for apportioning EOM.

Daisey and Kneip (1981) first developed an FA/MR model for the cyclohexane-, dichloromethane- and acetone-soluble fractions of respirable EOM in New York City (NYC, $D_{50} = 3.5~\mu m$). The models were developed using 62 weekly samples collected from January, 1978 through August, 1979. Satisfactory apportionment models could only be obtained for the CX and ACE fractions. Modeling was difficult since at that time Mn, the soil tracer, had also been added to gasoline as MMT, an antiknock compound. This pioneering work was continued and further developed with RSP weekly samples collected between January, 1979 and December, 1980 (Daisey and Hopke, 1984; Daisey et al., 1985). In addition to the elemental composition used during the previous study, five other elements were measured. Titanium was used as a soil tracer rather than Mn, as the latter was found to be also associated with residual oil emissions (MMT was no longer added to gasoline after 1978). Adequate models were obtained for the CX, DCM, and ACE fractions. More sources of EOM were identified and apportioned than in the previous work. These two studies demonstrated that FA/MR methods can be applied to source apportionment modeling of EOM sources. They also showed that different extractable organic fractions can originate from different source types. Daisey (1985) has more recently applied FA/MR methods to apportion sources of benzo(a)pyrene, benzo(b)fluoranthene, indeno(1,2,3-cd)pyrene, and benzo(ghi)perylene in New York City, utilizing 88 weekly samples of respirable particulate matter. Motor vehicles and oil burning were identified as the main sources of these four compounds. This study demonstrated that FA/MR methods can be used to identify sources of specific airborne mutagens and carcinogens.

The application of FA/MR techniques to EOM in ATEOS has the following distinctive characteristics: (1) first application of apportionment modeling techniques to IPM extractable organic matter; (2) partial resolution of the tracer multicolinearity limitation, a confounding factor in previous applications of this approach to airborne organic compounds, through the use of tracer apportionment; (3) use of 24-hr rather than weekly samples, thus reducing concerns related to sampling artifacts associated with long-term sampling; and (4) application to a more complex urban airshed than New York City.

Development of FA/MR EOM Models for Newark

Previous EOM sources modeling studies relied, to some extent, on either analysis of correlations between the various organic fractions and the different tracers, or on their exclusive association with particular factors in the FA procedure. The use of initial correlations between the dependent variables and the tracers may result in the exclusion of significant tracers from the model (i.e., as successive independent variables are entered in the stepwise regression model, correlations between the corresponding regression residuals and variables not included in the equation may be very different from those initially observed).

A small loading in the factor model does not necessarily correspond to low or no source contribution to the dependent variable in the regression model. Each EOM fraction will tend to factor with those variables that account for most of their respective common variance, and will have low loading in other factors. A more effective approach is to treat each EOM fraction as a dependent variable, equivalent to IPM. All the emission source types identified in Newark are known to have organic components and, therefore, they also probably contribute to ambient EOM concentrations in Newark. If a particular source does not contribute significantly to EOM, the corresponding tracer regression coefficient would not be significant. Thus the EOM FA/MR models were developed using forward stepwise regression of CX, DCM, and ACE on the same tracers used to apportion IPM.

Results

The CX, DCM, and ACE models are presented in Table 7.11. Actual source contributions are summarized in Figure 7.6. The regression coeffi-

Table 7.11.   CX, DCM and ACE Source Apportionment Models for Newark, NJ[a]

CX = (7.4 ± 0.8) PbA[b] + (23.2 ± 3.7) V + (49.5 ± 12.5) Mn + 1.4 ± 0.3 (7.11.1)
n = 135
Overall F = 58 (p = 0)
Multiple R = 0.76

DCM = (0.03 ± 0.001) SO_4^{-2} + (1.3 ± 0.4) PbA[b] + (0.9 ± 0.2) FeR[c] + (4.0 ± 1.7) V + 0.4 ± 0.2 (7.11.2)
n = 135
Overall F = 12 (p $\leq$ 0.000)
Multiple R = 0.52

ACE = (0.300 ± 0.005) SO_4^{-2} + (8.9 ± 2.0) PbA[b] + (137 ± 31) Mn + (18.7 ± 8.9) V + (0.5 ± 0.3) Zn   (7.11.3)
+ 0.38 ± 0.8
n = 135
Overall F = 25 (p $\leq$ 0)
Multiple R = 0.70

[a]Concentrations are expressed in $\mu g/m^3$. Coefficients are presented with their standard error.
[b]Motor vehicle-associated Pb (from Equation 7.4.1).
[c]Paint spraying/paint pigment associated Fe (from Equation 7.4.2).

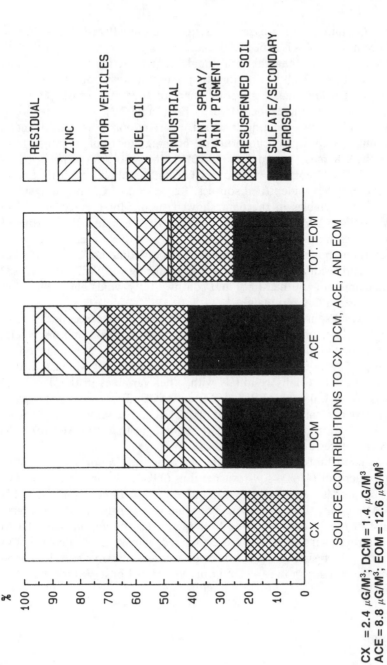

Figure 7.6.   Newark—Source contributions to CX, DCM, ACE, and EOM.

cients for CX and the other organic fractions were smaller than those found in the IPM model. This is expected because the organic mass associated with the tracers is smaller than the total inhalable particle mass. For example, elemental carbon, which is a major component of some source emissions, e.g., motor vehicle exhaust, is a component of IPM but not of EOM.

Of the probable sources identified by FA (Table 7.3), only motor vehicles, oil burning/space heating, and soil resuspension were significant in determining CX mass. Soil and fuel oil burning contributed similar fractions of the CX mass, approximately 20%, while motor vehicle contributions were 26%. Almost one-third of the CX mass could not be attributed to any of the previously identified sources. Regression of CX model residual against other variables in the data showed significant correlations ($p < 0.05$) with IPM, FPM, ACE, CcdP (66 cases), BeP, BjF, and PER. None of these variables were included in the CX model either because they were mixtures of compounds or because unique sources could not be identified at the time. CX residuals were slightly higher during the W82 and the S82 periods. Dominant southeasterly and southwesterly winds also resulted in slightly increased CX residuals.

The principal source contributors to DCM were sulfate/secondary aerosol (28%), followed by paint spraying/paint pigment (18%), motor vehicles (14%), and fuel oil burning (11%). The average residual was similar to that found in the CX model, approximately one-third of the DCM mass. Correlations of the DCM daily residuals with other variables in the data were significant ($p < 0.05$) with FPM, IPM, and ACE. There were also significant negative correlations with CcdP and CHRY. The seasonal and prevalent wind direction residual pattern was similar to that observed for IPM and CX model residuals.

Source contributors to ACE were, in order of importance, sulfate/secondary aerosol (41%), soil resuspension (29%), motor vehicles (15%), fuel oil burning/space heating (8%), and Zn (3%). In contrast to the CX and DCM models, the average ACE residual was nonsignificant, implying that most of the ACE sources had been identified and apportioned. DCM and alkylating agent activity were correlated with ACE model residuals ($p \leq 0.05$). The residuals were inspected on a seasonal and prevalent wind direction basis. They showed a similar pattern to that observed for the IPM, CX, and DCM model residuals.

Discussion

The CX fraction consists mostly of nonpolar compounds of primary rather than secondary origin, such as alkanes, alkenes, and aromatic and polycyclic aromatic hydrocarbons (Daisey, 1980). Thus the SO_4^{-2}/secondary aerosol formation source should not contribute significantly to overall CX levels, as the model results indicated. Instead, fuel oil burning and motor vehicle sources accounted for approximately half the CX mass. Polycyclic aromatic hydrocarbons are emitted by fossil fuel burning sources such as these and are extracted in the CX fraction. The soil resuspension contribution to CX may be related to contamination of soils by deposition of particles from these sources as well as the natural organic content of soils. Organic contamination of soils near highways has been documented (Blumer et al., 1977).

In contrast to the IPM model, a significant amount of the CX fraction (1.5 μg/m^3) could not be attributed to any of the identified sources. The nature of these sources is not known. Daisey (1985) has suggested that the unexplained CX mass may be in part due to natural sources, such as plant waxes. Transport of CX may also account for a fraction of the CX model residual. Daisey et al. (1984) estimated that transport from upwind sources may account for the 1.2 μg/m^3 average CX model residual observed in New York City. Sampling artifacts probably played a minor role in the magnitude of the Newark CX model residual. Also, there was no indication that temperature effects were important in the seasonal residual pattern (i.e., a clear summer/winter difference).

The significant correlation between the CX model residuals and several PAHs also suggested that the unexplained CX mass could be related to unidentified sources of EOM in Newark, for which elemental tracers were unavailable. Correlations between IPM model residuals and other variables in the data proved useful in identifying potential sources of IPM; they could be of similar significance in the CX model. The significant correlation between CcdP and the residuals may have been fortuitous. CcdP has been identified as being mostly emitted by motor vehicles, but it is rather reactive, so care must be taken during sampling, handling and storage (Greenberg et al., 1981). Daisey (1984) attributed this PAH to oil burning and motor vehicle emissions in New York City. However, tracers for both these sources were included in the Newark CX model; thus, there could be another CcdP source type present in Newark. Due to the mix of sources in the area, it is difficult to identify all source types which could emit BaP, BjF, and/or PER and account for the significant correlations between these PAHs and the residuals of the CX model. This question merits further investigation, as any of these compounds could be related to a source not yet identified. The association between the residuals of the CX and ACE models could be the result of the sequential method used for EOM extraction, and/or similarity of origin.

Dichloromethane-extractable organic compounds are more polar than cyclohexane-extractables. Moderately polar compounds, including some products of photochemical reactions, would be expected to be present in the DCM fraction. As expected, sulfate/secondary aerosol formation accounted for a large fraction (28%) of DCM mass in Newark. Fuel oil and motor vehicle primary and secondary emissions would also be expected to contribute to DCM, and indeed they do (11% and 14%, respectively), although proportionally less than to the CX fraction. There is some evidence that supports these results in the case of motor vehicle emissions. EOM samples obtained at the Caldecott Tunnel indicate that the relative CX:DCM:ACE proportions is 11:1:5 (Daisey and Hering, unpublished data, 1985). A 4:1:9 average ratio was observed for the Newark ambient EOM samples, indicating that motor vehicle exhaust is enriched in CX as compared with ambient EOM.

The most interesting feature of the DCM model is that it was the only organic fraction associated with the paint/paint pigment source. Many organic compounds formulated as solvents and additives in paints, such as polyester resins and fatty acids, are at least partially soluble in DCM. Butler (1985) has reported evidence of the presence of such compound classes in DCM extracts from airborne particulate matter obtained in several U.S. and foreign cities. As was the case with the CX model, approximately one-third of the DCM mass could not be attributed to any of the identified sources. In the case of the DCM model, sampling artifacts may be an important factor in determining the magnitude of this residual. Daisey et al. (1985) demonstrated that the amount of DCM collected on fiberglass filters during 24-hr periods exceeds that determined on Teflon® coated fiberglass filters by 40% on average. Therefore, this artifact could more than account for the DCM model residual value. Seasonal effects were not evident, as the pattern of the DCM model residuals was very similar to that observed for the IPM and CX models.

Significant negative correlations of the DCM residuals with CcdP and CHRY could be explained by parameters related to atmospheric photo-chemistry that may affect patterns of accumulation of these two PAHs. Depletion of PAHs via reactions and/or shifts in the vapor/particle distributions (i.e., photochemical smog situations) would reduce their relative amounts while increasing the concentrations of compounds extractable in DCM and not accounted for by sources already included in the model. In the absence of those conditions, CcdP and CHRY would accumulate while the DCM extractable mass decreased. If the explanation given for the correlations observed were correct, SO_4^{-2}/secondary aerosol might not account for all secondary aerosol formation, as this source type was already included in the model. At this point, the available data allow only speculation. This should be the object of further investigation. It is interesting, however, that a model of this type can uncover avenues of further inquiry into the physicochemical behavior of pollutants, not just identify and apportion sources.

Compounds contained in the ACE fraction are more polar than those present in either CX or DCM, and include oxidized hydrocarbons such as acids, aldehydes, phenols, etc. (Butler, 1985). Some of these compounds are of primary origin, but many are secondary (Daisey et al., 1984; Daisey, 1985). As expected, given the nature of the compounds found in this fraction, most of the ACE mass was SO_4^{-2}/secondary aerosol related. There is some evidence that partially supports these results. It has been shown that the ACE fraction increases significantly during periods of summertime regional accumulation and secondary aerosol formation in the Newark area (Daisey et al., 1984). Regional contributions to secondary EOM under episodic situations have been reported to be approximately 2 $\mu g/m^3$ in the northern New Jersey area. In Newark, an additional 4 $\mu g/m^3$ has been reported to be due to local secondary aerosol contributions (Daisey et al., 1984). However, a word of caution is in order. There is evidence suggesting inorganic ions, particularly NO_3^- and NH_4^+, are partially extracted in acetone. These ions are generally considered to be secondary in nature. On certain occasions, these inorganic ions can account for up to 25% of ACE (Lioy et al., 1982). Besides increasing the apparent concentration of ACE, these ions can produce a biased estimate of the SO_4^{-2}/secondary aerosol organic contributions to this fraction. Although this effect may be minor, it represents added uncertainty in the ACE model.

The presence of ACE in soil is probably due to natural sources, such as vegetation decay, and anthropogenic activities. Both fuel oil burning and motor vehicle emissions would be expected to produce acetone-extractable compounds. An interesting result of the ACE model is that while the Zn source was not a significant contributor to average IPM, it contributed significantly to the ACE fraction. Therefore, some of the more polar organic compounds are emitted by this source, but the day-to-day mass contribution is too small to have a significant impact on IPM concentrations. In contrast to the CX and DCM models, the ACE mass was almost totally accounted for by the FA/MR model. The ACE model residuals had a similar pattern to those of IPM, CX, and DCM in Newark, and also IPM in Camden and Elizabeth. This suggests that some large-scale variables, probably related to meteorology, need to be included in the model.

EOM Model Validation

Validation of organic model results is more difficult than for IPM apportionment because of a scarcity of source emission data and the few applications of this type of model to organic compounds. The Newark EOM model results were compared to those reported by Daisey and Hopke, (1984) and Daisey et al., (1985), for New York City. These previous studies modeled respirable rather than inhalable particulate matter. As previously stated, EOM is concentrated in the smaller particle sizes. Also, some of the tracers used in these studies differed from those used in Newark. Therefore the comparison of the various EOM model results should be viewed with caution.

A summary of New York City and Newark tracer regression coefficients model is presented in Table 7.12. The sources identified and apportioned in the CX models were similar in both cities. The CX soil regression coefficients are not directly comparable since Mn was used in Newark and Ti in New York City. However, the Mn regression coefficient in Newark was similar to previously reported values in New York City (46 ± 11) and within a factor of 2 of the Mn/EOM ratio estimated by Daisey and Kneip (1981). The CX motor vehicle tracer regression coefficients of these cities differ. Differences could be due to a couple of factors: (1) a larger proportion of leaded gasoline-powered vehicles at the time of the New York City study, which was reflected in a lower tracer regression coefficient for Newark; and (2) proportionally more diesel powered vehicles in Newark, resulting in overall lower Pb concentrations. Daisey et al. (1986) estimated the CX/Pb ratio in Allegheny Tunnel samples as a function of the percentage of diesel traffic. The ratio increases as the proportion of diesel vehicles in traffic increased. The regression coefficient for PbA in the Newark CX model is close to the 6.0 ratio estimated for a 12.5% diesel mix. The regression coefficient for V is similar in both cities, indicating similar source characteristics.

Differences were also found in the DCM models. Soil was a significant contributor to DCM in New York City, but not in Newark. The reverse occurred for the fuel oil burning and motor vehicle sources. The explanation for these differences are not yet known. Daisey and Hopke (1984) suggested that sampling artifacts may have been important for this fraction in New York City, since weekly samples were collected. In addition, only 23% of the DCM variance was accounted for in New York City, indicating that significant variables were missing from the apportionment equation. Fuel oil burning and motor vehicle exhaust would be expected to contribute to DCM. The regression coefficient for SO_4^{-2} in Newark was close to that in New York City. The ratio of SO_4^{-2} to secondary aerosol contributions in Newark was approximately 33, while the corresponding value for New York City was 27, assuming all S was present as SO_4^{-2}.

The ACE model results for both cities were comparable, with the exception of the motor vehicle and SO_4^{-2}/secondary aerosol sources. With respect to the motor vehicle tracer regression coefficient, the comments made for the DCM model apply. The SO_4^{-2} regression coefficients differed by a factor of 3, that is, the ratio of SO_4^{-2} to ACE secondary aerosol contributions in Newark was approximately 3, while for New York City it was 11. These results suggest that there was more secondary mass associated with ACE in the Newark data than in the New York City data. Since the New York City model included measurements for all four seasons during 1970–1980, the differences in coefficients may reflect real differences between the two data

Table 7.12. Comparison of EOM Modeling Regression Coefficient for Newark and New York City

| Source Type | Regression Tracer Coefficient[a] | | | | | |
| | CX | | DCM | | ACE | |
	Newark	NYC	Newark	NYC	Newark	NYC
SO_4/sec Soil	49.5 ± 12.5 (Mn)	20 ± 12 (Ti)	0.03 ± 0.001	0.037 ± 0.019 54.6 ± 13.1 (Ti)	0.03 ± 0.05 137 ± 31 (Mn)	0.09 ± 0.03[b] 42 ± 12.4 (Ti)
Fuel Oil Burning	23.3 ± 3.7 (V)	25 ± 3 (V)	4.0 ± 1.7 (V)		18.7 ± 8.9 (V)	29.4 ± 6.2 (V)
Motor Vehicles	7.4 ± 0.8 (PbA)	1.1 ± 0.4 (Pb)	1.3 ± 0.4 (PbA)		8.9 ± 2.0 (PbA)	

[a]All coefficients are presented with their standard errors.
[b]S Coefficients in NYC models adjusted to SO_4^{-2} for comparison.

sets. Daisey et al. (1984) have presented evidence indicating that organic regional background is an important contributor to secondary aerosol in the Newark area. Since different soil tracers were used, the model coefficients cannot be compared. The V regression coefficients were similar.

The average CX model residuals were similar in both cities, both in terms of absolute mass and as a percentage of EOM. This was not the case for the DCM and ACE models. In New York City, the average DCM model residual was nonsignificant, while the ACE residual was significant. The reverse occurred in Newark. The amount of EOM not explained by the model in Newark was negligible, while the EOM residual in New York City was 29 ± 12. This could be due to different source types and strengths impacting DCM and ACE in these cities, as well as the extent of photochemical activity.

A summary of source contributions to EOM in Newark and New York City is presented in Figure 7.7. Although two different particle sizes were used, the comparison with the Newark results illustrates the major differences in source contributors to EOM in these two cities. Fuel oil burning and soil resuspension were similar in both cities. In contrast, motor vehicle and SO_4^{-2}/secondary contributions to EOM were lower in New York City both in absolute and percentage mass. These observations were probably the result of a combination of factors, such as the particle size modeled, differences in source types and strengths, seasonal differences in sample collection, and perhaps also the height of the sampling sites used for each study.

The EOM model results indicated that approximately 30% of CX and DCM mass could not be accounted for by identified sources. The CX residual is probably related to primary contributions from unidentified sources. The DCM residual could be due to sampling artifacts and/or contributions from unidentified sources. Further research is needed to characterize these residuals. Soil, fuel oil burning and motor vehicle emissions were the main source contributors to CX in Newark. Sulfate/secondary aerosol, fuel oil burning, motor vehicles and paint spraying/paint pigments were the principal contributors to DCM. ACE was accounted for by the SO_4^{-2}/secondary aerosol, soil resuspension, fuel oil burning and motor vehicle emissions. The only IPM source types that did not contribute to any EOM fraction were industrial emissions. As shown by previous EOM models in New York City, these results indicate that the three EOM fractions have somewhat different origins. Analysis of model residuals indicated variables in the data that could be potential tracers for the unidentified EOM sources. Further qualitative and quantitative characterization of these fractions is needed. This need is imperative for motor vehicle emissions, since the use of unleaded fuel is placing serious limitations on the availability of Pb as a tracer.

The pattern of EOM model residuals was similar to those of IPM at all

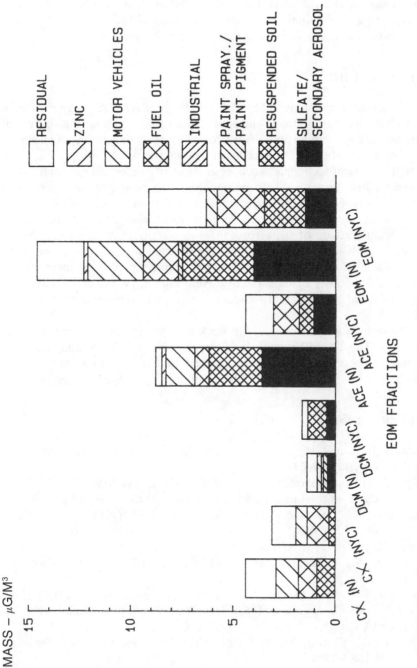

Figure 7.7. Newark—New York City source contributions to EOM.

the sampling sites. This is a strong indication that an important factor determining the residual values may be variables affecting the whole area in the study. The most likely candidate is meteorology.

CONCLUSIONS

The source apportionment models for the three ATEOS urban sites demonstrated that limitations to the application of FA to apportion sources of ambient aerosol can be partially overcome by analyzing ambient concentration data patterns and the variables affecting them, and using other traditional statistical techniques such as analysis of regression residuals. With these modifications, FA/MR methodology can be successfully applied to complex airsheds, where traditional elemental tracers, such as Pb, may be emitted by more than one source. The study also demonstrated that a significant fraction of the aerosol mass in certain urban areas may be the result of emissions from a large number of small sources rather than a few large ones. This was the case with the paint spraying/paint pigment source. Also, as previously demonstrated in New York City, the extractable fractions of EOM had different sources of origin, which may vary from city to city.

The techniques developed in this work may be applicable to similar urban airsheds. The FA/MR approach developed for the ATEOS study does not remove the need for unique tracers. The optimum number of available unique tracers to nonunique ones should be determined by future investigators.

REFERENCES

Adams, F., Dams, R., Guzman, L., and Winchester, J. W. (1977), *Atmos. Environ.*, 11:629–634.

Alpert, D. J., and Hopke, P. K. (1980), *Atmos. Environ.*, 14:1137–1146.

Alpert, D. J., and Hopke, P. K. (1981), *Atmos. Environ.*, 15:675–687.

Appel, B. R., Colodny, P., and Wesolowski, J. J. (1981), *Environ. Sci. Technol.*, 10:359–363.

Baier, R. E. (1972), *J. Geophs. Res.*, 77:5066–5075.

Bjorseth, A., Lunde, G., and Lindskog, A. (1979), *Atmos. Environ.*, 13:45–53.

Blifford, I. H., and Meeker, G. D. (1967), *Atmos. Environ.*, 2:147–157.

BMDP Statistical Software (1981), Department of Biomathematics University of California Press, Los Angeles, CA.

Blumer, M., Blumer, W., and Reich, T. (1977), *Environ. Sci. Technol.*, 11(12):1082–1084.

Butler, J. P. (1985), *Doctoral Dissertation*. New York University Medical Center, New York.

Cass, R. G., and McRae, G. J. (1983), *Environ. Sci. Technol.*, 17:129–139.

Commins, B. T. (1962), *Nat. Cancer Inst. Monogr.*, 9:225–233.

Commoner, B., Madyastha, P., Bronsdon, A., and Vithajathil, A. (1978), *J. Toxicol. Environ. Health* 4:59–77.

Cooper, J. A., and Watson, G. J. (1980), *J. Air Poll. Control Assoc.*, 30:1116–1125.

Daisey, J. M. (1980), In: *Annals N.Y. Academy of Sciences.*, 338:50–69.

Daisey, J. M. (1985), *Environ. Internal.* 11:285–291.

Daisey, J. M., and Hopke, P. K. (1984), *Proceedings of the 77th. Annual Meeting of the Air Pollut. Control Assoc.* San Francisco, CA, Paper No. 84-16.4.

Daisey, J. M., and Kneip, T. J. (1981), In: *Atmospheric Aerosol. Source/ Air Quality Relationships* ACS Symposium Series 167, 197–221.

Daisey, J. M., and Lioy, P. J. (1981), *J. Air Poll. Control Assoc.*, 31(5):567–570.

Daisey, J. M., Cheney, J. L., and Lioy, P. J. (1986), *J. Air Poll. Control Assoc.* 36:17–33.

Daisey, J.M., Hershman, R.J., and Kneip, T.J. (1982), *Atmos. Environ.*, 16(9):2161–2168.

Daisey, J. M., Leyko, M. A., and Kneip, T. J. (1979), In: *Polynuclear Aromatic Hydrocarbons*. Ann Arbor Science Publishers, Inc., Ann Arbor, Mich. 201–215.

Daisey, J. M., Lioy, P. J., and Kneip, T. J. (1985), *EPA-600-S3-85-014, PB 85-172 583-AS*. Office of Research and Development, Washington, DC.

Daisey, J. M., McCaffrey, R. J., and Gallagher, R. A. (1981), *Atmos. Environ.*, 15(8):1353–1363.

Daisey J. M., Allen, C. F., McGarrity, G., Atherholt, T., Louis, J., McGeorge, L., and Lioy, P. J. (1986), *Aerosol Sci. Technol.*, 5:69–80.

Daisey, J. M., Hawryluk, I., Kneip, T. J., Mukai, F. (1979), In: *Conference on Carbonaceous Particles in the Atmosphere*, University of California, Berkeley, CA.

Daisey, J. M., Morandi, M., Lioy, P. J., and Wolff, G. T. (1984), *Atmos. Environ.*, 18(7):1411–1419.

Dattner, S. L., and Hopke, P. K. (1983), *J. Air Pollut. Control Assoc.*, 33(4):302–303.

Delany, A. C., and Fenchelsky, S. (1976), *Soil Sci.*, 121:146–155.

DeWiest, F. (1978), *Atmos. Environ.*, 12:1705–1711.

Duce, R. A. (1978), *Pageph.*, 116:244–273.

Dzubay, T. G. (1980), In: *Aerosols: Anthropogenic and Natural, Sources and Transport*, Ann. N.Y. Acad. Sci. 338, 126–144.

Dzubay, T. J., Stevens, R. K., and L. W. Richards (1979), *Atmos. Environ.*, 13:653–659.

Feeney, P. J., Cahill, T. A. Flocchine, R. G., Eldred, R. A., Shadoan, D. J., and Dunn, T. *J. Air Pollut. Control Assoc.*, 25:1146–1147.

Fish, B. R., (1972), *Science* 175:1239–1240.

Friedlander, S. K. (1973), *Environ. Sci. Technol.*, 7:235–240.

Friedlander, S. K. (1981), In: *Atmospheric Aerosol. Source/Air Quality Relationships*, ACS Symposium Series 167, Washington, DC.

Gaarenstroom, P. D., Perone, S. P., and Moyers, J. L. (1977), *Environ. Sci. Technol.*, 11(8):795–800.

Gartrell, G., and Friedlander, S. K. (1975), *Atmos. Environ.*, 9:279–299.

Gatz, D. F. (1977), *J. Applied Meteor.*, 17:600–608.

Gordon, G. E. (1980a), *Environ. Sci. Technol.*, 14:792–800.

Gordon, G. E. (1980b), In: *Aerosols: Anthropogenic and Natural, Sources and Transport*, Ann. N.Y. Acad. Sci., 338:93–102.

Gordon, G. E. (1983), Lecture Presented at the NATO Advance Study Institute on the Chemistry of Multiphase Atmospheric Systems, Corfu, Greece.

Gorse, P. E., Salmeen, I. T., and Clark, C. R. (1982), *Atmos. Environ.* 16:1523–1528.

Greenberg, A., Bozzelli, J. W., Canova, F., Foastner E., Georgio, P., Stout, D., and Yokalyama, R. (1981), *Environ. Sci. Technol*, 15(5):566–570.

Grennberg, R. R., Gordon, G. E., Zoller, W. H., Jacko, R. B., and Mgebroff, J. S. (1983), *J. Air Pollut. Control Assoc.*, 33(10):937–943.

Greenberg, R. E., Gordon, E. G., Zoller, W. H., Jacko, R. B., Neuendorf, D. W., and Yost, K. J. (1978) *Environ. Sci. Technol.*, 12(2):1329–1332.

Harman, H. H. (1976), *Modern Factor Analysis. Third Edition*. University of Chicago Press, Chicago, IL.

Henry, R. C., and Hidy, G. M. (1979), *Atmos. Environ.*, 13:1581–1596.

Henry, R. C., and Hidy, G. M. (1982), *Atmos. Environ.*, 16:929–943.

Henry, R. C., and Lewis, C. H., Hopke, P. K., and Williamson, H. J. (1984), *Atmos. Environ.*, 18:1507–1515.

Hidy, G. M., and Friedlander, S. K. (1970) In: *Proceedings of the 2nd International Clean Air Congress*, Academic Press, New York, New York, 391–404.

Hoffman, D., and Wynder, E. L. (1977), In: *Air Pollution*. A. C. Stern, Ed., 3rd Edition, 2:361–455, Academic Press, Inc., New York.

Homoloya, J. B., and Lambert, S. (1981), *J. Air Pollut. Control Assoc.* 31:139–143.

Hopke, P. K. (1981), In: *Atmospheric Aerosol Source/Air Quality Relationships*, ACS Symposium Series 16, Washington, DC.

Hopke, P. K., Lamb, R. E., and Natusch, D. F. (1980), *Environ. Sci. Technol.*, 14:164–172.

Hopke, P. K., Gladney, E. S., Gordon, G. E., Zoller, W. H., and Jones, A. G. (1976), *Atmos. Environ.*, 10:1015–1025.

Hueper, W. C., Kotin P., Tabor, E. C., Payne, W. W., Falk, H., and Sawicki, E. (1962), *Arch. Pathol.*, 74:89–116.

Jacko, R. B., and Neuendorf, D. W. (1977), *J. Air Pollut. Control Assoc.* 27:989–994.

Jones, P. W., Wilkinson, J. E., and Hrup, P. E. (1977), *Environmental Sciences Research Laboratory, Office of Research and Development*, U.S. EPA., Research Triangle Park, NC.

Kleinman, M. T. (1977), *Doctoral Dissertation*, New York University Medical Center, New York.

Kleinman, M. T., Pasternack, B. S., Eisenbud, M., and Kneip, T. K. (1980), *Environ. Sci. Technol.*, 14:62–66.

Kneip, T. J., Mallon, R. P., and Kleinman, M. T. (1983), *Atmos. Environ.*, 17:299–304.

Konig, J. W., Funcke, E., Balfanz, B., Grosch, B., and Pott, F. (1980), *Atmos. Environ.*, 14:609–613.

Kowalczyk, G. S. (1979), *Doctoral Dissertation*. University of Maryland.

Kowalczyk, G. S., Chogoette, E. C., and Gordon, G. E. (1978), *Atmos. Environ.*, 12:1143–1153.

Lagerwerff, J. V., and Specht, A. W. (1970), *Environ. Sci. Technol.*, 4(7):583–586.

Lee, R. L., and Von Lehmdem, D. J. (1973), *J. Air Poll. Control Assoc.*, 23:853–857.

Lee, F. S., Pierson, W. R., and Ezike, J. (1980), In: *Polynuclear Aromatic Hydrocarbons. Fourth International Symposium in Analysis Chemistry and Biology* Batelle Press, Columbus, OH, pp. 543–563.

Lewis, C. W., and Macias, E. S. (1980), *Atmos. Environ.* 14:185–194.

Lioy, P. J., Mallon, R. P., Lippman, M., and Kneip, T. J. (1982) *J. Air Poll. Control Assoc.*, 32(10):1043–1047.

Lioy, P. J., Daisey, J. M., Greenberg, A., McGarrity, G., and Atherholt, T. (1984), *New Jersey Airborne Toxic Element and Organic Substances (ATEOS) Project Report*, New Jersey Department of Environmental Protection, Trenton, NJ.

Lioy, P. J., Samson, P. J., Tanner, R. L., Leaderer, B. P., Minnich, T., and Lyons, W. (1980), *Atmos. Environ.*, 14:1391–1407.

Lioy, P. J., Daisey, J. M., Atherholt, T., Bozzelli, J., Darak, F., Fisher, R., Greenberg, A., Harkov, R., Kebbekus, B., Kneip, T. J., Lewis, J., McGarrity, G., McGeorge, L., and Reiss, N. (1985), *J. Air Poll. Control Assoc.* 33:649–657.

Liu, C. K., Bradley, A. R., Severin, K. G., and Hopke, P. K. (1982), *Am. Indust. Hyg. Assoc. J.*, 43:314–318.

Malek, R. (1984), personal communication, Reichhold Chemicals, 525 N. Broadway, White Plains, NY.

Miller, W. P., and McFee, W. W. (1983), *J. of Env. Quality*, 12(1):29–33.

Miller, M. S., Friedlander, S. K., and Hidy, H. M. (1972), *J. Colloid. and Interface Sci.*, 39(1):165.

Morandi, M. T. (1985), Doctoral Dissertation, New York University, N.Y.

Morandi, M., Daisey, J. M., and Lioy, P. J. (1983), In: *Proceedings of the 76th Annual Meeting of the Air Pollut. Control Assoc.*, Atlanta, GA.

Morandi, M. T., Lioy, P. J., and Daisey, J. M. (1986), *Atmos. Environ.*, Accepted for publication.

National Academy of Sciences (1972), *Particulate Polycylic Organic Matter*. Printing and Publishing Office, Washington DC.

New York Times, April 8, 1983.

Nie, N. H., Hull, C. H., Jenkins, J. G., Steinbrenner, K., and Bent, D. H. (1975), *Statistical Package for the Social Sciences Second Edition*, McGraw Hill Company, New York, pp. 320–365.

Ondov, J. M., Zoller, W. H., and Gordon, G. E. (1982), *Environ. Sci. Technol.*, 16:318–328.

Parkinson, G. (December, 1980), *Chem. Eng. News*, 38–39.

Pierson, W. R., and Brachaczek, W. W. (1983), *Aerosol Sci. Technol.* 2:1–40.

Pitts, J. N., Jr., Grosjean, D., and Mischke, T. M. (1977), *Toxicol. Lett.*, 1:65–70.

Rasmussen, R. A. (1972), *J. Air Pollut. Control Assoc.*, 22:537–543.

Sawicki, E. (1962), *Nat. Cancer Inst.*, Monograph No. 9:201–219.

Severin, K. G., Roscoe, B. A., and Hopke, P. K. (1983), *Particulate Sci. Technol.*, 42:258–263.

Schwartz, G. P., Daisey, J. M., and Lioy, P. J. (1981), *Am. Ind. Hyg. Assoc. J.*, 42:258–263.

Shah, J. T., Kneip T. K., and Daisey, J. M. (1985), *J. Air Poll. Control Assoc.*, 35:541–544.

Stevens, R., and Pace, T. G. (1984), *Atmos. Environ.*, 18(8):1499–1506.

Stevens, R., Dzubay, T., Lewis, C., Pace, T., Currie, L., Johnson, D., Henry, R. C., Gordon, G., and Davis, B. (1982), *Mathematical and Empirical Receptor Models: Quail Roost II*. U.S. EPA Environmental Sciences Research Laboratory, Research Triangle Park, NC.

Stocks, P. (1960), *British J. Cancer*. 14:397–410.

Talcott, R., and Wei, E. (1977), *J. Nat. Cancer Inst.*, 58(2):449–451.

Thurston, G. D. (1983), Doctoral Dissertation, The Harvard School of Public Health, Boston, Mass.

U.S. Department of Commerce National Technical Information Service. (1983), *Compilation of Air Pollutant Emission Factors, Second Edition* U.S. EPA, Research Triangle Park, NC.

VanVaeck, L., and Vancauwenberghe, K. (1980), *Atmos. Environ.*, 12:2229–2339.

Von Lehmden, D. J., Jungers, R. H., and Lee, Jr., R. E. (1974), *Anal. Chem.*, 46:239–245.

Watson, J. G. (1979), Doctoral Dissertation, Oregon Graduate Center, Beaverton, OR.

Watson, J. G., (1984), *J. Air Pollut. Control Assoc.*, 34:619–623.

Watson, J. G., Henry, R. C., Cooper, J. A., and Macias, E. S. (1981), In: *Atmospheric Aerosol. Source/Air Quality Relationships*, ACS Symposium Series 167:89–106.

Weber, G. W., and Hunter, J. V. (1979), *J. Water Pollut. Control Fed.*, 51:2810–2811.

Willan, G. W., and Watts, D. G., (1978), *Technometrics* 20(4):407–412.

Winchester, J. W., and Nifong, G. D. (1971), *Water, Air, Soil Poll.* 1,50.

Yamaski, H., Kuwata, K., and Mijamoto, H. (1982), *Environ. Sci. Technol.*, 16:189–194.

CHAPTER 8

The New Jersey ATEOS Program: An Overview of Its Importance and Health/Regulatory Implications

Ronald Harkov

CHAPTER CONTENTS

The New Jersey ATEOS Program:
An Overview of Its Importance
and Health/Regulatory Implications

Introduction

Toxic air pollutants are of concern to the general public primarily due to their potential role in the induction of cancer. Recent reviews (Goldstein 1983; Harkov 1982) have presented information on a wide variety of substances with genotoxic capabilities that are found in ambient air, in addition to assessing various health impact methodologies. Besides the potential role of toxic air pollutants (TAPs) in the induction of cancer, these substances may have the ability to cause a wide variety of health-related impacts ranging from eye irritation to the induction of heart disease. Information on the role of pollutants and chronic diseases is expanding. For example, many TAPs have been shown to be teratogens (Kurzel and Cetrulo, 1981), immunosuppressors (Caren, 1981) and allergens (Kegg et al., 1977) when individuals or test animals are exposed to elevated doses of selected substances. At the present time the importance of environmentally (pollution) induced cancer is the subject of great debate (OTA, 1981). While many substances have carcinogenic properties at high dosage levels in animal studies, it is unclear what impact low-level, long-term exposures may have on selected population groups. Many recent reports (Gori, 1980; Squire, 1981; Hoel et al., 1983; Weinstein, 1983; Ames, 1983; IPC, 1984) indicate that knowledge is increasing about cancer, but this information presents little clarity in the development of regulatory policy.

The New Jersey ATEOS project can be used to give some indication of the health risks associated with atmospheric concentrations of toxic air pollutants (Harkov and Fischer, 1982), and such an analysis will be provided in this chapter. However, the project was not specifically designed to develop cause and effect relationships between specific substances or compound classes and a health response in a local population. Rather, the primary purpose of the ATEOS project was to gather high-quality information on the levels, variation, interrelationships, and sources for a select group of TAPs in New Jersey. This information provides a strong foundation to begin designing epidemiologic studies on specific TAP health effects.

With regard to the usefulness of the ATEOS project to assess the regulatory and health implications of selected TAPs, it will be necessary to review the ATEOS project goals, sampling strategies, quality assurance/quality control results, and selected monitoring data. Following this presentation, the significance of ATEOS results will be assessed, the health risks estimated, and the regulatory implications outlined. A bibliography of ATEOS research publications follows this manuscript.

OVERVIEW OF THE IMPORTANCE OF ATEOS RESULTS – MONITORING DATA ANALYSIS

ATEOS Project Goals

The basic goals for the ATEOS project were described by Harkov and Fischer (1982). These milestones included: (a) quantification of background concentrations of the selected contaminants in New Jersey, (b) developing an understanding of pollutant dynamics and distributions in the state, (c) assessments of sources contributing to measured ambient levels, (d) providing a data base to facilitate health risk assessments, and (e) establish background urban concentrations to aide in site-specific investigations.

Sampling Strategies

The ATEOS project was designed to measure both particulate and vapor-phase TAPs during the two seasons (summer, winter) that typically have the poorest overall air quality and which are associated with unique environmental conditions (space heating, photochemistry). The pollutants were assessed for their importance in New Jersey, and monitoring sites were chosen using criteria related to sources, population impacts, and typical sampling locale considerations (Harkov and Fischer, 1982; Lioy et al., 1983a). It is important to note that substances were primarily selected for inclusion in the ATEOS project based on the likelihood of their being present in the air environment and the possibility of some health consequences from low-level human exposure. The data base for assembling such a list of candidate monitoring substances was mostly based on late-1970s information. With the recent increasing information available about TAPs, perhaps different pollutant choices would have been made. For example, recent information on the carcinogenic nature of 1,3-butadiene (Huff et al., 1985) may have supported including this substance in the volatile organic compound portion of the program, particularly since it has been shown to occur in measurable quantities in urban air (Graedel, 1979).

The sampling strategy used during the ATEOS project (24 hr/day, 7 days/week for 6 weeks during four separate campaigns) allowed for certain types of comparisons in the data analysis portions of the project. These analyses include pollution episodes (Lioy et al., 1983b; 1985), day to day trends (Harkov et al., 1983) and seasonal comparisons (Lioy et al., 1983a; Greenberg et al., 1985; Harkov et al., 1984; Harkov et al., 1983). However, shorter sampling times would have facilitated the application of more detailed meteorological assessments (Delisi, 1985) and possibly better accuracy for receptor modeling (Morandi, 1985). In addition, because there was only one monitoring locale in each urban area, there is always some concern about the representativeness of the results to a portion of a city different than that surrounding the sampling sites.

The trade-offs that were available during the development of the sampling strategy phase of the program were carefully assessed. Final sampling strategy selection reflected the desire to be comprehensive and yet cost effective. Thus we did not measure all potential candidate substances nor monitor for short-sampling times in keeping with the constraints of the project.

Quality Assurance/Quality Control (QA/QC)

The ATEOS project included various quality assurance (QA) procedures that were used to help ensure that data was collected and subject to the highest possible standards for a specific measurement. Unfortunately, at the time the ATEOS project was initiated, QA guidelines for sampling and analysis for TAP were nonexistent. A recent EPA report (Riggin 1984) suggests some QA steps needed to measure organic TAP, although this document falls far short of providing adequate guidelines. In addition, until recently, very few researchers reported QA information in technical reports. Thus there is very little basis for comparison of ATEOS QA data with other air quality studies.

A summary of some QA information for selected pollutants measured during the ATEOS project are shown in Tables 8.1 and 8.2. All particulate-phase pollutant precision (P) and accuracy (A) values are based on analyses of selected National Bureau of Standards (NBS) standard materials for TM (#1648,P,A), PAH (#1647,P,A), EOM fractions (#1649,P), and SO_4^{-2}

Table 8.1. QA/QC Particulate-Phase Results from Three Urban Sites during the ATEOS Project

	IPM	FPM	SO_4^{-2}	CX	DCM	ACE	Pb	Cd	Cu	Ni	Fe	Zn	V	Mn	As
No. Possible	468	390	468	468	468	468	468	468	468	468	468	468	468	468	135
No. Taken	467	379	467	468	468	468	468	468	468	468	468	468	468	468	135
No. Analyzed	460	363	461	464	462	463	463	463	463	463	464	464	461	464	135
MDL[b]	0.270	0.270	1.300	0.109	0.236	0.423	0.021	0.0006	0.011	0.007	0.100	0.083	0.005	0.003	6×10^{-6}
NBDL	–	–	–	–	4	–	–	–	76	63	5	103	23	–	–
Precision(%)	±0.1	±0.1	±8.0	±2.1	±7.1	±9.8	±3.4	±12.0	17.0	±15.0	±2.5	±14.0	±17.0	±8.4	±4.2
Accuracy(%)	NA[a]	NA	NA	NA	NA	NA	0	–8.0	+1.6	–9.8	–17.4	+0.6	NA	NA	+0.6

	BaP	BeP	BjF	BbF	BKF	BghiP	COR	IcdP	DbahA	BaA	CcdP	BghiF
No. Possible	468	468	468	468	468	468	468	468	468	468	234	234
No. Taken	468	468	468	468	468	468	468	468	468	468	234	234
No. Analyzed	390	403	420	403	324	400	364	373	146	290	204	208
MDL[b]	0.06	0.10	0.08	0.02	0.08	0.05	0.01	0.05	0.01	0.03	0.04	0.01
NBDL	23	87	50	0	44	3	2	3	4	13	49	5
Precision(%)[c]	±6	NA	NA	±4	±5	±7	NA	±6	±8	±9	NA	NA
Accuracy(%)[c]	+1	NA	NA	–4	–3	–4	NA	+1	–3	–3	NA	NA

[a]NA = not analyzed.
[b]PAH MDLs calculated as ng/m^3; all others µg/m^3. Calculated as described in text.
[c]Precision and accuracy values based on NBS #1647 and #1648.

Table 8.2.   QA/QC Results for Selected VOC from Three Urban Sites during the ATEOS Project[a]

Analyte	No. Analyzed	NBQL[b]	Precision ($\pm$%)[c]
Vinyl chloride	218	215	–
Vinylidene chloride	179	18	58
Methylene chloride	190	11	36
Chloroform	212	24	25
Benzene	216	1	50
Carbon tetrachloride	209	79	50
Trichloroethylene	216	8	47
Toluene	216	0	49
Perchloroethylene	215	3	46
Chlorobenzene	215	8	76
Ethylbenzene	215	4	60
m, p-Xylene	215	1	57
Styrene	215	9	26
o-Xylene	213	3	10
p-Chlorotoluene	213	58	67
o-Chlorotoluene	213	16	29
p-Dichlorobenzene	211	36	53
o-Dichlorobenzene	211	32	21
Nitrobenzene	205	103	96

[a]Number of possible samples = 234. Number taken = 218 for vinyl chloride; 217 for the remaining substance.
[b]NBQL = number below quantitation limit.
[c]Based on thirty side-by-side samples with a mean individual VOC concentration of 0.67 ppbv.

(#1648,P). Some of the TM and PAH values in the standards are certified by NBS, thus facilitating accuracy estimates. For VOC measurements collected during ATEOS, certified standards materials for accuracy determinations were not available for environmental levels (ppb$_v$ or less), although U.S. EPA had recently begun a certified standard program for source level (ppm$_v$ or more) concentrations of selected VOCs (Jayanaty et al., 1983). The precision values for selected VOCs are based on approximately 30 side-by-side duplicate Tenax-GC samples.

The minimum detection limit (MDL) values for SO_4^{-2}, TM, and EOM were determined from analyses of blank filters. The method of Gabriels (1970) was used to calculate MDLs, and it should be noted that this estimate is more conservative than the U.S. EPA (1982) MDL procedure. The number of blanks varied for TM (19), EOM (20), and SO_4^{-2} (74). The MDLs for the PAHs were determined using the least sensitive (highest value) method of three studied; (a) successive dilution on the least sensitive detector using four times the signal-to-noise ratio, (b) blank quantitation at an appropriate retention time multiplied by six, (c) multiplication of the intercept of Beer's law plots by a factor of three. The VOC MDL values are based on three times the signal-to-noise ratio.

A general conclusion about the ATEOS measurements is that the inorganic pollutants were determined with a much smaller level of uncertainty than the organic contaminants, particularly the VOCs and PAHs. For the PAH measurements in the ATEOS project, NBS #1647 is the best standard for the laboratory analysis, since the laboratory that conducted the analysis (NJIT-APRL) received CX extracts for the separation and detection of these substances. Since NBS #1649 was not available until the end of the ATEOS project, the accuracy values in Table 8.1 are probably inflated. Five NBS #1649 samples analyzed by NJIT-APRL indicate an accuracy of 30–50%, with a precision similar to that of the NBS #1647 results. The higher degree of uncertainty in the PAH and VOC measurements was most likely a reflection of available collection, separation, and detection methodologies for complex environmental mixtures containing organic pollutants, and because these materials generally occur at concentrations in ambient air that are very low relative to the selectivity of current laboratory methods. Finally, a lack of certified standards precludes methods development to improve precision and accuracy estimates. Nevertheless, the level of data quality for the PAH and VOC measurements was at least as good and in most cases better than those typically found in the air pollution literature.

Pollutant Evaluation

Much of the present volume describes the results of the air sampling data collected during the ATEOS project. The purpose of the present review is to highlight the importance of particular sampling results. The entire data set results are summarized in Chapter 1, Table 1.5.

IPM/FPM

The IPM levels measured during the ATEOS project were generally low ($40\mu g/m^3$), and with the exception of extreme episode days, during which IPM concentrations reached $200\mu g/m^3$, the levels indicated that New Jersey would be in compliance with any new annual PM-10 standard proposed by the U.S. EPA (1984e). The FPM fraction included about 65–75% of the IPM measured at the four monitoring locales. Higher proportions of FPM were generally associated with periods of greater fossil fuel combustion in the winter and/or more pronounced periods of photochemical activity during the summer (Harkov et al., 1983; Lioy et al., 1983; Daisey et al., 1984).

Trace Metals

Most of the trace metals were found at very low levels compared with historical NASN data for New Jersey (unpublished U.S. EPA data). Because of this situation, and as a result of the relatively invariate nature of the day-to-day concentration trends, some trace metals measured during the ATEOS program were often unacceptable as tracers for individual IPM sources in receptor modeling studies (Harkov and Shiboski, 1985).

Sulfate

This pollutant, as $(NH_4)_2SO_4$, represented the largest fraction of IPM (20–45%) at all sites during the entire study (Tables 8.3a,b). In addition, SO_4^{-2} levels were highly correlated ($r \geq 0.70$) among all sites (Tables 8.4a,b) and the concentrations were not found to be significantly different using nonparametric analysis of variance (Table 8.5a,b). Thus the SO_4^{-2} data for New Jersey provides additional evidence for the regional nature of this portion of the acid deposition problem in the northeastern U.S.

Extractable Organic Matter

Of all the material measured during the ATEOS project, the EOM fractions were of greatest public health and regulatory concern. This conclusion is based on the fact that during the present study the EOM contained measurable quantities of mutagenic material at all locales for all campaigns, and also that the EOM represented 20–50% of the IPM mass during the entire study (Tables 8.6a,b). Comparison of the ATEOS EOM data with results from other studies is difficult because of the different solvents, extraction procedures, and sampling methods used by various investigators (Table 8.6). The levels of EOM recorded at the urban New Jersey sites were similar to those recently presented for three studies in the U.S. (Appel et al., 1976; Wesolowski et al., 1981, Daisey et al., 1982). In addition, historical benzene-soluble data (corrected to cyclohexane) from 1970 collected at NASN sites in the three urban areas used during the ATEOS program indicate that little change has occurred in the levels of these materials (Table 8.6). More broadly interpreted, this observation can be compared with the significant improvements in air quality over the last fifteen years for the criteria pollutants SO_2, TSP, CO, and Pb in the same urban areas. Thus it appears that regulatory controls and changing pollutant source composition have not resulted in much improvement in cyclohexane-soluble organic levels in New Jersey. Unfortunately, there is no way to estimate shifts in levels of the more polar DCM and ACE fractions of EOM over the same time period.

Table 8.3a.   Mass Balance of IPM at Three Urban New Jersey Sites during the 1981/1982[a] Summer ATEOS Campaigns—NEP vs EP Periods

Analyte	1981		1982	
Camden	NEP(%)	EP(%)	NEP(%)	EP(%)
$SO_4^{=}$ [b]	32	44	42	36
CX	6	4	7	4
DCM	2	1	3	3
ACE	15	15	14	15
EC[c]	6	6	3	3
TM[d]	4	2	3	2
IPM($\mu g/m^3$)	34.8	57.5	47.7	63.9
Elizabeth				
$SO_4^{=}$	44	47	36	39
CX	7	6	7	5
DCM	2	2	4	3
ACE	14	15	12	13
EC	4	4	5	5
TM	4	2	3	2
IPM($\mu g/m^3$)	28.3	53.3	42.3	71.1
Newark				
$SO_4^{=}$	28	38	29	33
CX	7	6	7	5
DCM	2	2	4	2
ACE	12	18	13	11
EC	6	6	6	6
TM	4	4	3	3
IPM($\mu g/m^3$)	39.1	68.2	51.4	84.4

[a]1981 EP dates, 7/18–21, 8/2–5, 8/10–13; 1982 EP dates, 7/10–19, 8/3–5.
[b]$SO_4^{=}$ as $(NH_4)_2SO_4$; EP = episode; NEP = non-episode
[c]Very few EC samples were analyzed: 4–5 samples/site by GM laboratory (G. Wolff) Summer 1981; 12 samples/site by Brookhaven National Laboratory (R. Tanner) Summer 1982. Thus the proportions were assumed the same during EP and NEP periods.
[d]TM = PbO, ZnO, and Fe_2O_3.

Polycyclic Aromatic Hydrocarbons

The PAH data collected during the ATEOS project represent one of the most comprehensive ambient air assessments of this pollutant class. During the present effort up to 26 PAHs, including 10 substances which are known animal carcinogens, were measured at the four monitoring locales. The

Table 8.3b.   Mass Balance of IPM at Three Urban New Jersey Sites during the 1982/1983[a] Winter ATEOS Campaigns—NEP vs EP Periods

Analyte	1982		1983	
Camden	NEP(%)	EP(%)	NEP(%)	EP(%)
SO_4^{-2b}	40	30	36	25
CX	8	9	10	12
DCM	3	3	2	3
ACE	17	22	23	25
EC[c]	4	4	4	4
TM[d]	3	3	4	4
IPM($\mu g/m^3$)	38.6	62.6	35.7	72.5
Elizabeth				
SO_4^{-2}	33	23	42	23
CX	12	17	15	15
DCM	3	4	2	3
ACE	10	19	20	23
EC	5	5	5	5
TM	3	3	4	5
IPM($\mu g/m^3$)	42.4	75.6	30.5	80.0
Newark				
SO_4^{-2}	33	21	30	22
CX	11	12	11	12
DCM	3	3	2	2
ACE	22	20	12	23
EC	6	6	6	6
TM	4	4	5	6
IPM($\mu g/m^3$)	43.3	82.2	36.7	103.5

[a]1982 EP dates, 1/19, 1/28–29, 2/5, 2/11, 2/15; 1983 EP dates, 1/21, 1/29, 2/1, 2/13–15, 2/21–22.
[b]$SO_4^=$ as $(NH_4)_2SO_4$.
[c]Very few EC measurements were taken from winter samples; 4–6 samples per site were analyzed by Brookhaven National Laboratory (R. Tanner) during the Winter 1982. Relative proportions were kept constant during NEP, EP, and different campaigns.
[d]TM = PbO, ZnO, Fe_2O_3.

PAH levels were generally below 1 ng/m³, while individual samples occasionally contained specific PAH concentrations in the 10–100 ng/m³ range. Detecting trends in PAH levels in New Jersey is difficult, although certain NASN TSP sites were used to quantify benzo(a)pyrene (BaP) levels in New Jersey during 1970. A recent New Jersey study (Harkov and Greenberg,

Table 8.4a.   Intersite Relationships[a] Between Selected Pollutants — Summers

	Summer 1981			Summer 1982		
Analyte	Newark	Elizabeth	Camden	Newark	Elizabeth	Camden
IPM						
SO_4						
CX						
DCM						
ACE						
Pb						
Mn						
Cu						
V						
Zn						
Ni						
BaP						
BghiP						
Cor						

[a]Spearman rank correlations. Sites underscored by the same line are highly correlated at the $p \geq 0.001$ level.

1985) using the same analytical and sampling procedures indicates that BaP levels have improved at Camden (0.47 vs 1.92 ng/m³) and Newark (0.71 vs 1.53 ng/m³) over this time period (Elizabeth was not sampled). This comparison can be contrasted with the apparent lack of change of ambient CX levels at three urban New Jersey sites, which is in some part related to nonpolar compounds from natural sources. Thus, using this rough comparison, long-term CX and PAH trends do not coincide.

Analysis of the PAH data indicates that this pollutant class was not correlated with CX concentrations, nor the Ames test results for the cyclohexane fraction. Only during the Summer 1981 campaign did the PAH data relate to the Ames test results for the CX fraction. Thus, analysis of the PAH, CX and Ames testing results indicates that (a) PAHs and the CX fraction are probably produced from different combustion sources and/or formed following dissimilar mechanisms within a source, (b) the atmo-

Table on page 263 should read as follows:

Table 8.4b. Qualitative Analysis of Intersite
             Relationships[a] Among Selected
             Pollutants--Winters

	Winter 1982			Winter 1983		
Analyte	Newark	Elizabeth	Camden	Newark	Elizabeth	Camden
IPM	_____			_____		
SO_4	_____			_____		
CX	_____			_____		
DCM	_____			_____		
ACE	_____			_____		
Pb	_____			_____		
Mn	_____			_____		
Cu	_____			_____		
				_____		
V	_____			_____		
Zn	_____			_____		
				_____		
Ni	_____				_____	
				_____		
Fep	_____			_____		
BaP	_____			_____		_____
				_____		
BghiP	_____			_____		
Cor	_____			_____		_____
				_____		

[a]Spearman rank correlations. Line lengths indicate
sites with highly significant correlations
($p \geq 0.001$ level).

Toxic Air Pollution
Published: 1987

ERRATA

Table on page 262 should read as follows:

Table 8.4a. Qualitative Analysis of Intersite
Relationships[a] Among Selected
Pollutants--Summers

Analyte	Summer 1981			Summer 1982		
	Newark	Elizabeth	Camden	Newark	Elizabeth	Camden
IPM						
SO$_4$						
CX						
DCM						
ACE						
Pb						
Mn						
Cu						
V						
Zn						
Ni						
BaP						
BghiP						
Cor						

[a]Spearman rank correlations. Line lengths indicate
sites with highly significant correlations
(p$\geq$ 0.001 level).

Table 8.4b.   Intersite Relationships[a] Between Selected Pollutants —
Winters

	Winter 1982			Winter 1983		
Analyte	Newark	Elizabeth	Camden	Newark	Elizabeth	Camden
IPM						
SO$_4$						
CX						
DCM						
ACE						
Pb						
Mn						
Cu						
V						
Zn						
Ni						
Fep						
BaP						
BghiP						
Cor						

[a]Spearman-rank correlations. Sites underscored by the same line are highly
correlated at the $p \geq 0.001$ level.

spheric fates of PAHs and the CX fraction as a whole are not the same, (c)
PAHs are not necessarily the only or most important class of mutagens in
the CX fraction (the CX contains a complex mixture of compounds and
chemical classes), and (d) because of the presence of mutagens within the
two more polar extracts, the PAHs only represent a small fraction of the
total airborne mutagenic burden in the ambient air in New Jersey.

Table 8.5a. Multiple Comparisons of Combined Summer Data Found Significant in One-Way Nonparametric Analysis of Variance[a]

IPM

Site[b]	12	11	10
Mean Score	71.72	92.17	115.48

CX

Site	12	11	10
Mean Score	77.85	110.95	163.71

DCM

Site	11	12	10
Mean Score	103.98	114.51	134.01

ACE

Site	11	10	12
Mean Score	97.33	126.77	128.40

Pb

Site	12	11	10
Mean Score	84.91	129.10	136.58

Mn

Site	11	12	10
Mean Score	81.74	116.26	152.99

Cu

Site	12	11	10
Mean Score	79.05	127.74	139.88

V

Site	11	12	10
Mean Score	94.98	124.80	125.49

Zn

Site	11	12	10
Mean Score	100.28	103.10	144.06

Fe

Site	12	11	10
Mean Score	87.84	102.99	159.79

Ni

Site	11	12	10
Mean Score	87.28	124.55	136.66

BaP

Site	11	12	10
Mean Score	86.48	90.81	118.20

BghiP

Site	12	11	10
Mean Score	81.72	97.91	130.31

Cor

Site	12	11	10
Mean Score	73.89	104.01	125.17

[a]One-way nonparametric ANOVA evaluated using the Chi-square approximation to the Kruskal-Wallis test for rank sums. Multiple comparisons between all pairs of mean rank sums by the Dunn large-sample approximation. Pairs of mean scores not significantly different at the 0.05 level are underscored.
[b]10 = Newark; 11 = Elizabeth; 12 = Camden.

Table 8.5b. Comparison of Combined Winter Data Found Significant in One-Way Nonparametric Analysis of Variance[a]

Cd

Site[b]	10	11	12
Mean Score	127.3	109.4	90.3

Cu

Site	11	10	12
Mean Score	130.5	117.5	101.6

Fe

Site	10	12	11
Mean Score	133.3	109.2	107.1

Mn

Site	10	12	11
Mean Score	127.3	124.6	97.5

Ni

Site	12	11	10
Mean Score	131.9	109.3	108.1

Pb

Site	10	11	12
Mean Score	131.1	121.8	96.9

Zn

Site	10	11	12
Mean Score	150.9	99.7	99.1

CX

Site	11	10	12
Mean Score	129.4	125.1	92.5

BaP

Site	10	12	11
Mean Score	111.7	86.0	90.0

[a]One-way nonparametric ANOVA evaluated using the Chi-square approximation to the Kruskal-Wallis test for rank sums. Multiple comparisons between all pairs of mean rank sums by the Dunn large-sample approximation. Pairs of mean scores not significantly different at the 0.05 level are underscored.
[b]10 = Newark; 11 = Elizabeth; 12 = Camden.

Table 8.6. Some Recent EOM Information

Site	Study	Date	Solvent	Sampler	µg/m³	Author(s)
Los Angeles, CA	ACHEX	7/73–10/73	CX	<3.5 µm	6.3	Appel et al. (1976)
			BSO	<3.5 µm	11.1	
			Meth/cform	<3.5 µm	20.6	
ContraCosta, CA	Contra Costa Study	11/78–10/79	BSO	TSP	4.9	Wesolowski et al. (1981)
NYC	–	8/77	CX	TSP	4.9	Daisey et al.(1982)
			DCM	TSP	0.9	
			ACE	TSP	7.1	
		1/78–2/78	CX	TSP	4.0	
			DCM	TSP	0.6	
			ACE	TSP	5.4	
NASN	Newark	1970	BSO	TSP	5.5[a]	NA[b]
	Elizabeth	1970	BSO	TSP	4.7	
	Camden	1970	BSO	TSP	6.1	

[a]CX has approximately 84% of the extraction efficiency of benzene, so adjusted values are 4.6 µg/m³, 3.9 µg/m³, 5.1 µg/m³ for Newark, Elizabeth, and Camden, respectively. Average CX values for these sites during ATEOS were 4.4 µg/m³, 4.1 µg/m³, and 3.0 µg/m³, respectively.

[b]Data supplied by U.S. EPA Region II Air Branch.

Mutagenicity

The use of biological assays (such as the Ames test) as part of an overall air quality study allows for a holistic assessment of the organic data set. During the ATEOS project, the mutagenicity results yielded some very important information pertaining to airborne extractable mutagens in the New Jersey environment. The three most important findings from the Ames testing portion of the ATEOS project were (a) an urban/rural (rev/m^3) difference in mutagenic activity was found during all campaigns, (b) mutagenic activity was found in all fractions at all sites during each campaign, and (c) the PAHs make up a small fraction of the total airborne mutagenic burden in the New Jersey atmosphere. An additional result which was of some interest was the role of pollution episodes in altering the mutagenic nature of the EOM. These results taken in toto indicate that we have a poor appreciation of the nature of the mutagenic substances occurring in the New Jersey atmosphere, as well as any source or environmental fate relationships to the airborne mutagenic load present at any particular point of time or space within the state.

Volatile Organic Compounds

Of all the pollutants measured in the ATEOS program, the VOCs represent the most unique data set. The VOC data established certain specific observations as key points in the understanding of the relationships of this class of pollutants to the dynamics of the New Jersey atmosphere. These observations include: (a) day-to-day changes in compound concentrations, (b) importance of pollution episodes in raising ambient VOC levels, (c) role of local sources in influencing ambient concentrations of selected VOCs, and (d) the relationship between VOCs and other noncriteria air pollutants.

ASSESSMENT OF HEALTH RISKS

General Description of Methods

The assessment of health risks associated with low-level multiple-pollutant environmental exposures is extremely complex and is subject to many uncertainties. For example, one could ask a very simple yet difficult question: What is an adverse health effect? In the present context, an adverse health effect will be defined as a biological change that reduces the level of well being or functional capacity in the human organism (Higgins, 1983). To adequately investigate the health implications of environmental chemicals, it is necessary to resolve questions related to (a) exposure, (b)

Table 8.7.   Some Uncertainties in Health Risk Assessment of Inhaled Chemicals in the Community

о Deposition Rates and Patterns
о Absorption Rates
о Metabolic Alteration
о Environmental Modification of Exposure
о Antagonism between Pollutants
о Individual Variations
о Age Variables
о Sex Differences
о Ethnic Differences
о Diet
о Extrapolation from Animals to Man

environmental and population variation, (c) health end points, and (d) extrapolation from animal to man and/or high- vs low-dose effects. Consideration of these questions can implicate an entire series of uncertainties in the overall health risk assessment (HRA) process (Table 8.7).

In general, the process of HRA requires four steps: (a) establishing that a hazard exists, (b) estimating exposure, (c) low-dose extrapolation, and (d) calculating excess risk. To date, multiple-pollutant exposures and interactions are seldom addressed, although there is substantial information concerning pollutant interactions (Goldstein, 1983). Thus the problem of HRA is commonly accomplished using a pollutant by pollutant approach. For the purpose of this discussion, the principles for exposure and risk assessment outlined by the Office of Science and Technology Policy (OSTP, 1984) for establishing health impacts of chemical carcinogens will be adopted (Table 8.8). Those principles discussed by OSTP provided a basis for the recent EPA (1984a–d) proposals for HRA of chemical carcinogens, mutagens, teratogens and exposure assessments, but tend to be more conservative than the later guidelines. While it may be beyond the scope of this discussion, it is important for regulatory agencies utilizing HRA to have the necessary technical expertise to understand the consequences of the additional principles established by OSTP (1984) for mechanisms of carcinogens, short- and long-term assays and human epidemiological studies when dealing with a specific hazard. Finally, although methods are available to assess carcinogenic risks, there are no accepted techniques to establish risks for other chronic diseases as, for example, those related to developmental abnormalities, respiratory infections, and/or neurological impairments (EPA, 1984d). Thus our hazard assessment tools need some serious improvements.

Application of available carcinogen HRA techniques was attempted for selected pollutants from the ATEOS program. Concentrations of selected particulate-phase pollutants were compared between the urban sites for the

Table 8.8. Principles of Exposure and Risk Assessments for Carcinogens[a]

Exposure Assessments

1 – Animal route should be comparable to the human route
2 – Integrated exposure assessments should be done on a case by case basis
3 – An exposure assessment should include a delimitation of strength, weakness, limitations, and assumptions
4 – An array of exposure values is preferable to a single value

Risk Assessments

1 – Weight of evidence approach should be adopted

    a – Factors to be included are:

        1 – Long-term animal studies
        2 – Epidemiological studies
        3 – In vivo, in vitro short-term bioassays
        4 – Structural activity
        5 – Metabolic differences between test animals and man
        6 – Use of more than one low-dose extrapolation model

2 – Quantification of uncertainties

    a – Statistical
    b – Models
    c – Converting animal to human data

3 – Consideration should be given to high-risk groups
4 – Qualitative consideration of the strengths and weaknesses related to hazard and exposure data, and animal extrapolation methods

[a]Adapted from OSTP (1984).

combined summer and winter campaigns, while the VOCs were compared on an individual campaign basis. Comparisons are only discussed related to potential genotoxic pollutants. For the combined summers, only significant differences were found between Cd, BaP, BkF, BgF, BbF, IcdP, COR, Ni, Pb, and the three EOM fractions (Table 8.5a). During the combined winters, Cd, BaP, CX, Ni, and Pb were found to have significant concentration differences between the three monitoring sites (Table 8.5b). For the VOCs, only trichloroethylene and perchloroethylene were found to be different between monitoring sites for the first two campaigns.

These comparisons indicate that there were very few actual differences in the concentrations of most of the genotoxic substances measured at the three urban sites. However, the urban particulate pollutant levels were significantly elevated compared to the rural site, with the exception of SO_4^{-2} and As. From these comparisons, three types of substances will be assessed for health risks associated with site-specific exposures. The selected substances will include perchloroethylene, Pb, and carcinogenic PAHs such as BaP. Monitoring data for the selected substances are presented in Chapter 1. The data utilized will allow comparisons between sites, seasons, and substances. The assessment for Pb will be focused on noncarcinogenic effects, and thus will be unique compared with the other two substances.

Hazard Identification

Perchloroethylene

This substance is a high-use chlorinated hydrocarbon and a common contaminant in urban air (EPA, 1982a). Perchloroethylene is used primarily in textile cleaning and to a lesser extent as a metal degreaser. In a single animal bioassay, perchloroethylene has been shown to be a liver carcinogen, while other studies have produced negative results (EPA, 1982). Although this substance can have other impacts on human health, such as teratogenicity, neurotoxicity, and liver and kidney dysfunction, the primary concern is as a carcinogenic agent. Because perchloroethylene is lipophilic and has been shown to concentrate in mothers' milk, young children are perhaps a high-risk group.

Benzo(a)pyrene

The polycyclic aromatic hydrocarbons include the largest number of documented animal carcinogens and suspected human carcinogens. Epidemiological studies of coke oven and gas retort workers have linked lung cancer mortality incidence to the extent of benzo(a)pyrene (BaP) exposure (CAG, 1978). IARC (1982) lists soots and tars as human carcinogens, but the evidence for BaP is inadequate. Since soots and tars are complex mixtures containing many substances and various proportions of PAH compounds, it is very difficult to ascribe the carcinogenic potential of these materials to any compound or class of substances.

Lead

Lead is a well documented human toxicant (EPA, 1983). Some of the health consequences of Pb exposure include dysfunction of the renal, blood, and neurological systems. Recently a review has summarized much of the important environmental data related to Pb (EPA, 1983). From most past Pb studies, it is clear that young children are a high-risk group with regard to environmental exposures.

Table 8.9. Exposure Assessment Assumptions for Air Pollutants

Parameter	Adult	Child
Weight	70 kg	16 kg
Exposure Time	70 yr	2 yr
Breathing Rate	20 m³/day	7 m³/day[a]
Deposition Rates	See tables or text	
I/O	See text	

[a]Assumes tidal volume of 10 mL/kg, 30 breaths per minute.

Estimation of Exposure

Most ambient air pollution measurements may not be an adequate description of individual exposures (Spengler and Soczak, 1984). Individual exposures to air pollutants are affected by the person's level of activity, proximity to sources, time spent indoors vs outdoors, occupation, and specific characteristics related to inhalation patterns (Yocum, 1982; Moghissi et al., 1980; EPA 1982b). Uncertainties exist for any exposure assessment, and some of these items include relationships of pollutant concentration to biological dose, impact on high-risk populations, and alternate routes of exposure.

The basic approach recommended by the Carcinogen Assessment Group (1980) and followed here is to compare exposure in carcinogenic assessments using a 70-kg man, over a 70-year period and assuming a 20-m³ breathing rate per day. An additional method will be described for a high-risk population (children) in the Pb assessment. To help improve the accuracy of the present exposure assessment, estimates are made of pollutant deposition and/or absorption in the respiratory system and percentage of time spent indoors. From these figures an exposure estimate can be made for the selected substances (Table 8.9).

It is apparent that the exposure assessments described here are very crude approximations. Lifetime breathing rates should be described as a function of body weight/day, and deposition should include consideration of deposition area per unit body weight as a person ages. An obvious additional shortcoming in the present assessment includes the limitation of discussion to a single exposure route. Finally, personal monitoring could better establish actual exposure relationships than those developed using stationary sampling sites.

Table 8.10.   Human Lung Absortion Rates for Selected VOCs

Pollutant	Rate	Author
Perchloroethylene	39%	Monster et al. (1979)
Trichloroethylene	36–75%	EPA (1982)
Dichloromethane	31–75%	EPA (1982)
Toluene	40–60%	EPA (1982)
Benzene	46%	Snyder et al. (1978)

Perchloroethylene

Most VOCs appear to have human lung absorption rates of 30–60% when individuals are exposed to high concentrations during short exposure periods (Table 8.10). While human perchloroethylene lung absorption rates have been infrequently measured, the estimate from Monster et al. (1979) is approximately 39% for individuals at rest. While low-level exposures to perchloroethylene may not follow absorption and clearance patterns observed by these researchers, in the absence of additional information the above estimate will be used. As a basis of comparison, CAG has utilized a 50% absorption rate for perchloroethylene (EPA, 1982). The deposition rate is assumed to be 100%. The amount of time spent indoors for the assessment will be adopted from Dockery and Spengler (1980), that is, 83% for winter and 75% for summer. Differences between indoor/outdoor (I/O) levels of perchloroethylene are not known, although it should be pointed out that some common over-the-counter consumer items contain substantial quantities of this solvent. In the absence of this information, indoor levels were assumed to be 80% of the outdoor concentration. This estimation is taken from the Six City Study and is based on I/O ratios (0.7–0.8) for SO_2 in low-pollution areas (Spengler et al., 1979). In the EPA Total Exposure Assessment Methodology the source of indoor exposure was from dry cleaned clothing (Pellizarri, 1984). Since concentrations of perchloroethylene will generally be low, and since SO_2 and perchloroethylene primarily are associated with outdoor pollution sources, this assumption is somewhat reasonable.

The exposure model for perchloroethylene and for the other substances is:

Dose (mg/kg/day) = Concentration × breathing rate × 1/bodyweight × Deposition Rate × Absorption rate × I/O × Duration of Exposure

Because perchloroethylene levels were similar between summer and winter, the mean values were used to estimate annual exposure. Exposure estimates are shown in Table 8.11.

Table 8.11. Exposure Estimates for Three Selected Pollutants from the ATEOS Program

Perchloroethylene

	Annual (mg/kg/day)
Camden	0.178×10^{-4}
Newark	0.280×10^{-4}
Elizabeth	0.262×10^{-4}

BaP/PAHs

		Summer	Winter	Annual (mg/kg/day)
Camden	BAP	1.1×10^{-8}	6.5×10^{-8}	3.8×10^{-8}
	PAHs	8.8×10^{-8}	39.7×10^{-8}	24.2×10^{-8}
Newark	BaP	1.5×10^{-8}	8.7×10^{-8}	5.1×10^{-8}
	PAHs	11.4×10^{-8}	56.3×10^{-8}	33.8×10^{-8}
Elizabeth	BaP	1.0×10^{-8}	7.1×10^{-8}	4.0×10^{-8}
	PAHs	7.1×10^{-8}	50.5×10^{-8}	28.8×10^{-8}
Ringwood	BaP	0.3×10^{-8}	1.8×10^{-8}	1.1×10^{-8}
	PAHs	3.2×10^{-8}	14.8×10^{-8}	8.7×10^{-8}

Pb

	µg/m³/day	mg/kg/day
Camden	0.222	1.8×10^{-5}
Newark	0.303	2.4×10^{-5}
Elizabeth	0.275	2.2×10^{-5}
Ringwood	0.092	0.7×10^{-5}

Table 8.12. Concentrations (Geometric Mean) of BaP and Seven Carcinogenic PAHs[a] at Four New Jersey Sites

Site		Summer '81	Winter '82	Summer '82	Winter '83
	(ng/m^3)				
Newark	BaP	0.23	1.63	0.21	1.05
	PAH	1.71	9.59	1.54	5.17
Elizabeth	BaP	0.14	1.01	0.14	0.96
	PAH	0.95	10.32	1.09	3.69
Camden	BaP	0.20	0.87	0.11	0.94
	PAH	1.75	6.57	0.77	4.45
Ringwood	BaP	0.06	0.32	0.04	0.17
	PAH	0.43	2.83	0.49	1.13

[a]BaP, BbF, BjF, BaA, ICDP, DbaeP, and DbacA.

BaP and Selected PAHs

Human lung absorption rates for BaP or selected PAHs are unknown, although it has been shown that the nature of the absorbent the compounds are associated with has a great impact on lung absorption in animal exposure models (NAS, 1983). Most PAHs are found in the fine particle-size range ($\leq 2.5\mu$) (Miguel and Friedlander, 1978; Van Vaeck et al., 1979), thus in the absence of specific absorption information (assumed 100%) only deposition rates for fine particles will be utilized. Since a large portion (at least 80%) of the PAH appear to be less than 1.5 μ in size (Van Vaeck et al., 1979), deposition will be primarily in the pulmonary region of the lung. Deposition rates for particles $\leq 1.5\mu$ in the pulmonary regions of the lung are in the range of 20–30% (Raabe, 1979). For the purpose of this report deposition rates will be set at 30%. Finally, a 70% I/O ratio for fine particulate matter will be used (Dockery and Spengler, 1980), while the percentage of time indoors will be the same as for perchloroethylene. Table 8.12 presents concentrations of BaP and seven carcinogenic PAHs measured during the ATEOS project, and Table 8.11 includes the exposure estimates for these substances.

Lead

Without question, Pb is a pollutant with multiple exposure pathways. Primary inhalation exposure results from motor vehicle emissions and, to a lesser extent, from municipal solid waste incinerators and various nonferrous metal industries. A recent review (EPA, 1983) provides basic exposure relationships between lead inhalation and blood concentrations for children. Population-based studies indicate that at Pb levels ≤ 3.2 $\mu g/m^3$ and blood levels $\leq$ 30 μg/dL, the blood lead inhalation relationship is linear, with a value of approximately 2. It can be assumed that most of the Pb measured during the ATEOS program was inhalable. The I/O relationships are assumed to be similar to BaP. Lead absorption by adult lungs has been shown to vary from 20 to 80%, and for our purposes the levels will be set at the upper portion of this range, since children are thought to have about a twofold greater Pb absorption rate than adults (EPA, 1983). Exposure estimates are shown in Table 8.11.

Quantitative Estimates of Risk

The assessment of risks from exposures to carcinogenic agents is normally done by utilization of some numerical models that relate animal or human occupational studies to low-dose environmental exposures (Fishbein, 1980). Levels of uncertainty for each model proposed in the literature are unknown, thus placing a large degree of dubiety on a particular assessment. The purpose of this assessment is not to present the pros and cons of various models, although it is important that regulators and others using these tools have a qualitative understanding of their limitation as they pertain to specific substances. The values established by the U.S. EPA CAG are utilized for the perchloroethylene and PAH assessment. The CAG utilizes the linear, multistage, nonthreshold model for low-dose extrapolation. This model is one of the most conservative, that is, it can lead to a higher level of risk for each estimated exposure than other models, such as the Weibull or log-probit (Fishbein, 1980).

Perchloroethylene

The results of a mouse study indicated that high-level exposure to perchloroethylene led to elevated liver cancer incidence in male mice. The slope for the carcinogenic potency for humans is 5.31×10^{-2} (mg/kg/day), and the calculated risks are shown in Table 8.13. It is important to note that because perchloroethylene has failed to elicit a carcinogenic response in other assays, it is generally considered a suspect carcinogen. In addition, the potency of perchloroethylene is considered much lower (by as much as three orders of magnitude) than other known animal carcinogens, such as BaP. The risks associated with perchloroethylene exposure at the three urban sites were in the range of 1×10^{-6}, which is generally considered to be an acceptable leve of risk for exposures to environmental carcinogens.

Table 8.13. Estimated Risks for Three Selected Pollutants from the ATEOS Program

Perchloroethylene

	Cancer Risk
Camden	1.0×10^{-6}
Newark	1.4×10^{-6}
Elizabeth	1.5×10^{-6}

BaP/PAH

BaP

	Annual[a]	Annual[b]
Camden	0.4×10^{-4}	3.1×10^{-4}
Newark	0.6×10^{-4}	4.5×10^{-4}
Elizabeth	0.5×10^{-4}	3.3×10^{-4}
Ringwood	0.1×10^{-4}	0.8×10^{-4}

PAHs

	Annual[a]	Summer[a]	Winter[a]
Camden	2.5×10^{-4}	0.9×10^{-4}	4.0×10^{-4}
Newark	3.3×10^{-4}	1.2×10^{-4}	5.4×10^{-4}
Elizabeth	2.9×10^{-4}	0.7×10^{-4}	5.1×10^{-4}
Ringwood	0.9×10^{-4}	0.3×10^{-4}	1.5×10^{-4}

Pb

	Blood Pb (µg/dL)	% of mean U.S. Blood Pb level[c]	% total daily dose[d]
Camden	0.444	4.0	0.5
Newark	0.606	4.3	0.6
Elizabeth	0.550	4.0	0.6
Ringwood	0.184	1.3	0.2

[a]Based on estimated animal risk for BaP, 3.5×10^{-4}/ng/m^3; PAHs are assumed equal potency to BaP.
[b]Based on estimated human risk for BaP, 2.8×10^{-3}/ng/m^3.
[c]Assume national blood Pb levels for children are 14 µg/dL (EPA, 1983).
[d]Based on a comparison of data in Table 8.13 with daily Pb dose of children (61 µg/Pb/day), assuming 2-year-old weighing 16 kg, the mean Pb dose was set at 3.8×10^{-3} mg/kg/day.

BaP/PAHs

There is more evidence for the carcinogenicity of BaP in animals than perhaps any other carcinogen. In human epidemiological studies of lung cancer incidence, PAHs, expressed as BaP, have been shown to have a slope of $2.8 \times 10^{-3}/ng/m^3$. Animal studies with BaP alone led to a slope of $3.5 \times 10^{-4}/ng/m^3$. Thus the results from the animal experiments suggest that BaP can account for roughly 13% of the total risk associated with PAH exposures in the epidemiological studies.

Since the BaP/PAH results show clear-cut urban/rural and seasonal differences, this class of pollutant is amenable to a multiple comparison of risks (Table 8.13). On an annual basis, the health risks are in the range of 1×10^{-4} to 1×10^{-5}, with urban risk levels four to five times rural values. Also, in a comparison of estimated exposure levels, annual total carcinogenic PAH risk values are found to be 6 to 9 times BaP values alone, while winter risk levels are 4 to 7 times summer values.

These estimates suggest that BaP/PAH levels at all sites in New Jersey pose an unreasonable level of risk to the population in the state. However, it is probable that BaP has become less acceptable as a carcinogenic surrogate for extractable organic matter (EOM) exposures as air quality has improved. The air pollution matrix that BaP is now measured in is far different than that which existed twenty years ago or in past occupational studies. Thus risks determined for high-level exposures to pollutant mixtures (as in the workplace) and then extrapolated to low-level exposures in the environment may be very inaccurate. There are additional observations from this assessment that are important. First, while the numerical risk may not be accurate, BaP/PAHs (and probably EOM as a whole) have the highest level of attributed risk of all classes of materials measured in the ATEOS project. Second, BaP appears to correlate fairly well with the total carcinogenic PAH levels at each site. Thus, it may be an accurate surrogate for this class of materials in cities with similar combustion sources. Finally, health assessments based on short sampling periods may under- or over-estimate exposures and risks by a large margin.

Lead

Utilizing a blood Pb exposure assessment for 2-year-old children, the dose received from airborne Pb at the four sites was very small, ~1–4% of the total daily blood burden. Also, it was estimated that the ambient Pb levels represented less than 1% of the total daily Pb dose for the 2-year-old children near these monitoring sites. Thus the present Pb levels are not likely to have any significant impact on children in the urban areas studied during the ATEOS project.

REGULATORY IMPLICATIONS

The regulatory implications of the ATEOS project can be described in three general areas; survey, assessment and enforcement, and rule-making. Each of the tasks will have broad impacts on the air pollution control activities of the New Jersey Department of Environmental Protection (DEP).

Survey

Inhalable particulate matter is made up primarily of three fractions, SO_4^{-2}, carbon, elemental, and crustal factors. The DEP needs to develop a comprehensive inventory of in-state sources of SO_4^{-2} and particulate carbon-related pollutants. These surveys will serve two purposes: (a) provide the necessary information for rule-making if the state is out of compliance for any proposed inhalable particulate (PM-10) standard, (b) with the assumption that the state will meet any proposed PM-10 standard, DEP will have the ability to reduce the environmental and health consequences of locally emitted acidic and carbonaceous aerosols in the state.

Assessment

The ATEOS project highlighted certain limitations in our knowledge of TAP. Perhaps the greatest limitation was the lack of emission measurements for specific substances or classes of substances. Thus it appears that a comprehensive source assessment program is needed, particularly for trace metals, EOM, and SO_4^{-2}. Based on the data produced on genotoxic agents in the EOM, ambient monitoring studies should be directed to define the nature of mutagenic material in the EOM. The VOC data assessment indicated that near source-based ambient monitoring programs are necessary to adequately define the extent of the population exposure problem associated with this pollutant class. Also, better exposure assessment data are needed to fine tune quantitative health evaluations. Finally, a trends network for TAP should be established at a minimum number of sites in the state and elsewhere so that the DEP and other agencies will be better able to determine the level of success associated with any new regulatory program designed to control TAP. At the present time, the DEP has initiated a limited number of projects directed at all of the above points, but a higher level of effort is needed to adequately address these issues.

Enforcement and Rule Making

The ATEOS project results do not specifically lead to a series of rule-making recommendations. Generally, levels of most types of TAPs measured were low enough to dismiss the notion of a statewide air toxics problem. The problems are probably directed toward situations in which a population subgroup is in close proximity to a source or group of sources (Lioy and Daisey, 1986). However, through the development of a source survey and assessment and an ambient monitoring program for carbon-containing particulates, it may ultimately be necessary to develop a rule for these materials. At this particular point in time, it would be premature to outline any structure for such a rule. Finally, it was apparent by the occasional spikes in TAP levels that a better enforcement system is necessary for this class of pollutants. Perhaps the most pressing need in this area is the development of monitoring tools for enforcement investigations. With simple, field-orientated instruments, DEP enforcement personnel will be able to determine whether or not an operation is in compliance with their permit for specific TAPs.

CONCLUSION

The New Jersey project has provided a substantial amount of information related to TAPs in the environment. In toto, this project developed a foundation for future TAP research effects in New Jersey and elsewhere in the U.S. Clearly, the many uncertainties concerned with the measurement, sources, human exposures, and risks of TAPs place a series of caveats in the study of this class of contaminants. Yet if we are to better understand the role of air pollution in human health, it is necessary to rigorously explore this research area. The interpretation of the ATEOS project results has led to some broad health and regulatory implications from this study. To make certain that these implications are seriously addressed on a state or federal level it will be important to present the data in peer-reviewed scientific journals, and also to present the study results in a form that is useful to policymakers. This summary chapter is an attempt to address the latter point. As is obvious from this book as a whole, data from the ATEOS project are well represented in the peer-reviewed air pollution literature.

ACKNOWLEDGMENT

The ATEOS project was funded in its entirety by the New Jersey Department of Environmental Protection. The views expressed by the authors do not necessarily reflect those of the Department and have not been officially reviewed by an internal publication board.

REFERENCES

Ames, B. N. (1983), *Science* 221:256.

Appel, B. R. et al. (1976), *Environ. Sci. Technol.* 10:359.

CAG. (1978), Carcinogen Assessment Groups Preliminary Report on EOM Exposures. Unpublished U.S. EPA Report, 15 pp.

CAG. (1980) Carcinogen Assessment Groups Method for Determining the Unit Risk Estimate for Air Pollutants. Unpublished U.S. EPA Report, 17 pp.

Caren, L. D. (1981), *Bioscience* 31:502.

Daisey, J. M., et al. (1984), The Mutagenic Activity of the Ambient Aerosol during Summertime: A Comparison of Photochemical Pollution Episodes with Other Periods. Proceedings of 77th annual APCA meeting, San Francisco, CA, #84-801.

Daisey, J. M., et al. (1982), *Atmos. Environ.* 16:2161.

Delisi, M. P. (1985), The Use of Meteorological Data in Locating Pollutant Sources. MS Thesis, Rutgers University, 120 pp.

Dockery, D. W., and J. D. Spengler. (1981), *JAPCA* 31:153.

EPA. (1984a), Proposed guidelines for Carcinogenic Risk Assessment, *Federal Register* 49:462941.

EPA. (1984b), Proposed Guidelines for Exposure Assessment. *Federal Register* 49:46304.

EPA. (1984c), Proposed Guidelines for Mutagenicity Risk Assessment. *Federal Register* 49:46314.

EPA. (1984d), Proposed guidelines for health assessment of suspect developmental toxicants. *Federal Register* 49:46324.

EPA. (1984e), Proposed revisions to national ambient air quality standards for particulate matter to control particles 10 micrometer less *Federal Register* 49:10408.

EPA. (1983), Air Quality Criteria for Lead. EPA 600/8-83-028A.

EPA. (1982a), Health Assessment Document for Tetrachloroethylene. EPA-600/8-82-005.

EPA. (1982b), Air Quality Criteria for Particulates and Sulfur Oxides. EPA-600/8-82-029a,b,c.

Fishbein, L. (1980), *J. Environ. Path. Toxicol.* 5:1275.

Goldstein, B. D. (1983), *JAPCA* 33:454.

Gori, G. B. (1980), *Science* 208:256.

Graedel, T. E. (1978), Chemical Compounds in the Atmosphere. Academic Press, NY 440 pp.

Greenberg, A., et al. (1985), *Atmos. Env.* 19:1325.

Harkov, R., and Shiboski, S. (1986), *J. Environ. Sci. Health.* 21:177.

Harkov, R., et al. (1984), *STOTEN* 38:259.

Harkov, R., et al. (1983a), *JAPCA* 33:1177.

Harkov, R., et al. (1983b), Comparisons between Summer and Winter

Inhalable Particulate Matter, Fine Particulate Matter, Particulate Organic Matter and Sulfate Levels at Urban and Rural Locations in New Jersey. In Proceeding Meas. and Mont. of Noncrit. Poll. in Air. APCA-Publ. SP-50. 538pp.

Harkov, R. (1982), *STOTEN* 26:67.

Harkov, R., and Fischer, R. (1982), Development and Initiation of an Integrated State Monitoring Program for Airborne Toxic Substances. Proceedings 75th annual APCA meeting, New Orleans, La. #82-1.1.

Higgins, I. T. T. (1983), *JAPCA* 33:661.

Hoel, D. G., et al. (1983), *Science* 219:1032.

Huff, T. E., et al. (1985), *Science* 227:548.

IARC. (1982), Chemicals, Industrial Processes and Industries Associated with Cancer in Humans. IARC, Lyons, France, Supp #4,292pp.

IPC. (1984), *Science* 225:682.

Jayanaty, R. V. M., et al. (1983), *Environ. Sci. Technol.* 17:257A.

Keg, M. M., et al. (1977), Occupational diseases: A guide to their recognition. US-DHEW, DHS-NIOSH Pub. No. 77-181.

Kurzel, R. B., and Cetrulo, C. L. (1981), *Environ. Sci. Technol.* 15:626.

Lioy, P. J., et al. (1985), *Atmos. Environ.* 19:429.

Lioy, P. J., et al. (1983a), *JAPCA* 33:649.

Lioy, P. J., et al. (1983b), *Atmos. Environ.* 17:2321.

Lioy, P. J. and J. M. Daisey (1986), Env. Sci. and Tech., 35, 8–15.

Miguel, A. H., and Friedlander, S. V. (1978), *Atmos. Environ.* 12:2407.

Moghissi, A. A., et al. (1980), Methodology for Environmental Human Exposure and Health Risk Assessment. In, Dynamics, Exposure and Hazard Assessment of Toxic Chemicals. Ann Arbor Press, Mi. 496 pp.

Monster, A. C., et al. (1979), *Int. Arch. Occup. Environ. Health* 42:311.

Morandi, M. T. (1985), Development of Source Apportionment Models for Inhalable Particulate Matter and Its Extractable Organic Fractions in Urban Areas of New Jersey. Doctoral dissertation, NYU Medical Center, NY, 286 pp.

OSTP. (1984), Chemical Carcinogens: Notice of Review of the Science and Its Associated Principles. *Federal Register* 49:21594.

OTA. (1981), Technologies in Determining Cancer Risks from the Environment. OTA, U.S. Congress 240 pp.

Pellizzari, E. D., et al. (1984), "Total Exposure Assessment Methodology (TEAM) Study: First Season—Northern New Jersey," Report RTI/2392/03-035; Research Triangle Institute, Research Triangle Park, N.C.

Raabe, O. G. (1979), Deposition and Clearance of Aerosols. UCD 472-503.

Riggin, R. M. (1984), Compendium of Methods for the Determination of Toxic Organic Compounds in Ambient Air. EPA-600/4-84-041.

Spengler, J. D., et al. (1979), *Environ. Sci. Technol.* 13:1276.

Squire, R. A. (1981), *Science* 214:877.

Van Vaeck, L., et al. (1979), *Environ. Sci. Technol.* 13:1494.

Weinstein, M. C. (1983), *Science* 221:17.
Wesolowski, J. J., et al. (1981), *J. Aer. Sci* 12:208.
Yocum, J. E. (1982), *JAPCA* 32:500.

APPENDIX
PUBLICATIONS FROM THE ATEOS PROJECT

1. Lioy, P. J., et al. (1983), The New Jersey project on Airborne Toxic Elements and Organic Species (ATEOS): A Summary of the 1981 Summer and 1982 Winter Studies. *JAPCA* 33:649–657.
2. Lioy, P. J., Daisey, J. M., Reiss, N. M., and Harkov, R. (1983), Characterization of Inhalable Particulate Matter, Volatile Organic Compounds and Other Chemical Species Measured in Urban Areas in New Jersey, I. Summer Episodes. *Atmos. Environ.* 17:2321–2330.
3. Harkov, R., Kebbekus, B., Bozzelli, J. W., and Lioy, P. J. (1983), Measurement of Selected Volatile Organic Compounds at Three Locations in New Jersey during the Summer Season. *JAPCA* 33:1177–1183.
4. Harkov, R., Daisey, J. M., and Lioy, P. J. (1983), Comparisons between Summer and Winter Inhalable Particulate Matter, Fine Particulate Matter, Particulate Organic Matter and Sulfate Levels at Urban and Rural Locations in New Jersey. In: *Proceedings of Conference on Measurement and Monitoring for Non-Criteria (Toxic) Contaminants in Air.* APCA Publ. SP-50. 538 pp.
5. Daisey, J. M., Morandi, M., Wolff, G. T., and Lioy, P. J. (1984), Regional and Local Influences on the Nature of Airborne Particulate Organic Matter at Four Sites in New Jersey during the Summer. *Atmos. Environ.* 18:1411–1419.
6. Harkov, R., Greenberg, A., Darack, F., Daisey, J. M., and Lioy, P. J. (1984), Summertime Variations in Polycyclic Aromatic Hydrocarbons at Four Sites in New Jersey. *Environ. Sci. Technol.* 18:287–291.
7. Harkov, R., Kebbekus, B., Bozzelli, J. W., Lioy, P. J., and Daisey, J. M., (1984), Comparison of Winter and Summer Volatile Organic Compound Levels at Urban New Jersey Sites. *Sci. Tot. Environ.* 38:259–274.
8. Lioy, P. J., Kneip, T. J., and Daisey, J. M. (1984), The Measurement of Particulate Organic Matter in a Rural Area of the Northeastern United States, *J. Geophys. Res.* 89:1355–1359.
9. Lioy, P. J., Daisey, J. M., Greenberg, A., and Harkov, R. (1985), A Major Wintertime (1983) Pollution Episode: Analyses of the Accumulation and Spatial Distribution Inhalable Particulate Matter, Extractable Organic Matter and Other Species. *Atmos. Environ.* 19:429–436.
10. Greenberg, A., Darack, F., Harkov, R., Daisey, J. M. and Lioy, P. J.

(1984), Comparison of Seasonal Differences in Polycyclic Aromatic Hydrocarbon Levels in New Jersey. *Atmos. Environ.* 19:1325–1339.

11. Harkov, R., and Shiboski, S. (1985), Can Extractable Organic Matter be Used as a Motor Vehicle Tracer for Multivariate Receptor Models? *J. Environ. Sci. Health* 21:177–190.

12. Harkov, R., Lioy, P. J., Daisey, J. M., Greenberg, A., Darack, F., Bozzelli J., and Kebbekus, B. (1986), Quality Control for Non-Criteria Air Pollutants. Results from the ATEOS Project. *JAPCA* 36:388–392.

13. Lioy, P. J., Avdenko, M. A., Harkov, R., Atherholt, T., and Daisey, J. M. (1985), A Pilot Indoor-Outdoor Study of Organic Particulate Matter and Particulate Mutagenicity. *JAPCA* 35:653–657.

14. Atherholt, T. B., et al. (1985), Mutagenicity Studies of New Jersey Air Particulate Extracts. In: Short-Term Bioassays in the Analysis of Complex Environmental Mixtures *IV*, Eds., Waters, M. D. et al., Plenum Press, New York, pp. 211–231.

15. Harkov, R. (1983), Toxic Air Pollutants in New Jersey. Office of Science and Research. New Jersey Department of Environmental Protection, 49 pp.

16. Morandi, M. (1985), Development of Source Apportionment Models for Inhalable Particulate Matter and It's Extractable Organic Fractions in Urban Areas in New Jersey. PhD Thesis, NYU Medical Center, New York, New York. 286 pp.

17. Butler, J. P. (1985), Separation and Characterization of Biologically Significant Chemical Classes in Airborne Particulate Organic Matter. PhD Thesis, NYU Medical Center, New York, New York. 144 pp.

18. Lioy, P. J., and Daisey, J. M. (1986), Airborne Toxic Elements and Organic Substances. *Environ. Sci. Technol.* 20:8–14.

19. Daisey, J. M., Allen, C. F., McGarrity, G., Atherholt, T., Louis, J., L. McGeorge, and Lioy, P. J. (1986), Effects of Filter Type or the Organic Composition and Mutagenicity of Inhalable Particulate Matter. *Aer. Sci. Technol.* 5:69–80.

20. Daisey, J. M., Kebbekus, B., Bozzelli, J., and Lioy, P. J. (1986), Exploratory Application of Factor Analysis to Volatile Organic Compound Concentration Data from Urban Sites in New Jersey. In: *Transactions, Methods for Source Apportionment, Real World Issues and Applications*, TR-5, T.G. Pace, Ed., Air Pollution Control Association, Pittsburgh, PA. pp. 149–160.

21. Butler, J. P., T. J. Kneip and J. M. Daisey. (In Press) An Investigation of Interurban Variation in the Chemical Composition and Mutagenic Activity of Airborne Particulate Organic Matter Using an Integrated Chemical Glass/Bioassay System. *Atmos. Environ.*

22. Morandi, M. T., J. M. Daisey and P. J. Lioy (In Press) Development of a Modified Factor Analysis/Multiple Regression Model to Apportion Suspended Particulate Matter in a Complex Airshed. *Atmos. Environ.*

List of Abbreviations

AAS — atomic absorption spectrometry

ACE — acetone-soluble fraction of particulate matter (polar organics)

ACN — acrylonitrile

ALK — alkylating activity of the acetone-soluble fraction

ANTH — anthracene

APC — absolute principal component(s)

ATEOS — Airborne Toxic Elements and Organic Species Study

BaA — benzo(a)anthracene

BaP — benzo(a)pyrene

BbF — benzo(b)fluoranthene

BENZ — benzene

BjF — benzo(j)fluoranthene

BkF — benzo(k)fluoranthene

BghiP — benzo(ghi)perylene

BaP — benzo(a)pyrene

BeP — benzo(e)pyrene

BSO — benzene-soluble organics

C — cold period, October to March

C — coastal area of New Jersey

CcdP — cyclopenta(cd)pyrene

CCl₄ — carbon tetrachloride

CEB — chemical element balance

CFOR — chloroform

CHRY — chrysene

CLBZ — chlorobenzene

CMB — chemical mass balance

COH — coefficient of haze

COODD — cooling degree days

CO_{max} — daily maximum of 1 hr averages of carbon monoxide concentrations

COR — coronene

CPM — coarse particulate matter

CX — cyclohexane-soluble fraction of particulate matter (nonpolar organics)

CX(Son) — cyclohexane-soluble fraction of particulate matter determined by sonication extraction

CYC — cyclohexane

DBacA — dibenz(a,c)anthracene

DBaePY — 1,2,4,5-dibenzopyrene

DBahA — 1,2,5,6-dibenzanthracene

DCE — 1,2-dichloroethane

DCM — dichloromethane-soluble fraction of particulate matter (moderately polar organics)

DIOX — dioxane

DMSO — dimethyl sulfoxide

DNA — deoxyribonucleic acid

EC — elemental carbon

ECD — electron capture detector

EOM — extractable particulate organic matter

EP — episode period

ETBR — 1,2-dibromoethane

ETBX — ethylbenzene

FA — common factor analysis

FA/MR — factor analysis/multiple regression

FeR — ambient concentration of Fe from paint spraying/paint pigment sources

FID — flame ionization detector

FPM — fine particulate matter (D_{50} = 2.5 μm)

GC — gas chromatography

HEADD — heating degree days

IPM — inhalable particulate matter

HPLC — high-performance liquid chromatography

IcdP — indeno(1,2,3-cd)pyrene

IPM — inhalable particulate matter (D_{50} = 15 μm)

MAXT — maximum daily temperature (°F)

MECL — methylene chloride (gaseous phase)

M_G — geometric mean concentration

MINT—minimum daily temperature (°F)

MMAD—mass median aerodynamic diameter

MMT—methylcyclopentadienyltricarbonyl

MnR—ambient concentration of residual Mn, i.e., Mn which could not be attributed to any known source

MS—mass spectrometry

MX—m-xylene

N—Newark

NBLD—number of samples below the detection limit

NBQL—number of samples below the quantitation limit

NBS SRM—National Bureau of Standards Standard Reference Material

NBZ—nitrobenzene

NEI—northeastern industrial area of New Jersey

NEP—nonepisode period

Nitro-PAH—nitro derivatives of polycyclic aromatic hydrocarbons

NR—not reported

N.Y.C.—New York City

OC—organic (volatilizable) carbon

OCLT—o-chlorotoluene

ODB—o-dichlorobenzene

O_{3max}—daily maximum of the 1-hr average ozone concentrations

OX—o-xylene

P1 — percent of time on a given day with prevalent winds from the NE

P2 — percent of time on a given day with prevalent winds from the SE

P3 — percent of time on a given day with prevalent winds from the SW

P4 — percent of time on a given day with prevalent winds from the NW

PAH — polycyclic aromatic hydrocarbons

PAH Profiles — a display of a group of PAH relative to one index PAH

PbA — ambient concentration of Pb from motor vehicles

PCA — principal components analysis

PCLT — p-chlorotoluene

PDB — p-dichlorobenzene

PECIP — daily precipitation (inches of water)

PER — perylene

PERC — tetrachloroethylene (perchloroethylene)

PIC — products of incomplete combustion

PUF — polyurethane foam

PYR — pyrene

RI — rural interior area of New Jersey

R_{sp} — Spearman rank correlation coefficient

RSP — respirable particulate matter (D_{50} = 3.5 μm)

S9 — Aroclor 1254-induced liver homogenate

SO_{2avg} — average daily sulfur dioxide concentration

STY — styrene

SURE — Sulfate Regional Experiment

SWI — Southwestern industrial area of New Jersey

TA-98 — strain of bacteria used in the Ames test for mutagenic activity; other strains used include TA-100, TA-1537, TA-1538, etc.

TCANE — 1,1,2-trichloroethane

TCE — 1,1,2,2-tetrachloroethane

TLC — thin-layer chromatography

TM — mass concentration of selected trace metals as oxides, PbO + ZnO + Fe_2O_3

TOL — toluene

TRJC — trichloroethylene

TSP — total suspended particulate matter

TTFA — target transformation factor analysis

VCL — vinyl chloride

VENC — vinylidene chloride

VISMD — mean daily visibility (miles)

VOC — volatile organic compounds

WKDAY — day of the week

WSPINV — inverse of the average daily wind speed (miles-hr^{-1})

Index